Praise for *Between Inca Walls*

"They call the Peace Corps 'the hardest job you'll ever love!' And Evelyn learns just what this means as she tirelessly serves others and finds multiple varieties of love, from indigenous children who touch her heart to a dashing young man who steals that heart away. A great read for all ages."
—**Charles David Kleymeyer, PhD,** author of the triple award-winning *YESHU: A Novel for the Open-Hearted*

"Evelyn LaTorre tells a story that becomes that of the readers. I was amazed to find myself turning page after page, absorbed in a world I didn't know and would never otherwise know. Scenes remain in my mind, as if these stories are my own. I found myself caught up in adventure after adventure, from busy cities with cobblestone streets to roads that clung to the sides of mountains. I became captivated by Evelyn's community of students and peers and the man who became Evelyn's big love."
—**Charlotte Robin Cook, MFA,** former publisher, current story editor, and head fiction judge for the Next Generation Indie Book Awards

"Travel with Evelyn LaTorre during the chaotic early days of the Peace Corps as she arrives in Peru and must navigate finding housing and suitable volunteer jobs in an unfamiliar land whose language she barely speaks. Along the way, she also finds friends, love, and respect for a new culture. An inspiring journey."
—**Tish Davidson,** editor of the *California Writers Club 2019 Literary Review* and author of *African American Scientists and Inventors* and *The Vaccine Debate*

"Walls typically keep people and things both in and out. In this memoir of her days as a Peace corps volunteer, Evelyn LaTorre breaks down those walls and tells a story of establishing relationships and projects in the mountains of Peru in the sixties—a ͏ in learning about oneself through t̶ start reading, you won't want to pu
—**Dr. Jackie M. Allen, MFT,** assc University of LaVerne and coauth̶ *Using the PDSEA Protocol*

"One of the most enjoyable aspects of my position as President and CEO of the National Peace Corps Association is hearing stories of Peace Corps Volunteers, especially those from the early years. In *Between Inca Walls,* Evelyn Kohl LaTorre describes her many adventures serving as a community development volunteer in rural Peru in the 1960s. It's fabulous. I really enjoyed it!"

—**Glenn Blumhorst,** President and CEO, National Peace Corps Association

"All [Peace Corps] Volunteers will appreciate the negotiation process for her site in an isolated community in the Andes. Once Evelyn and her roommate, Marie, finally did find an acceptable home base they worked for eighteen months in a hospital, started 4-H clubs, attended campesino meetings, and taught P.E. in a rudimentary school with a dirt floor. A number of black-and-white photos and a map help bring the author's story to life."

—**Mark D. Walker,** author of *Different Latitudes: My Life in the Peace Corps and Beyond*

"Evelyn LaTorre made two trips. The first, in 1964, was an expedition to Perú with the Peace Corps. The second, more recent, was in her memory, recounting that transformative experience. This book is a trip into a part of Perú not many people tour. As a Mexican, I also enjoyed reading of her experiences in my country during a forgotten time."

—**Alaíde Ventura Medina,** author of *Entre Los Rotos,* winner of the 2019 Mauricio Achar Prize

"This book is very engaging and well written. Evelyn has a way of finding drama in interesting and ordinary events alike. Like when she tries to find the Tres Estrella bus station while fearing missing the departure and losing her travel companions—I felt her sweat-soaked dress and brow."

—**Jackie Reid Dettloff,** author of *My Mexico*

Between Inca Walls

Between
Inca
Walls

*A Peace Corps
Memoir*

Evelyn Kohl LaTorre

SHE WRITES PRESS

Published 2020
Printed in the United States of America
Print ISBN: 978-1-63152-717-3
E-ISBN: 978-1-63152-718-0
Library of Congress Control Number: 2020904043

For information, address:
She Writes Press
1569 Solano Ave #546
Berkeley, CA 94707

Interior design by Tabitha Lahr

She Writes Press is a division of SparkPoint Studio, LLC.

All company and/or product names may be trade names, logos, trademarks, and/or registered trademarks and are the property of their respective owners.

Included photographs are from the author's personal archive, save those on page 143, provided by Ken S.

This book has been recreated from the author's journals and documents that she's saved for over fifty years. For the sake of readability and brevity, separate incidences have sometimes been combined or presented in altered timeframes. In some instances, the author changed the names of individuals either at their request or her discretion.

When the author lived in Peru from 1964 to 1966, Cuzco, spelled with a "z," was the name of both the province and the city. City officials now spell the name of the city as Cusco. In this book the author has chosen to refer to the city as Cusco and the province as Cuzco.

This book is dedicated to my sons, Tony and Tim. May you value your origins in love—discovered in the blending of cultures

❧ *Contents* ❧

Searching for the Source 1

Precarious Places 4

Adventures in Apaseo 16

Goodbyes 23

Cracked Mirror 31

Trips and Trip-ups 37

Roughing It 47

Detour 56

A New Country 61

Finding a Place 66

Saved 72

Abancay 78

Work 89

First Holidays 96

Over the Andes 105

Unexpected 110

Beginning 118

Strong Women 123

Falling 128

Preparing 134

Suncho 145

Potato Caper 150

Finding a Purpose. 158

Working on Ranches .165

Back and Forth. 171

A Choice 182

Retreating. 194

Growing Up 200

Competitions. 206

Wedding. 215

Tensions 221

Letters 227

Love Letters 234

Demonstrating. 242

Touchy Situation 248

Birthday Present for Daddy 257

Worry and Work. 266

Selling and Packing. .274

Back on Track. 278

Chance Card 283

Goodbye Abancay 290

Leaving Peru. 297

Beginning in Ruins. .306

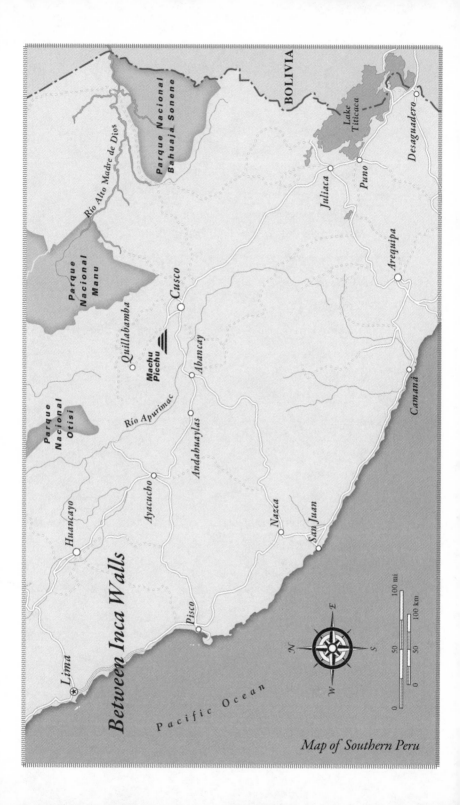

Map of Southern Peru

Searching for
the Source

E ach spring a torrent of muddy water raced through the ditch and over the four-plank bridge in front of my Ismay, Montana, schoolhouse. The strong current forced most of the seventy first-through-twelfth-graders and the four teachers to detour to the far corner of the playground. There, all but the boy daredevils entered the two-story brick building from the gravel road where the water rushed through a culvert. Most of the year the four-foot deep ditch stood bone dry, like everything else in my corner of southeastern Montana.

One sunny April Saturday in 1949, when I was six, I put on my white rubber overboots and teddy-bear coat with the red trim that Mom had made me. I crossed the road next to our first house a block uphill from the school and squeezed through the barbed-wire fence at the base of the nearby hill. My mission—to find the origin of the angry waters that spilled over the school bridge.

I clambered up the hill through ankle-high grass and stepped around mud puddles. Small piles of snow crunched under my feet. I jumped over small streams that rushed around limestone boulders and emptied into deep gullies. Water snaked from every direction as if an imaginary faucet were open behind each sagebrush. When I reached the top of the hill, I looked around in amazement. No rushing waters.

Quiet rivulets gurgled under my boots. Tiny streams ran together into little rivers and hurried down the hill. The muddy waters rushing over the plank bridge that drove us to take an alternate route into the school began as calm, clear waters from melting snow. I took off my coat and leaned against a sandstone boulder to take in the astonishing sight. A surge of satisfaction welled in my chest. I had made a discovery. I would make many more as I moved from Ismay's small hills to the mountains of Mexico, Puerto Rico, and Peru.

My Catholic religion and small-town upbringing dictated for me a traditional future of marriage and motherhood. Ismay girls planned for the horse and the man they wanted, in that order. My parents, teachers, movies, and books presented me alternative streams of possibility that led to a more independent future.

When I graduated from college in 1964, the world was in turmoil. We were still in a cold war with the U.S.S.R. Young men my age left to fight in the growing Vietnam conflict. Others protested the war, and still others turned to drugs and dropped out of traditional society. Reading Betty Friedan's *The Feminine Mystique* in college reinforced my belief that despite the world's turmoil, I could obtain what I wanted. I yearned for a life of excitement and adventure. I got it.

From innocence to sexual awakening to passion. The emotional eddies that flowed through the hills and gullies of my Montana childhood began as silent streams of religious reverence and family protection. My social development crept along at a slow creek's pace when I was a teen in California, then erupted like a storm-stirred ocean as I entered my twenties and lived in Latin American cultures that awakened my body and soothed my restless soul.

I found different languages, customs, and levels of emotional openness in the Hispanic culture. I discovered how I could contribute to the world and live a stimulating life. Idealistic and eager to fulfill a noble purpose, I joined President Kennedy's recently founded Peace Corps. I believed my community development work in Peru could make a difference for poor people there. Little did I suspect the moral and spiritual challenges that would confront me during my two-year experience.

I questioned beliefs from my early life and doubted whether I had the strength to navigate the turbulent currents I encountered. But close friendships, letters from home, and a caring environment helped me gain self-confidence and knowledge.

In the majestic Andes, rivers rushed through deep valleys toward the mighty Amazon. I hurried above, tossed back and forth on precarious mountain switchbacks, struggling with the new emotions surging within me. A desire I didn't comprehend compelled me to risk body and soul for country, adventure, and love. From rivulets to streams to a torrent, the forces of nature shaped my life—and at age twenty-two, a tsunami of passion swept me away.

Precarious Places

I wiped the dust from the window of the Peace Corps truck and looked down. The Apurimac River meandered five thousand feet below me. My stomach fluttered. On November 4, 1964, a day before my twenty-second birthday, I was in the Andes Mountains with my new roommate, Marie, on my way to Abancay, Peru. After a month's delay, we'd finally been sent to fulfill our Peace Corps assignment in the capital of the Apurimac Province. The dirt road reminded me of those in southeastern Montana, where I grew up—except the roads in my part of Montana were flat. No wrecked vehicles there clinging to steep mountainsides.

I looked up just as we rounded another sharp curve—and screamed. A fast-moving semi-truck emerged from a swirling cloud of dust and headed straight for us. Norm, a veteran Corpsman driver, pulled the truck close to the unfenced edge and stopped. The vehicles passed, inches apart. The smell of hogs on their way to the Cusco market drifted into our truck. I wondered what I'd gotten myself into this time.

Encountering new places had always filled me with excitement. Despite the dangers, the anticipation of a new discovery left me breathless. I'd wanted to explore more Hispanic cultures ever since living in Mexico, the summer after my junior year in college. That 1963 adventure landed me in my current situation. And though I had numerous pleasant memories of that time, the trip to Mexico also had a perilous beginning.

∘·◦·◦·◦

In the early 1960s, my consciousness had been awakened by significant news events. Men orbited the earth, Jane Goodall went to observe chimpanzees in Africa, and hundreds of young American men died fighting in Vietnam. Too many civil rights activists were jailed in the South. Americans' spirit of adventure had risen alongside their desire for change. I, too, wanted to make my mark in the world.

I joined a group called Amigos Anonymous made up of students from San Francisco Bay Area colleges and coordinated by Father O'Looney out of Newman Hall at the University of California, Berkeley. Many of us had spent weekends in the Central Valley helping César Chávez organize the area's migrant workers by going door-to-door to take a census. Our work motivated us for our next step in healing the world—developing needed services in rural Mexican towns. We were joined by hundreds of new Amigos, twenty-something-year-old college students like me, who planned to spend our two-month vacation performing good works among Mexico's poorer residents.

On a warm mid-June Sunday morning, nine college coeds, including myself, departed from the San Diego home of one of our members and headed to the San Ysidro Greyhound bus station in her parents' van. My group's schedule called for us to catch the

Sunday 1:30 p.m. Tres Estrellas bus from Tijuana and arrive in Guadalajara on Tuesday morning. After two days' rest from two nights on the bus, we would continue eastward from Guadalajara to the small town of Apaseo el Grande in central Mexico. Twenty-eight pieces of luggage filled with our clothes, plus the books, medicines, and supplies needed for our work, lay heaped in the back of the van. All went well until the van broke down.

We lost precious time loading our suitcases and bags into a rented station wagon and arrived at the San Ysidro bus depot close to 12:30 p.m. When the bus agent saw our huge collection of baggage, he enforced the "one piece of luggage per person" rule. But we had thirteen suitcases and fifteen Navy sea bags filled with supplies essential for the school and library we expected to start. None of this could be left behind without jeopardizing our projects. So I, the co-director of our group, took charge.

I bought tickets for eight more seats and located our bus. Next, I convinced several men about to board to carry one of our overflow bags and place it on an empty seat. The bus, full of chattering women, helpful men, and luggage as passengers, pulled out of the San Ysidro station at 1:00 p.m., everything in place.

Greyhound personnel said the bus would drop us near the Mexican Tres Estrellas bus station in Tijuana. Imagine our surprise when the bus left us at a taxi stand on the border near the edge of Tijuana. None of us had ever been to this crossing before. A passerby said the Tres Estrellas station was four miles away. We looked at one another in dismay.

Now 2:00 p.m., half an hour past our bus boarding time, we waited somewhere outside central Tijuana surrounded by our luggage. For the past four months of planning, our group had looked forward to living in Apaseo el Grande. Nine American girls now stood in the hot June sun at the Mexican border wondering if we'd ever get to our destination.

Finally, a lone rickety taxi stopped in front of us. Obviously, nine girls plus our luggage couldn't fit in the one vehicle. No one seemed to know what to do. So I volunteered to take the taxi into town to tell the Tres Estrellas people we would be late. I grabbed my suitcase and said I'd be back, *pronto*. I prayed that our bus hadn't already left.

The taxi limped along a paved road through an area strewn with garbage and vehicles in various states of disrepair. Small one-story cement brick homes squatted next to one another along the pavement. A sign said, WELCOME TO TIJUANA in Spanish, but I didn't feel very welcome. I felt alone and out of place.

The cab inched along a beehive-busy main street past swarms of men with bright striped *serapes* slung over their shoulders and women in ballooning skirts of bright yellow, eye-popping red, and sea blue. Dirty-faced children in rags worked the street too. Most everyone on foot seemed to be a vendor who shouted at the slow-moving vehicles to buy his or her wares. Lively salespeople hawked roasted corn, Chiclets chewing gum, and embroidered shirts while weaving in and out among exhaust-spewing cars and colorfully decorated trucks. The scene was like nothing I'd ever experienced. I longed to continue on into the heart of this fascinating country to live my dream—helping Apaseo's residents better their lives. But instead I was caught in a colorful but chaotic traffic jam.

The scent of corn tortillas grilling at a nearby taco stand reminded me of meals I'd had in the Mexican communities of California's Central Valley. Today the vibrant colors and the food smells didn't attract me as they had in Parlier. I had a critical job to do—get my group to the town that waited for us to start a school and a library. But first, I had to find the Tres Estrellas bus station *pronto*.

Pronto didn't come soon. After ten minutes in the taxi searching for the station, I spied what looked like the letters of a big neon sign flashing TRES something on the top of a four-story office building. The sign had to be the one designating our bus station. I told the taxi driver to stop and let me out. I paid, grabbed my suitcase, and hurried down the crowded sidewalk. Then I lost sight of the neon sign I'd seen just minutes ago. I swore under my breath at our adult leaders who hadn't given us sufficient information to get to our destination. I'd come to Mexico to help our group perform good works—not get lost in the first Mexican city I drove into. We couldn't help others if we missed our bus. I'd have to reach out to the Tijuana residents I saw.

"*¿Dónde estación de autobuses?* Where is bus station?" I asked a passerby in my uncertain Spanish.

The man shook his head. He either couldn't understand me or didn't know the answer. After searching the sky for ten minutes, I spotted the complete neon sign blinking, TRES ESTRELLAS DE ORO with the three gold stars signifying the bus company's name. Relieved, I found the ticket agent and asked whether the 1:30 p.m. reservations for the "*muchachas Americanas*, American girls," were still valid.

"Sí," he said, pointing to two young men loading cargo onto a bus.

"The girls will be here," I said, "*en un momento*, soon."

"Thank God for '*hora Mexicana,*' Mexican time," I muttered to myself and handed my suitcase to the baggage helper.

Now maybe our Amigos group could resume our charitable mission. Knowing our bus hadn't yet left us, tension drained from my body. I had to let my fellow volunteers know where to find the Tres Estrellas station. I hailed another taxi to rush me back to the border.

A surprise awaited when I arrived at the taxi stand where I'd been less than an hour before—no girls and no luggage. Could my colleagues have found enough cabs to take them to town? I asked my taxi to return me to the downtown bus station.

Once again, I could see no order to the mass of honking buses, cars, and pickups. The previous hour, inside the rickety taxi, I'd inched my way through Tijuana's commercial center. This time traffic didn't move. Exasperated, the taxi driver pulled over to the side.

"The station is right there," he said, pointing his index finger westward. "But it's on a one-way street going the other way. You can get there faster on foot."

I exited the cab and hurried west but saw no bus station. This time I didn't even see a neon TRES ESTRELLAS sign. Confused, I looked around at the totally unfamiliar area. The clock ticked past 4:20. My heart sank. I thought our 1:30 bus, three hours behind its original departure time, might now be on the road to Guadalajara. If so, I wouldn't be accompanying the others for a summer of missionary-type work. I redoubled my efforts to find my colleagues and accosted random people on the street.

"Where is the Tres Estrellas bus station?" I asked in Spanish, breathing hard now. One person directed me down an alley and several blocks to the left. The next pointed me in the opposite direction, and I retraced my steps. Outstretched arms motioned me west, then east. From the puzzled looks on the brown faces and their varying directions, I gathered there must be more than one Tres Estrellas bus station. My heart beat fast, and sweat poured down my face. Where was I?

Me, a blue-eyed, brown-haired, twenty-year-old college student from an all-women's Catholic college, on my own in the middle of this border town full of bars and brothels. Until now I'd only traveled to a handful of western states for fun and never gone out of the country. Four months of once-a-week Spanish classes at the University of California's Newman Center had given me only a rudimentary vocabulary in this new language. And in my fear of never finding the bus station, I forgot what little Spanish I knew.

My eyes searched up and down the streets for the taco stand I thought I'd recognize, or any other landmark. The bus station had to be somewhere. My Timex now showed 4:35 p.m. I felt like I'd been lost for hours. What if the bus left without me? By now, my luggage and friends must be on the road. And I had nothing but my purse and the tan dress I wore. And the dress dripped wet with perspiration.

I darted up and down unrecognizable streets asking, "*¿Dónde estación de autobuses?* Where bus station?" Breathing hard and near tears, I mustered all the Spanish I knew and asked the question to a young woman in a business suit.

"*¿Dónde está la estación de Tres Estrellas?* Where is the Tres Estrellas bus station?"

The woman seemed to sense my desperation, took my arm and walked me through an alley and around a corner. And there it stood—the beautiful Tres Estrellas bus station. In my happiness I could have kissed my rescuer. Big green letters on the side of a cream-colored bus spelled out TRES ESTRELLAS DE ORO. I headed toward the bus and recognized my director, Kay, hauling duffle bags from the waiting room. My breathing and heartbeat slowed.

"We were starting to worry about you," Kay said, handing me my ticket. "Taxis came by for us right after you left. The bus is about to pull out."

The vehicle's luggage compartment bulged with our twenty-eight pieces of luggage. The baggage checkers complained to Kay and me that we were way over our limit. This time I couldn't buy extra seats for our bags. The bus looked full. The passengers waited while Kay and I argued with the station manager about how much we owed for our excess luggage.

The driver gunned the engine ready to leave. We'd already caused more than a three-hour delay. In desperation, we paid twenty-three dollars, 10 percent of our total budget, and boarded the bus. Exhausted, I crawled up the steps. I could feel sweat pouring down my face.

I looked for the seat number on my ticket. A young Mexican girl sat in my spot. Then toward the rear of the bus I spied the curly black hair of my friend, Barbara, a fellow Sociology major from my Holy Names College classes whom I'd convinced to join Amigos.

"Come sit here," she said, motioning to me. "I guess the buses in Mexico aren't on a strict time schedule."

"Just like seat numbers don't mean anything," I said, plopping down. Barbara's brown eyes lit up, and the worry wrinkles of her brow disappeared. I felt comforted to be with a friend. The bus pulled out of the station. I looked around.

The thirty-six Mexican passengers didn't look upset by the long delay caused by nine tardy American girls. Our Mexican traveling companions passed around food they'd brought. When nighttime approached, we all sang "Celito Lindo" and other songs in Spanish. Everyone on the bus cooperated like one big family. I'd never experienced anything like this camaraderie.

One of the friendliest passengers, Flavio, sat in front of Barbara and me. He spoke English and said he was twenty-one and single. He was headed home to Guadalajara. His brown round face and mop of black hair turned backward more than forward as we became acquainted. Each time the bus stopped for refreshments, our new short and handsome Mexican friend disappeared out the door to buy us sodas. He refused our offer of reimbursement.

The next morning we passed rows of buildings made of sticks held together with mud. I'd seen run-down houses in Montana and even parts of California but never like the ramshackle structures in these towns. Mile after bumpy mile, out the window I viewed nothing but wooden hovels, cacti, and dirt. The poor quality of the buildings, land, and roads shocked me.

I liked the view inside the bus better. My attention turned to the more pleasing scene near me.

Flavio strummed his guitar and led the passengers in singing Mexican favorites. They fell silent when my male admirer crooned romantic tunes like "Pretty Blue Eyes" to me. I blushed when his big brown eyes fixed on me and he translated from Spanish into English, "Your happy smile makes me vibrate and soothes my wounded heart." Sunday night he pulled out a harmonica, which he played as beautifully as he had played the guitar.

Then we Amigos sang American songs like "Row, Row, Row Your Boat" and "Red River Valley" for our new Mexican friends. Between music performances, Flavio gave Barbara and me Spanish lessons, and we became confident enough to talk to the families around us. They welcomed our attempts to speak their language.

On Monday afternoon, I noticed a change in the landscape. The bus climbed into the mountainous area of Mexico. The scenery improved from desert to green foliage, from impoverished dwellings to modern, sturdy houses made of brick. By 9:30 Tuesday morning we were in Flavio's bustling hometown of Guadalajara.

Flavio offered to show Barbara and me his city the next day. We accepted. Our new friend helped us find our host family's chauffeur, then left for his home in the center of town.

Our hosts, wealthy friends of our Amigos founder, lived in an elegant area of the city. I welcomed the luxury of the family's three-story, fifteen-room house. Two nights trying to sleep upright on a bouncing bus had earned me a good night's sleep in a bed. Several of us took a dip in the family's pool. That night I slept soundly. I awoke Wednesday morning eager to see Guadalajara's sights—and Flavio.

My friend collected Barbara and me in his brother's red 1938 vintage hot-rod. The three of us squeezed onto the car's one long front seat, laughing at the close fit. Then we drove around the city where we marveled at the size of the soccer stadium and gloried in the brilliant red-and-blue stained glass windows of Guadalajara's churches. We stopped at a marketplace where Barbara and I purchased sandals for two dollars a pair. Flavio's city delighted me with its colorful sights and great bargains.

At lunchtime, Flavio took us to his four-room wood-framed home to meet his mother and eat pineapple pie. His petite mother, sweeter than the pie she served, had the same sparkling deep brown eyes and bubbly personality. I could see where he got his good looks. Mother and son entertained us with lively Mexican songs. Then we three young people got back in the hot rod and drove to a placid blue lake.

We circled the lake in a rowboat until an afternoon shower forced us to disembark. We laughed, running from the wharf to shelter ourselves in a nearby coffeehouse. For dinner, Flavio treated us to a seven-course meal accompanied by mariachi music at the Capri Restaurant.

With my stomach and heart full, Flavio drove us home. He stayed at our mansion for hours chatting with the women of our Amigos group. Our aristocratic host, acting superior, frowned when interacting with my Mexican friend. I figured the owner looked down on Flavio because he wasn't rich, had coffee-colored skin, and came from a lower class. I winced at the mansion owner's coolness.

Flavio asked for my address in Mexico, which I gave him. Then he begged me to go on one more ride with him. Barbara and I met him around the corner from the rich people's house so as not to incur our host's further disapproval. For the next hour I listened to the sincerest outpouring of love I'd ever heard.

"I have never met a girl like you," Flavio said to me, tears welling up in his eyes. "You are like Mexican people because you are generous and selfless."

Barbara cried. I couldn't say anything, overcome with embarrassment and pleasure at the same time. I liked Flavio, but his outpouring of emotion unsettled me. I'd heard such sweet words only in the movies. With my American dates, I usually went out three times then, bored, I dropped the guy, feeling I could wrap him around my little finger. I couldn't recall them saying anything romantic to me. Flavio was different. He had a more expressive and emotional personality. Of the handful of American guys I'd dated, none had expressed even a fraction of the affection that Flavio conveyed. And this cute Mexican guy seemed sincere. I was discovering the warmth and caring of Latin men. Their tenderness excited me. Despite my enchantment with my Mexican friend, I was wary of what sexual favors he might be after.

"I like you," I said. "But I'm confused by all this attention. I need time to sort out my feelings."

"That's because you are a woman," he said, "I'm a man and must express what I feel."

"You've done that," I said. "More beautifully than anything I've ever heard."

"I won't let you go until you promise," he said caressing my hand, "that you'll return to Guadalajara."

"I will," I said, "and soon."

Flavio's analysis of how men expressed their feelings and women didn't was the exact opposite of how I'd experienced the two sexes in the U.S. His warm Spanish words swept me away. At the same time, I viewed his motives with skepticism. Flavio must have noticed distrust in my voice.

"I want nothing from you," he said, looking at me lovingly. "Just knowing you for the past few days and being with you has brought me much happiness."

I felt like a woman in a romance novel. At the same time, my head filled with the warnings from our Newman Center trainers.

"Watch out," Father O'Looney had said, "for those fast-working Mexican boys."

I had to think about the reason I'd come to Mexico—to do the work that Apaseo needed done. It was time to be on my way.

Thursday morning Flavio, dressed in a gray suit, arrived at the bus station on his motor scooter. He wrote down each woman's California home address and, after hugging each of us, wished us well on the remainder of our journey. Then we boarded the bus for Celaya, the next stop on the road to Apaseo. And Flavio followed our bus out of town—until a flat tire on his scooter stopped him.

The bus traveled east across central Mexico, where I drank in the beauty of the green, verdant, landscape and pondered my experience so far. My encounter with Flavio left me feeling special. He and the other friendly people I'd met made me forget the difficulties I'd first had when beginning my journey south of the border.

Getting lost had not resulted in disaster. In fact, never before had I experienced such intense emotions—both within myself and in those around me. I cherished these newfound feelings and looked forward to more experiences with the people of this strange new land.

Adventures in Apaseo

The bus from Guadalajara headed toward Celaya, two hundred miles away, and ten miles from my summer home, Apaseo el Grande. I peered through the rain-streaked windows at the serene beauty of rolling green hills sprinkled with pine and oak trees. Lime-colored pastures dotted with brown bushes slid by. Singing inside the bus turned my attention from the scenery outside.

Everyone sang "Guadalajara, Guadalajara." We nine American girls joined the others when we could remember the words. When the Mexicans asked us to sing one of our songs, we sang, "When Irish Eyes are Smiling." Between songs we laughed and joked our way down the highway. The eight-hour trip felt like three. I warmed to the blending of known and unknown—companions and strangers laughing and singing together.

In a Celaya restaurant that evening, I was finishing dinner with three others from our group when four young men pulled their chairs up to our table. One of the black-haired youths, a bullfighter, offered to demonstrate how not to get hooked by a bull's horns. One of my colleagues served as the bull. We laughed at the evasive antics of the toreador, graceful in his tight, tapered pants. He invited us to see him fight a real bull in Mexico City. We accepted his invitation but said we'd have to wait for a weekend free from our work. These handsome, dark-haired, dark-eyed, friendly young men had me hooked.

❖ ❖ ❖ ❖

Four more coeds from the States joined us the following morning, for a total of thirteen of us assigned to Apaseo el Grande. None of the guys I'd trained with over the past eight months had been assigned to work in Apaseo. For three years I'd attended Holy Names, an all-women's college, and I'd looked forward to working in the Amigos program with men during the summer. No such luck. They'd all been assigned to other towns. The Señor Cura, head priest of Apaseo, didn't want a mixed group of men and women in his town. Their young hormonal bodies might mingle in unholy ways.

Apaseo el Grande, turned out to be not *grande* but rather *pequeño*, small. Five dusty cobblestone thoroughfares flowed out from the hedge-bordered central plaza past wall-lined streets and ended in fertile fields a mile away. On three sides of the main square, tall stucco arches formed porticoes in front of businesses. On the fourth side, the town's major church overlooked two small courtyards and a revolution era monument.

A change of color on the stuccoed walls bordering the long streets indicated where one family's property ended and another's began. The entry doors to each home varied in type, size, and ornamental knocker. Some had big, round brass fixtures, and others sported unpainted wooden handles. Giant entrances often had smaller human-sized doors set into them. Inside, past the front entry, the rooms of each house surrounded a patio. The homes felt private and secure inside their eight-foot-high walls. They didn't look like the single-family dwellings back home, where fences, not walls, separated homes.

The local organizers for Amigos assigned me to live with Dr. Hernández, a physician, his wife, and their five dark-haired children ages one to six. The doctor spoke fluent English and asked me in which language I preferred to communicate, English or Spanish. "Spanish," I responded, wanting to improve my fluency. From then on he spoke to me in his native language. I soon forgot I had the option of speaking English with him.

My new home bordered Apaseo's main square and had indoor plumbing and heated water. I slept in the living room on a comfortable sofa, which I made into a bed each evening. When I visited others from my group, I saw that they had their own bedrooms. I didn't mind. My home had fewer flies in the kitchen than theirs.

Señor Cura had requested that the Amigos develop a new library in his town. Father O'Looney assigned me to be director of the project. Back home I'd worked as a book shelver in the local public library. Apparently, that qualified me to set up a library in Apaseo, despite the fact that the town already had one. But Señor Cura said it was a communist one, and he wanted his own, less political reading room.

Father O'Looney had named me spiritual director for our group. He must have thought that because I attended a Catholic college I could lead our group in inspiration and prayers. Uncomfortable preaching aloud, I didn't fulfill that role well. I preferred to concentrate on more tangible projects.

The town's organizing couple sent us to work in La Villita, a poor area on the outskirts of Apaseo. Residents of the La Villita community lived in huts alongside a rutted dirt road that marched up the hill to a small Catholic church. The suburb had no school, running water, or sewage system. We couldn't do much about the latter two deficits, but we could renovate a warehouse owned by the church and give the local children a school. The male Amigos' muscles would have come in handy to help with the lifting, sawing, hauling and painting we had to do. Nevertheless, our group of young women managed fine.

Every morning we thirteen female volunteers gathered for breakfast in the dining room of two spinster sisters. The homeowners went elsewhere while we prepared scrambled eggs, black beans, and *pan dulce* sweet bread, in their kitchen. Between sips of orange juice, tea, or coffee, we made plans for the day, and then set about our work.

One group took the bus to Celaya to buy poster board and school-decorating materials. Another unit, alongside local girls, cleared the building's backyard of discarded bricks and cement pieces. My duties changed from day to day. One day I made alphabet letters for a schoolroom, the next I laid stones for the school's patio. We used the supplies we'd carried from the U.S., plus money and materials raised by local families, to turn the warehouse into an attractive elementary school.

With the assistance of young women from Apaseo, we opened a medical dispensary in the kitchen of the school. Together, we patched the gashed feet of residents injured from stepping on cacti in bare feet. Some of us gave smallpox and oral polio vaccines under the direction of a local doctor. The same physician gave weekly talks on nutrition and hygiene to the local women. Several members of our group set up a program through the Catholic Relief Services to distribute dry milk and flour to La Villita residents. Being so immersed in helping others gave me meaning in a way I'd only glimpsed at when volunteering the previous year working with farm workers in the Central Valley.

The teachers in our party began classes for the children at La Villita School using an elementary curriculum. I helped teach sewing to mothers in the area during the day. Some evenings I taught adult literacy. Pride filled my heart whenever an adult pupil recited the Spanish alphabet or sewed a child's skirt the way I'd taught her. By the end of July, fifteen local women, previously illiterate, could read and write.

For several weeks, Señor Cura, who ran the town, couldn't decide on a room where Barbara and I could establish the library he wanted. During that time, we visited the communist library. More flying insects perched on the shelves than books. I insisted we have window and door screens built for our room to keep flies out and readers in.

Several times the town held fiestas in the church courtyard. Lively mariachi music flowed through my body, urging my feet to move in time to the polka-like rhythms. I danced with Juan, then Sergio, both handsome and interesting dark-haired local college students. Señor Cura, or his appointees, reminded dancing couples to maintain a proper distance between one another. And there were other rules designed for young females.

The elderly head priest of Apaseo forbade girls from riding horses—unless they rode sidesaddle. Where I grew up in Montana I'd always straddled horses and sometimes rode bareback, without a saddle. I'd never heard of riding any way but astride a horse. Further instructions for female Amigos included that we wear dresses, never slacks. But I'd packed a pair of culottes. The split skirt came in handy when I encountered a horse I wanted to ride.

On a ranch outside Apaseo, away from the church and its watchers, I found a friendly pinto pony. With a leg on each side of the horse, I galloped across a hand-plowed field, delighted to feel the wind blowing through my hair. I'd broken two of Señor Cura's rules. I didn't believe I'd be damned to hell for enjoying myself.

◇·◇·◇·◇

Most weekends Barbara and I took a local bus to the transportation hub in Querétaro. From there, we hopped onto other buses to visit different cities. We traveled to Mexico City, Acapulco, Oaxaca, San Miguel de Allende, Guanajuato, Morelia, and Guadalajara. In Mexico City we watched a bullfight, but we couldn't find the toreador we'd met in Celaya. In Guadalajara we went by Flavio's house, the boy I'd met on the Tres Estrellas bus from Tijuana to Guadalajara. He wasn't home, so I left a note inviting him to visit Apaseo el Grande. In Acapulco, I met a young, slim engineering student named Inocente, who taught me to body surf in the warm waves of the Pacific Ocean. Before I returned to Apaseo, he and I agreed to correspond.

◅◦◅◦◅◦◅◦

In mid-July, Señor Cura finally gave Barbara and me a small, unfinished room off the main church in which to establish the new library. In the span of two weeks, we painted the bookshelves we'd ordered earlier and installed window and door screens. Then the two of us cataloged 150 books in Spanish that had been donated by friends, schools, libraries, and private homes in the U.S. and Mexico. At long last we'd established the noncommunist library.

On August 6 we invited everyone, including the mayor, to a ceremony for the library's grand opening. The mayor said Señor Cura should officiate. In the end both the mayor and the priest said a few words, as did I. Recalling that Dr. Hernández spoke English, I asked him to help put my fractured Spanish into appropriate sentences. I was proud of the result.

"This is your library," I waxed eloquent to those gathered before me. "Its existence depends upon your support. Its first purpose is for the children because it is most important to instill a love of books at an early age . . ."

I was proud of all that my Amigos Anonymous group had accomplished for the town. Local young people who'd worked with us would carry on what we'd begun. Apaseo's residents had shared their lives. The Mexican culture embraced me and captured my heart and soul. Sergio danced with me most of the evening. Señor Cura made certain we maintained a proper distance between us.

Goodbyes

On August 10, 1963, the time had come for me to leave Apaseo el Grande and head back to California for my senior year at Holy Names. The college had named me its representative to the National Federation of Catholic College Students, NFCCS, convention in Minneapolis, and I needed to be on my way. I'd worked with twelve other college women and would leave early, alone. The others would continue our work for another two weeks.

Juan, a premed student in the capitol, and Sergio, enrolled at a college in a nearby city, stayed by my side in the library to help put the books in order. I'd become fond of the two dark-haired young men, like I'd become attached to so many of Apaseo's residents. We exchanged addresses with promises to stay in touch.

I didn't want to take leave of my adopted, caring Mexican community. But after a summer of work and fun, I needed to return to my studies. So much had happened. It seemed like I'd left the States a lifetime ago.

Three of my American colleagues accompanied me out of town to the stick-and-mud hut home of my Mexican family's servant. Poor as her home was, she insisted I pack pieces of the delicious-smelling bread she'd made for my two-day bus trip. My heart filled with gratitude at the generosity of the poorest people. I hated to leave this newfound culture that loved me and I loved back.

More hugs of farewell enveloped me after the 6:30 a.m. mass on Sunday. Then, I went off to visit special families. Mr. Mendoza the town photographer, his wife, and daughter had wet eyes as they gifted me a bag of photos of the town. I asked them where I could buy rope to tie around my now-bulging cardboard suitcase. Their twenty-year-old son ran off to buy more rope than I needed. I added a box to my baggage to hold the many gifts. Tears streamed down my face at the Hernández residence as I tied the donated rope around my yellow plaid pasteboard suitcase for the last time. Including two bags and a purse, I now had five pieces of luggage to manage.

The bus bound for Guadalajara arrived in Celaya at 11:45 a.m., over an hour late. By now I was accustomed to Mexico's late buses. But I might miss my connection if the bus from Guadalajara to Tijuana left at its scheduled 8 p.m. time. I hugged each of the seven members of my Mexican family, boarded the bus, and waved goodbye. The trip back to the U.S. felt different than my trip down. Now, instead of taking charge of loading luggage, attendants took care of my box and suitcase. I sat in my seat and cried.

"Are you sick?" the bus driver asked, concerned, as he drove us out of town.

"No, I'm not," I said through my tears. "I'm leaving Mexico."

"You'll be back," he answered.

The bus made up time, until it came to a halt as we entered Tepotitlan. There had been a big rainstorm. Muddy red water five feet deep ran over the road. We waited half an hour for the storm water to subside. When it didn't, the driver told his helpers to bring the luggage inside the bus from the bins underneath. With the luggage protected, the driver revved the engine and we plowed through the flood like a boat. The sludgy water-mud mix rose halfway up the side of our bus but didn't come inside. A pickup we passed sat in the water where it had been abandoned. I marveled at the ingenuity of our driver.

The bus reached Guadalajara at 7:40 p.m. I must have looked nervous because the woman in the seat next to me asked if I needed assistance. I told her I'd be fine.

"Are you sure you don't need any help?" she asked again as we filed out.

"If I can just catch the 8 p.m. bus to Tijuana," I said trying with two hands to balance three bags, a box, and a suitcase, "I'll be alright."

I lugged my five pieces of luggage up to the Guadalajara–Tijuana bus window. My heart stopped racing. This time I'd arrived just in time, not three hours late. But when I went to pay for my ticket, the ticket agent refused to accept my traveler's cheque. My body tightened. The ticket-seller said my bus would leave at 8:30 p.m. and suggested I try to cash the cheque at the restaurant next door. I bought a 7-Up and cashed the cheque minus an extra five *pesos* for the service. I didn't like paying extra but thanked my lucky stars I'd obtained the cash needed to buy the bus ticket.

After signing my name on the passenger list, I read the names of those traveling with me. I squealed with delight when I spotted my friend Jackie's name. She had spent the summer working at a different Amigos Anonymous worksite near Morelia. Now I wouldn't have to make the two-night trip alone.

Jackie and I embraced one another at the bus station and compared notes about our summer experiences. Her placement in Zinapécuaro had been unorganized but as life-altering as mine had been. Two differences—she didn't think she had contributed much to the people in her community, and Amigos guys had been assigned to her town. I knew we thirteen women had made a difference in Apaseo without the help of Amigos guys. And, a new world had opened to me because of my experience.

The only seats available together were across the aisle from one another. That didn't last long. As soon as the lights went off in the bus, Jackie jumped out of her seat.

"That guy next to me," she whispered as she headed toward a seat near the back, "has his hands all over me."

I sympathized with her. On a weekend excursion to Acapulco a few weeks before, I had been in the same situation on a night bus. Movement from the young man seated next to me had awakened me from a deep sleep an hour out of Mexico City. His sneaky fingers climbed up my back like a spider. I froze. What should I do? I couldn't scream and awaken the entire bus. I pushed his hands away. That didn't help—he put them right back. I couldn't say anything. Speaking to him would elevate our relationship. I did what I usually did in times of severe stress. I prayed. The guy's hands moved to my front. I jerked his tentacles off my breasts with a violent tug. I could see no empty seats available. After an eternity the bus stopped for a break and the lights came on. I darted up and sat down between two girls in a two-person seat. We traveled uncomfortably the rest of the way to Acapulco with no complaints from the two girls. Maybe they understood.

Tuesday morning at the border, customs agents said they would confiscate Jackie's Mexican liquor because she possessed three bottles over the limit. We sat down on a nearby curb and drank as much of it as we could, not wanting to waste the drink. A bit tipsy, we caught the 9:20 a.m. bus to Los Angeles.

The difference between the U.S. and Mexico struck me as soon as we crossed the border. The bus clerks who sold us tickets in L.A. were crabby, unlike the friendly, helpful attendants in Tijuana. We paid a whopping $3.15 for the American bus that would take us from Tijuana to Los Angeles. To travel the same distance in Mexico it cost less than a dollar. I had mixed feelings about reentering my country.

For the first time I noticed how our cities were laid out in neat blocks. Bus stations had signs directing us to the right terminal. No refuse or nasty smells filled the streets or bathrooms. And there were bathrooms—clean ones. Modern buildings clustered together without poor barrios in between or vendors hawking their merchandise. No bugs flew around. Everything in the States looked super organized. I didn't know which I preferred, friendliness or order. Why couldn't a country have both?

◇ ◇ ◇ ◇

At home my mother said I needed to get a move on. I had to unpack and be ready in three days to drive to North Dakota with them. We'd save money, the folks said, by camping on the way. From North Dakota, I could take buses to get to the NFCCS convention in Minneapolis. I washed my clothes and repacked my weathered, pasteboard suitcase.

I felt like a stranger in my own country. No one seemed interested in my life-changing experience. The Mexicans had been more welcoming than my California family. Everyone at home was too busy, like all Americans. Then I, too, began to rush. I thought we'd drive all the way to North Dakota in two days, but plans changed.

My cousin Barbara Ann, a year older than me, was traveling from New England, North Dakota, to Billings, Montana, with her parents, Joe and Mary. Barbara Ann had been excited by my work in Mexico and to support my endeavor, had sent me a package of homemade fudge and cookies. I'd paid more duty than the food was worth, but I appreciated her thoughtfulness.

Now, Barbara Ann and her friend were on their way to teach Eskimos for two years in the snowy frontiers of Alaska. They would catch a plane from Billings. When Barbara Ann and her family met up with us near Ismay, where I'd grown up, I jumped at the opportunity to accompany my cousin and her parents back to Billings to see her off on her adventure. Barbara Ann listened with rapt attention to my Mexican adventures. We chatted nonstop all the way to the airport. I loved that my cousin saw me as a fellow adventurer. Finally, someone else was interested in my exciting summer. We understood one another.

After the plane to Alaska took off, Aunt Mary, Uncle Joe, and I drove in silence to North Dakota. Nontalkers like my dad when I'd left for Mexico, they too grieved over letting their daughter go so far away. In Alaska, only bush planes could reach Barbara Ann's town. The fact that she would be teaching in a Catholic school, however, seemed to be a comfort to my relatives.

From Joe and Mary's, I caught a ride to Grand Forks, North Dakota, with a newly married cousin on my mother's side. Her new husband slept on the floor in their living room so I could sleep in the bed with my cousin. I felt terrible dislodging my cousin's husband from their marital bed, but that's what people in Mexico would have done. I realized that Midwesterners were just as hospitable as my Mexican friends. The main difference—my relatives of German or English backgrounds, didn't give hugs or kisses like my affectionate Mexican friends.

I caught a bus to Fargo, North Dakota, to stay with Barbara Ann's older sister, Mary Catherine, and her new husband, just back from their honeymoon. A few years before I'd made mud pies and played dolls with this newly married cousin. Now Mary prepared edible food for a real husband. Marriage seemed to be happening for everyone my age. Not for me, though. I enjoyed seeing the world. And I had lots more to see.

I hopped on a bus to Minneapolis. My mother's youngest sister collected me at the bus station for a short stay with her family of five active children. We drove around the beautiful, green countryside to the University of Minnesota. Wider boulevards and greener lawns and trees than California's filled the city. Two weeks ago, I'd been in Mexico, then in California and now, Minnesota. My culture shock at being back had subsided. Each place I visited had its own kind of beauty.

❖ ❖ ❖ ❖

At the NFCCS convention, Sargent Shriver, Director of the Peace Corps, gave the keynote speech to the assembled Catholic college representatives. He expressed his belief in the idealism and responsibility of young people like me.

"They say the flame of idealism which illuminates the first pages of our history, is being smothered by the weight of material plenty which has made America the richest country in the world. They argue that young Americans have gone soft. . . . Today the record that American youth has made in Peace Corps service stands as a dramatic refutation of these charges."

Only a few weeks before, I'd experienced firsthand the difference my work could make and how caring and fascinating another culture could be. Sargent Shriver's challenge to my generation to use our idealism and make the world a better place inspired me. Not used to riches, I could easily reject the material plenty he spoke about and dedicate my efforts for the next two years to helping the poor of another country better themselves.

The charismatic director said that 5,000 Peace Corps Volunteers now served in impoverished countries overseas. The

Kennedy administration planned to have 13,000 volunteers in the field by the end of 1964. I vowed to be one of them.

California, Mexico and—who knew what part of the world I would explore next. Since I'd first begun exploring the hills and streams of Ismay, Montana, I'd ventured far.

Cracked Mirror

I grew up in Ismay, a southeastern Montana town of 200 people, 50 miles from the North Dakota border. Our first house sat atop a small hill across the road from the Catholic church, which we attended every Sunday until it closed for lack of parishioners. Cowboys on horses trotted down our gravel Main Street past false-fronted buildings. Three cattle trucks could fit side by side on our main thoroughfare, though I'd seen only one at a time parked there. The place looked like the Wild West towns I saw at the Sunday night movies in the school auditorium. But Wild West life in Ismay didn't have exciting holdups and dangerous shootouts with gunslingers like John Wayne and Tom Mix—just the occasional cowboy fight.

I longed to witness the goings on in the saloons like my peers did, but had to settle for my classmates' reports. Once, I heard that Stub, a short-statured cowboy, didn't like what another cowboy bar patron said to him. So after too many drinks, Stub shot up the big mirror behind the counter with his six-shooter. I peeked through the open door of the saloon on my way to school soon after the incident. Sure enough, the cracked, wall-sized mirror looked like a giant, shiny spider web.

Another time, Stub's adult son, Hunter, bit off a guy's ear in a bar fight. A friend told me the story, but I didn't get to see the one-eared cowboy. Several times I heard about bad parents who'd left their kids in the car while they spent hours drinking in the saloon.

Shootings, bar fights, and kids abandoned in cars were far from my existence. We had no TV until the early 1950s, so I knew only my small world. My parents kept a close eye on my three sisters, my brother and me. My 5'7" dark-haired father might not look threatening to others, but when his piercing blue eyes scrutinized us as he bellowed a command, we listened in fear. Daddy backed up his orders, like having to be home by dinnertime, with a razor strap held in his strong hands, though I don't think he ever used it on any of us.

Other town residents had adventures, but not me. Life within our home acreage distanced us from any wildness in Ismay. My siblings and I stayed away from the townspeople's misdeeds. We were corralled within our home's fences. My adventures happened when I ventured alongside characters I viewed in movies, heard on the radio, or read about in books. I sang in the rain or rode along with the cowboys in the movies projected Sunday nights in the school auditorium. Weekday evenings I followed Lassie to save Timmy and flew with Sky King, my ear glued to the small radio in the kitchen. Mama managed to reduce my summer tedium by convincing the school to open its library to me during the three-month hiatus. Then I mentally traveled to Spain, Italy, and England by reading *Captain from Castille, The Robe,* and *Wuthering Heights.* My world in Ismay was too small for me.

The town's designation came from combining the names of the railroad superintendent's daughters, Isabell and Mabell. I imagined them to also have sedate lives. The railroad company placed a water tower for its passing steam engines in the middle of the prairie, and Ismay was founded. In my town, dogs ran free and neighbors' pigs rooted among weeds in vacant lots. Our family's pig didn't roam the streets. It was corralled at home like me.

We five—Evelyn, Charlene, Patricia, Buddy, and Teri Ann—children of Charles and Ila Kohl, saw a different side of life. Crosses, pictures of the Sacred Heart, and statues of Mary decorated our home and reminded us of important religious rules and rituals.

Each week I confessed my sins and attended mass in Ismay's St. Francis Catholic Church which sat a few feet from the front door of our first house. Sunday school and summer catechism classes taught us that children should behave and adhere to the Ten Commandments. As the eldest of the Kohl siblings, I had to set a good example, but sweets presented a particular challenge.

One Saturday, just after I'd started second grade, the family sat down for supper. Mama remarked that a "juicy roll," the name for the caramel buns she made, had gone missing from the bunch for the following morning's breakfast. I'd sneaked the delicious roll that afternoon from the shelf where they cooled. When I took my place at our round oak table, Mama noticed my sticky hands. Slim at 5'3", she couldn't comprehend my sweet tooth.

"Evelyn," Mama, said, her short blonde curls jiggling around her heart-shaped face, "did you eat one of the juicy rolls?"

"No," I said, hesitating to look at the frown on her slender lips.

"If you disobey or lie," Mama said, hands on her hips, "you won't go to heaven."

I couldn't help it if I found Mama's baked goods irresistible. I thought for a bit, not wanting the sweetness in my mouth to be replaced with the unpleasant taste of soap, the punishment for lying.

"Oh, yes, I will too go to heaven," I said, determined to find a way. Then, looking into my mother's accusing hazel eyes, I said, "I'll just hang onto your hand to get there."

From the sounds of my parents' laughter I understood I'd been forgiven this time.

◇·◇·◇·◇

My angelic behavior continued in summer catechism class the June before I turned ten. Father Hanrahan, a Maryknoll priest, looked at the twelve Catholic children perspiring in the sweltering classroom. His deep brown eyes and furrowed brow indicated a serious topic.

"Who," Father said, standing in front of the class, "has never committed a mortal sin?"

Father held in his hand a rosary he said would shine in the dark—the prize for the right answer. My mind knew what to say. I was a good girl, if looking for adventure wasn't bad. I'd committed plenty of venial sins like talking about others, teasing my sisters, and sassing my mother, but never one of those big ones like stealing, killing, taking God's name in vain, or adultery, whatever that was. I raised my hand for Father's attention.

"I never have," I said, batting innocent blue eyes.

No one else raised a hand. Father smiled and placed the string of prayer beads on my fingers. I skipped home to see if this rosary would really shine in the dark. Like magic, the beads shone bright in the night.

The next week Father asked a different question with another prize. I paid close attention. I loved winning and collecting prizes.

"Who thinks they have a religious vocation," Father Hanrahan said, "to become a priest or a sister?"

I looked longingly at the crystal rosary dangling from his hand. This new set of beads sparkled like a diamond necklace. The pretty trinket called to me as much as Mama's juicy rolls and the shine-in-the-dark rosary. Father sought candidates who wanted to enter his line of work. My parents would be proud if I aspired to join a religious order. And I'd be proud to own another beautiful rosary.

"I do, Father," I said, the first to raise a hand. "I want to be a nun."

The priest passed the glittering object to me. I added the reward to a growing accumulation of religious tokens. The piles of holy keepsakes in my dresser drawer proved my saintliness.

Why, I didn't even swear. Other Ismay kids could cuss, but not my siblings and me. If anyone in Ismay said, "Damn" or worse, "God Damn," when I, or any of my siblings were present, our peers quickly corrected them.

"Oh, you can't swear," they'd say, "when the Kohl kids are here."

The offender then apologized and changed his choice of words. Our religion and our parents didn't permit taking the Lord's name in vain. I figured Mama and Daddy must have made a local rule about not swearing in front of us, and everyone in town agreed.

Each time I won a rosary or other award for my answer in religion class, I marched upstairs to deposit my newest prize in my dresser drawer. The beads lay next to a stack of holy cards and a pile of religious medals embellished with the faces of familiar saints. I compared the bigger and shinier crystal rosary to the one with the pea-sized beads. I fingered the white rosary that glowed in the dark, and I, too, felt radiant. My accumulated wealth of religious items showed I'd recognized the priest's reward system. I could figure out just how much effort I needed to obtain a desired goal.

I prayed with one of my rosaries every Saturday evening when the family knelt in the living room around the sofa my parents had built. I used another on Sundays when we drove eighteen miles to mass at St. Anthony's Catholic Church in Plevna, after our church in Ismay closed. My winning rosaries, praying, and church going added up to a well-known fact—I followed the religious, home, and school rules and set a good example for my younger siblings. I thought I had a religious calling.

Mama read to us every weeknight from *The Lives of the Saints*. I shivered after she'd finished a gory story about a martyr. Visions of Saint Catherine of Siena starving herself, or Saint Sebastian standing in the woods bleeding from arrows stuck into his bare body, flooded my mind. I would jump into bed and huddle under the covers for fear a saint or the Blessed Virgin would appear like ghosts in my bedroom. Religious objects accumulated like the money I saved but didn't protect me from my vivid imagination. They left me content and ready for a time when my life would be mine—unless I decided to become a nun.

Trips and Trip-ups

I'd thought I wanted to enter the religious life from the age of nine. My choice pleased my parents and won me awards from the priests. Adults in my life praised me for saying I had a religious vocation. Based partly on that commitment, I was awarded a four-year scholarship to a Catholic college. I graduated from Holy Names College on June 6, 1964.

On June 14, 1964, I looked around the sparsely furnished cell-like room. The tiny space held a straight-backed wooden chair, a twin-sized bed, and a corner sink. I couldn't see out of the small, high-set windows. Conventlike silence surrounded me.

But I wasn't in a convent. I was in New York City for four days on my way to Peace Corps training at Cornell University in Ithaca. I looked forward to two years of new, stimulating experiences instead of a life filled with chanting, praying, chastity, and obedience. Two of those activities I could have tolerated and two I couldn't.

I enjoyed singing and sometimes praying, if the prayers didn't last too long. I felt less certain about the vows of chastity and obedience. My attraction to young Mexican men made me question remaining celibate the rest of my life. And obeying orders from a Sister Superior would kill my independent spirit. I dreamed of an adventurous, more than a spiritual, future. When the time came to apply for entry into a religious order, I didn't. I applied instead to the Peace Corps.

First, I had to be investigated. The FBI conducted a background check asking my college instructors, neighbors, and employers about me. The government needed assurance I had committed no crimes and would be a successful volunteer. The answers to the FBI's questions must have been acceptable because in February 1964, I received a letter from the Peace Corps assigning me to my first choice, Peru.

I'd requested to go to Peru because of Tom, a student at Stanford. We had walked door to door, weekends during my junior year in college, taking a migrant worker census in small towns near Fresno. I liked handsome, guitar-playing Tom. But one weekend he didn't arrive in Parlier. When I asked Father Cowan, our host, why Tom hadn't come, his answer surprised me.

"Oh, Tom joined the Peace Corps," Father said, "and is in Peru."

So when my Peace Corps application asked to what country I'd like to be assigned, I wrote "Peru." That quick decision affected the rest of my life.

My acceptance letter said that Peace Corps training for Rural Community Action work in Peru would begin on June 18 at Cornell University in New York. Volunteers who were successful during nine weeks at Cornell would go on to three weeks of physical challenges at Camp Radley, Puerto Rico, then two weeks living with families in small Puerto Rican towns. I hadn't been to either New York or Puerto Rico. Now I'd get to to know two new parts of the U.S. I'd never seen.

Mary, my good friend and college carpool buddy, planned June 20 nuptuals to her boyfriend, Dave, and asked me to be her maid of honor. I'd introduced them the year before and wanted to be in the wedding. But the Peace Corps had sent me a $160 plane ticket to fly to New York so I could begin training on June 18. Duty to the U.S. government and traveling adventures meant I couldn't be part of my friend's important day.

Mary asked another friend to be her maid of honor, and I filled my suitcase for a trip to New York City. Into my graduation-gift blue suitcase I packed old and new sneakers, swim and gym suits, casual clothes, and hair rollers. I sewed a couple dresses for Sunday mass and social events and bought a couple more. Immunization records and passport photos went into my new big brown purse along with another graduation gift, an Instamatic camera. A week after college graduation, on June 13, I flew off to New York. I checked into the Barbizon hotel for women in the Big Apple and went up to my small convent-type room. I had four days to tour the city on my own before reporting for Peace Corps training.

I stepped out onto Central Park West Boulevard to the New York noise of honking horns and shouting people. I strolled into Central Park and followed meandering pathways past ponds, bridges, playgrounds, and statues. All around me birds chirped, children laughed, and baby carriages squeaked. Inside the park I found life as peaceful as a Montana hillside.

I walked the park's two-mile length, then stepped back into the bustle of the city. I dropped in at the Metropolitan Museum of Art and viewed a model of the Parthenon and some Rembrandt and Van Gogh paintings. At the Guggenheim, abstract Picasso paintings and the strange gray geometric shapes of Robert Morris puzzled me. I walked south from the museums and looked up at the pure symmetrical beauty of the Empire State Building. I loved the contrast between modern and traditional paintings—and buildings. This city left me breathless. Attending someone's nuptials couldn't compete with the thrill of exploring this city.

I hurried like the fast-walkers on the sidewalks, knowing I had only a few days to see everything. One day I took a ferry to the Statue of Liberty. The cool breeze and water from the harbor bathed my face. I looked at the woman holding a torch and realized her hypnotic quality. Then I said to her, "I understand liberty. Thank God for mine."

Another day I boarded a subway going north to visit the Cloisters. Touring the old monastery brought to mind my childhood decision to become a nun. I contemplated my life in a place away from the world. I appreciated the unique French arechitecture of the chapels. But I felt happy not to have to stay and pray in the beautiful surroundings. Other women could do this but not I.

Upon exiting the medieval structure, the subway system overwhelmed me. How would I get back to my hotel?

"What train," I asked a woman sitting on the stoop of a two-story brick building, "goes to Midtown?"

"Go a few blocks over to 190th Street," she said pointing. "From there take the A train." I thanked her. Contrary to their reputations, I found New Yorkers helpful and friendly.

On June 17, I paid the Barbizon $8 a day for my stay and boarded a Mohawk Airlines flight to Ithaca. My luggage weighed 13 pounds over the 40-pound limit for the small plane. I had packed too much. I paid the extra $1.17 without regret. My pleasure grew when, on my same flight, I met other excited Peace Corps volunteers.

❀

Green vines climbed over old stone buildings at Cornell. Gnarled oak trees dotted the parklike university campus. I walked across expansive green lawns to a rocky cliff on the edge of the grounds and found a creek meandering below. Creeks attracted me. Nature's beauty plus the co-ed setting gave me the right balance of outer beauty and inner anticipation. Cascadilla Hall, a mid-1800s ivy-covered six-story building, housed my Peace Corps group. I liked my East Coast summer home.

One-hundred-and-two new Peace Corps recruits lined up for photographs on Day One. Our faces would be published alongside autobiographical sketches in the Peru RCA/Tools directory and in our hometown newspapers. To my amazement, 20 percent of the volunteers came from California.

On Day Two we received the first of twenty immunizations. My arms hurt and the typhus, smallpox, and some other shots administered at the same time made me sick. Then came more challenges. The next day instructors told us to swim a lap around Cornell's Olympic-sized pool.

I'd never learned to swim in Montana. Mama hadn't allowed my siblings and me to enter Fallon Creek for fear we might contract polio from sewage dumped into the stream. Still, I leapt into Cornell's pool and stayed afloat by dog paddling along the circumference. Others volunteers zoomed past me. Panting and paddling, I managed to finish the swim. Surely I'd passed the test. Not the case.

"Now do the backstroke," the instructor barked. "All the way around."

Surprised, I took a deep breath, turned onto my back and moved my arms like I saw the others doing as they quickly sliced through the water before they hopped out of the pool. I slogged along. Water sloshed into my mouth. I grabbed onto the pool's side and stopped to cough liquid from my lungs. Above me, an instructor holding a long pole followed along the deck. He appeared ready to fish me out at any minute.

"Do you want to get out?" he said after one of my coughing spells.

"No," I sputtered, "I can make it."

No way would I quit. He'd send me home just because I couldn't swim. Not what I wanted. So I continued inching my way to the end, then lifted my tired body from the pool. I felt like a drowned rat.

"You're going to take swimming lessons," the man with the pole said.

"Yes," I said coughing up more water. I wanted to learn to swim the right way.

The most physically challenging part of my days happened every morning at 6:30 a.m., when we gathered in the parking lot for calisthenics after which we ran two miles up and down the campus hills. A girl from Oregon usually led the runners. She was a welcome example to me that women could be good athletes. I managed to keep up with the pack. Much to my surprise, after a month, I'd lost weight from all the exercise—without dieting.

Much of our training turned out to be everything I'd done growing up in Montana—raising and butchering animals, growing vegetables, baking bread, and understanding small communities. Another class, First Aid, I already knew from my recent experience in Mexico. Other lessons consisted of hours of Spanish language training and lectures about Peruvian history and culture. I took it all in, though staying awake during the thirteen-hour days became a challenge.

Week One, we took a series of psychological tests, such as the Minnesota Multiphasic Personality Inventory. The MMPI repeated similar, differently-phrased, questions. I'd encountered the test in my college psychology classes. I gave each item my full attention. One guy from our group said he wrote, "See my previous answer" next to the similar questions. The program sent him packing. His attitude would never be mine.

All trainees had two individual sessions with mental health professionals. I had few concerns. The prospect of an assigned psychologist asking me questions interested me.

"What do you think of your father?" the doctor asked.

A truly Freudian inquiry, I thought. I didn't have to ponder long for an answer. "My father and I have a close relationship," I responded. "He supports my studies, and I help him build things."

We talked about family, school, and my opinions. My session seemed to be going well. Still the process of remaining in the program was unclear.

"How does one get selected out?" I asked.

"The mental health professionals recommend whether or not a volunteer has the mental fortitude to do well in an undeveloped country," he said. "If someone appears unlikely to be successful, he or she gets deselected and has to leave."

I felt anxiety well up inside me. I frowned. More than anything, I didn't want to have to leave. I enjoyed everything about this new endeavor.

"I don't think," the psychiatrist added, "you have anything to worry about."

His words reassured me and I breathed a sigh of relief. Our syllabus for for rural community development said volunteers would need to develop projects in their future placements. To do that, we needed to be ambitious, outgoing, and tolerant. If we weren't, we'd likely be unhappy in a foreign country. The assessment team looked for resourceful volunteers who had some technical skills and knew the culture and language of the country they'd go to. I kept this in the front of my mind taking in whatever was taught. I wanted to demonstrate my determination.

I hadn't been in classes with men at Holy Names, an all-women's college. Now fifty-seven males surrounded me daily in our courses. I felt too self-conscious to speak up in class, but I enjoyed discussing current events with the guys individually. We discussed the bombing of Vietnam and the anti-U.S. riots in the Panama Canal Zone. Like me, they agreed we Peace Corps volunteers had found a more constructive way to help solve world differences. We would begin by getting to know the people in far-off countries.

Several guys on campus asked me on dates, like Larry, a fellow Californian. I enjoyed their innocent attentions, but not that of Señor Alfonso, my first Spanish teacher. The first day in his class, when I couldn't translate a phrase, he changed my seat to one next to him.

"I don't understand," I complained to Eliot, "why the instructor moved me to the desk right next to him. My performance is no worse than others in class."

"If you don't realize why," Eliot answered, smiling, "you are quite naive."

A few days later the instructor asked me to translate a sentence I thought suggestive.

"Will you go to the theater with me?" the instructor asked. I resisted giving a response. Maybe this was an actual invitation. Señor Alfonso's head nodded for me to answer "*Sí.*" I felt relieved when he didn't follow up by insisting I go somewhere with him.

How could I persevere under the duress of this aggressive teacher? Spanish lessons filled half our day and even our lunch and dinnertimes. It seemed our language instructors accompanied us day and night. Teachers made certain we spoke Spanish at all times, even in the cafeteria. Our first meals were surprisingly silent as we attempted to communicate our thoughts in a new language. My class headed to the cafeteria one day for lunch. My Spanish teacher walked next to me.

"Five foot two, eyes of blue," Señor Alfonso sang.

My face warmed with embarrassment. The description fit me, but I didn't like his attention. It seemed juvenile and I wanted to run.

My instructor's caramel-colored face and dark eyes made him attractive, but he was my teacher. His behavior seemed too aggressive. He found ways to be near me at breakfast, lunch, dinner, and evenings in the dorm lounge. I expressed annoyance when he grabbed my camera and refused to return it. He invited me to his weekend parties. I didn't go. Señor Alfonso went beyond his duties. A teacher should keep us practicing the language, I thought, not asking provocative questions and pestering female students.

One evening as the class ate dinner together, a female volunteer approached our table. She had a message for my Spanish teacher.

"Your wife called," the girl said. "She left a message for you to call back."

Señor Alfonso frowned. He'd been found out. Married. His antics with me ended. Señor Alfonso's behavior reinforced my opinion that Latin men tended to be unfaithful. They enjoyed the pursuit and the conquest but not the commitment. The following week, the powers that be moved me to a higher-level Spanish class. I welcomed the change.

❖❖❖❖

The Peace Corps assigned Judy as my roommate in Cascadilla Hall. She seldom slept in our dorm room and acted more worldly than I did. At first, I couldn't figure her out. Judy's scrawny body and long face didn't make her especially attractive, but apparently she possessed other qualities men liked. When we got to know one another better, she explained.

"Evelyn," Judy said tossing her long, stringy, brown hair. "I sleep with whatever man is interested in me."

I tried not to look shocked by her statement. I had crushes on guys and often appreciated their attention, but I didn't pursue them. Seven years in Catholic schools had left me wary about intimacy with the male species.

"I'll be spending tonight with Señor Alfonso," Judy announced one evening in our Cornell dorm room.

I'd heard rumors about Judy sleeping with our instructors, but I didn't know she'd moved on to my former Spanish teacher. Apparently, marriage didn't keep Señor Alfonso from dating and sleeping with other women.

Shortly after Judy spent that night with Señor Alfonso, she was sent home for being "too friendly with staff." She'd slept with one too many of the instructors. Others had left, too, for different reasons. Eighty-one remained. Which of our group would be left for our next set of challenges in Puerto Rico?

Roughing It

Twenty-three of the original one-hundred-two trainees had departed the program by the end of two months at Cornell. Two female students returned home to boyfriends. Another's allergies became a medical liability. A few decided they couldn't live for two years without running water, electricity, or bathrooms. Why they hadn't realized this before applying for "the toughest job you'll ever love" I didn't understand. I'd certainly considered these "inconveniences" and determined that one sometimes had to suffer a bit in order to do good. Small sacrifice for a life of adventure and noble purpose.

The rumor mill reported various reasons for volunteers being selected out. "Too young," stated the letter of dismissal to a nineteen-year-old guy who hadn't gone to college. Five male volunteers were deemed "immature." One of them "didn't get along with others." Another was said to be "obnoxious." One female volunteer changed to a group going to Africa, her choice when she'd first applied. In another case, the volunteer should have switched countries. She had "an inability to learn Spanish," a prerequisite for service in South America. I suspected some of the males had applied to the Peace Corps to avoid being drafted and sent to Vietnam.

Camp Radley, Puerto Rico, would be the next stop for the remaining seventy-nine of us. We flew from Kennedy Airport and arrived in San Juan, just as Hurricane Dora left. Our ground transportation couldn't get through the flooded roads to the Camp in the Arecibo countryside so, to my delight, we had a free day in the Puerto Rican capital. Larry and I toured the 400-year-old El Morro fort, then Old San Juan where we went shopping. Larry found the perfect pair of pearl earrings for me to buy.

Camp Radley lay sixty-seven miles west of San Juan in a lush tropical forest preserve. Ferns, giant bamboo groves, and palm trees shaded wood barracks and an open-air dining hall. Tiny inch-long coqui frogs sang "*ko-kee*." Their songs lulled me to sleep each night in my dorm-type screened cabin. During the day, I stepped over sunning iguanas on my way to the latrines.

Our days started at 6 a.m. with calisthenics and a mile run up and down the hills, a routine similar to Cornell's, except the camp had dirt roads, not paved. We had no flush toilets or hot water. No matter. I'd been without conveniences at the first ranch where I worked in Montana. Here, showering in cold water wasn't so bad if done during the hot, muggy daytime. I relished the opportunity to live on this tropical island. I didn't feel the same about rock climbing.

On a hot afternoon I looked up with trepidation at a cliff-face made of solid rock. Eliot had scampered to the top with little problem. Now he had to help get me up to where he sat. He had been in my Spanish classes and played host to a group of us at his Boston home over the July 4 holiday. But this climbing exercise proved harder than conjugating a Spanish verb or finding the Boston Esplanade. I'd clambered up the sides of dry gullies with ease in my childhood in Montana, but these cliffs in Puerto Rico's Cordillera went straight up. And they had sharp, protruding rocks.

I hesitated. I usually depended on myself. Our handsome redheaded instructor told me to have faith in my colleagues. But Eliot didn't look strong enough to pull me up thirty feet. Others on my team stood at the top encouraging me. I didn't want to fail them. So I put my feet through the two rope loops that formed a harness around my bottom. From there, the cord threaded through a couple of carabiners and into Eliot's hands at the top. I tied my end of the cord tightly around my waist and took a deep breath.

"Belay up!" I shouted to Eliot and braced my feet horizontally so my body made an "L" shape against the rock. Eliot pulled on the rope. My boots slipped, and I jerked back down. Rats!

"Whoa," I yelled.

Maybe I weighed too much, or wore too-new footwear, or Eliot was too weak to pull me up. Thank heavens I fell a short enough distance to land on solid soil. If I slipped farther up I could bang my face into the rock.

"Come on," Eliot encouraged, peering down at me through his glasses. "You can do it."

"I want to," I answered, my face perspiring and hot. "But I might be too heavy for you."

"I am heavier than you are," he said, "and Larry pulled me up."

Of course Larry did. Larry was bigger and probably stronger than Eliot. I doubted Elliot was any heavier than me. How could he pull up someone of equal size?

"OK," I said, looking up into the hot Puerto Rican sun. "Belay up."

This time I planted my feet firmly against the cliff's jagged edges. I pulled on the rope above me with my left hand, fed the bottom portion to my right hand, and inched my way to the top, walking up the cliff face like I was striding on a ramp. Group members clapped when I arrived. I felt relief and surprise at the same time, but I didn't have time to revel in my accomplishment—my turn to pull up the next team member.

Over the next days we summited ever higher rock faces and after that rappelled ninety feet down a cliff. Each new task tested my mental and physical limits and challenged my fear of heights. However, with each success, my confidence and skill grew. I learned I could be both self-reliant and dependent upon others.

Our final challenge, rappelling down the face of Dos Bocas Dam, was optional. Descending the concrete wall of a dam would be like plunging down the side of a thirty-story skyscraper. I looked three-hundred-fifty-feet down from the narrow walkway at the top of the dam. Volunteers standing at the bottom looked like ants. I pulled back. Whenever I peered over the edge, I experienced vertigo and a churning in my stomach. Unlike climbing the cliffs, not every volunteer attempted this challenge. I would. I just wouldn't look down.

I trussed up in the harness and slipped over the edge of the walkway, trembling. The technique of loosening the rope as I descended was now familiar. I pushed my body a few feet away from the slab of concrete with my boots. The rope slid through my gloved hands faster and faster. Within minutes I landed on solid ground and let out a whoop of victory. I had conquered another fear and accomplished more than I thought possible. My decision to join the Peace Corps had opened me to new understanding of what I could do.

I'd only recently learned to swim. In Puerto Rico, I managed to swim a lap with my legs tied and "drown proof" by remaining afloat for hours. Others in my group had grown up swimming and somehow swam with all their limbs tied. I couldn't believe their accomplishments in the water—or mine.

Repelling Down the Dam

Members of each team had to dive down eleven feet to the bottom of the pool and retrieve a foot-long tire fragment. Everyone on the team was required to complete all the dives. Other members of my group dove to the bottom with ease and retrieved the piece of rubber on the first try. I couldn't dive deeper than a few feet. Each time I grew close to the bottom, I panicked and feared I would drown. Time after time, I aborted my effort. Triumphing over my fear of heights seemed easier than overcoming the panic I felt in deep water.

Finally, with my team's encouragement, I held my breath, dove down and grabbed the damn piece of tire. The team showered me with praise. I could be brave in the face of great obstacles. I'd gone from not knowing how to swim two months before to diving deep into the pool. I'd pushed against my mental and physical limits.

Toward the end of our month in Puerto Rico, we hiked five miles through the jungle, eating only what we could find. We dined on green bananas, plant tubers, sweet limes, oranges, breadfruit, and guava juice. I couldn't bring myself to eat the snails. This was preparation for our final jungle challenge.

Each of us was dropped off alone to spend a night in the tropical forest to survive on what we found. First, I wove myself a hammock from vines that hung from the palm trees. No lizard, frog, or other creepy crawler would slither over me in my high-up platform. I felt like a queen, lying safe on my bed three feet above the jungle floor, eating the contraband chocolate bar I'd smuggled in my pocket. Then morning dawned. I shook out my sleeping bag and out dropped a scorpion. The poisonous insect must have slept at my feet all night without biting me. I figured the scorpion hadn't injected me with its venom because Scorpio is my astrological sign. Lucky me!

⊸·⊂·⊃·⊂

We left Camp Radley for a two-week stay with a Puerto Rican family. Four of my fellow female volunteers and I were sent to the west side of the island to live in Aguada. Our host was a young-looking woman who lived with her three children in a small four-room wooden shack with a shower and an outdoor latrine. The children gave their bedroom to us and they slept in the combination dining-living room.

We five volunteers slept together in three beds. The first morning, loud crowing awakened me. I looked between the wood slats of the wall to see a large red rooster with long tail feathers strutting like he owned the place. Then I noticed the huge, four-inch, hairy, gray spiders crawling across our bedroom walls. I'd had roosters wake me and often chase me in Montana, but here I needed to become accustomed to giant spiders. And the spiders and other insects came in too many numbers to kill. I hated the insects and the fowls but liked the family.

The family's yard looked a mess, with garbage thrown into many pits. I saw rats running from some holes. One day I decided to surprise the mother of the family with a clean yard when she returned from work. With the help of the children I removed much of the garbage from the ground depressions and swept the dirt yard with a broom. The mother didn't look as pleased as we were when she saw her spruced-up domain. I found out later that Puerto Ricans composted leftover food by putting it into yard pits. We'd undone much of the mother's work, and the children hadn't known how to tell me. This incident taught me not to impose my standards on other cultures before first determining their customs.

Two of my Peace Corps roommates had majored in Spanish in college but rarely spoke the language. They feared making mistakes. I, on the other hand, didn't always know the errors I made in Spanish. Furthermore, I took the lead in projects, eager to use what Spanish I knew. I read books in Spanish to the local children who corrected my pronunciation without criticism. Their nonjudgmental ways made me less hesitant to talk to townspeople.

One such local was Gilberto, a young man my age who had recently served in the U.S. Navy. The helpful, protective, dark-haired young man always seemed to be by my side. He guided me around his community teaching me new Spanish vocabulary and expressing his political views. I liked Gilberto's intellectual curiosity and detected that he seemed lost about what to do next with his life. I encouraged him to finish college. When the time arrived for me to leave Aguada, my Spanish had improved, and Gilberto had enrolled in college. My friend told me he wanted me to stay. Thinking of Larry, I said I already had a boyfriend.

"I hope you become Mrs. Larry," he said, "and have eleven children."

"I don't think that's going to happen," I said, as I packed my suitcase and headed toward the garbage with a pair of my dirty canvas sneakers. "I have too many places I want to go."

"If you're going to throw away your worn-out tennis shoes," Gilberto said watching, "give them to me as a remembrance. I'm going to wash them and keep them forever."

I gave him the shoes. I wondered if he would have them bronzed.

◦─◦·◦─◦

An additional nine members of our training group were selected out after Puerto Rico. Reasons varied. A young man, obsessed with bull fighting, apparently had a death wish. One woman, said to be "too dependent on the group," left. She had run with a tight clique called "The Bobbseys," nicknamed after a popular series of juvenile novels. One woman left to marry the trek master we had in Puerto Rico. We didn't learn the reasons for the others' eliminations.

The seventy remaining members of our Rural Community Action group scheduled our flights home from San Juan. Each of us had two weeks to pack and return to New York by October 8. Then we would fly together to Peru. I was given the choice of a stopover on my way home to California. It took me only a moment to decide—I'd visit the friends I'd made in Mexico the previous summer. But I did a poor job of calculating how much time I had to visit both Mexico City and Apaseo el Grande and had trouble meeting my family commitments and leaving for Peru on time.

Detour

I stepped off Pan Am flight 255 into a Mexico City night. I looked above the crowd for the tall, slim, black-haired university student I'd met on a weekend excursion a year ago. Inocente had taught me to body surf in the warm waters off Acapulco. Over the past year we'd written letters to one another—Inocente's in English and mine in Spanish. Our relationship had grown faster than our fluency in one another's native tongues.

In a telegram I'd sent from Puerto Rico, I told Inocente that my plane from Puerto Rico would arrive in Mexico City at eleven o'clock. Shortly after that hour, I entered the airport lobby and spotted my friend's tired, smiling face.

"Hola," I shouted to him with glee when his brown eyes met mine.

Inocente hurried toward me and gave me a hug. I'd forgotten what broad shoulders he had. He looked more handsome than I remembered.

"Finally you're here," he said. "Your telegram only said you'd arrive at eleven. You didn't say it was eleven at night. I've been waiting since eleven this morning."

My delight at seeing him turned to embarrassment. I'd neglected to tell him in which part of the day I'd arrive. But Inocente didn't look upset. He escorted me to a nice hotel—so respectable that men were not allowed to accompany single women beyond the lobby. Consequently, my friend kissed me goodnight at the entrance and said he'd call for me in the morning.

The next two days we rode buses around the city in a whirlwind of sightseeing and shopping. Inocente took me to see the University of Mexico where he studied engineering. I gazed in awe at the mosaic on the library façade that Inocente said represented ancient Mexican culture. The complex, colorful designs fascinated me.

When I said I needed to shop for clothes, Inocente took me to a marketplace he knew and then waited patiently while I found just the right garment and tried it on. Next, he bargained with the vendor so I could pay the cheapest price. He found bookstores where I stocked up on children's books and phonograph records I could use in Peru.

Evenings he took me to dinner where the mariachis played. My head lay on his shoulder as I dozed on the bus ride taking us back to my hotel. I loved being with this polite, considerate, and helpful young man.

Shopping expenditures began to deplete my cash supply. I had enough currency to buy the pretty pink suit I tried on if I moved from my expensive hotel to a cheaper place. I explained my financial dilemma to Inocente. He suggested I move to a hotel near the bus station. I'd be leaving on a Tres Estrellas bus from the station the following day to visit Apaseo el Grande. I didn't question my companion's choice of accommodations.

My final evening in Mexico City, the local bus dropped my friend and me off in front of a dingy, battered-looking hotel. Inocente registered the room in his name. I thought that strange.

"It isn't good for a single girl," he said, "to check into this type of place by herself. Now, no matter what you do, don't open the door for anyone tonight."

Puzzled, I didn't question my protector. He kissed me good-bye outside my room and wished me well in Peru. We promised to continue corresponding. I bolted my hotel room door. The next morning, I received surprised stares and some remarks upon leaving my room. I'd stayed in a hotel frequented by prostitutes.

◦·◦·◦·◦

In Apaseo I renewed acquaintances with girlfriends and the Hernández family with whom I'd lived the summer before. I'd forgotten how much I missed my caring Mexican friends. I had no time to search for my male friends, Sergio and Juan. My heart now belonged to Inocente.

One of the girlfriends told me my mother had called and left messages with a family in Apaseo. Mama didn't sound happy on the line when I reached her.

"Are you coming home anytime soon?" Mama asked, irritation in her voice. "I've sent out invitations for an October 4 farewell party for you."

I hadn't realized until then that she didn't know my precise whereabouts or when I'd return to California. I'd made the decision to swing by Mexico on my way home from Puerto Rico because the stopover cost me nothing. But I'd upset Mama's plans.

"I just want to see some of my friends," I said, "then I'll fly back in plenty of time. I still have to pack my trunk for Peru, you know."

◦·◦·◦·◦

I flew across Mexico and Southern California, back to my family. Friends wished me goodbye at my farewell party. I packed their gifts and items I'd need for the next two years into a trunk and a suitcase. The suitcase held mostly dresses I'd made and a couple warm jackets and pairs of slacks. The new sturdy trunk was filled to the brim with suggested items from a list handed out in training—rubber boots, a typewriter, a battery-powered phonograph, a hectograph for making copies, and small cooking utensils. I added a few classical music LPs to the Spanish language records and children's books I'd bought in Mexico.

Packing for Peru

Letters awaited me in California from Flavio, the young man who'd serenaded me during the bus trip from Tijuana to Guadalajara the previous summer. I'd received a few friendly letters from him during the past year, but nothing he'd written prepared me for his declaration.

"Very soon I will come to California," Flavio wrote, "to ask your father for your hand in marriage."

His letter startled me, but I didn't have time to write him or any of my Mexican suitors. I had to ship the trunk full of necessities to Peru, then fly there myself. And I needed to make peace with my constant distraction of the enticing, young Latin men who passed through my life. Was this something I could manage better in Peru?

A New Country

The Peace Corps Director for Peru distributed a partial list of area assignments at the beginning of Day Two of our group's weeklong orientation in Lima. Under the heading "Cusco Area," I read my name and smiled. Five women and seven men from our group of seventy would be sent to the mountains. Several volunteers assigned to coastal cities complained, saying they preferred appointments to the Andes. They probably didn't realize there were fewer conveniences in Sierra areas compared to those in the developed coastal cities. I welcomed the challenge.

My assignment wouldn't throw me into culture shock. In fact, a less developed area of the country would be an ideal assignment for me. After all, I'd been raised in a small Montana town and had lived in rural Mexico for a summer.

At 6 a.m. the morning of October 13, 1964, I boarded the Faucett Airlines DC-6, relieved to leave the humidity and darkness of Lima behind. We lifted off and the plane's propellers drilled a path through the thick, gray haze hanging over the city. As soon as the plane broke through the bank of clouds, we faced a rising sun that flooded the cabin with its warm rays. In another two hours I'd be in the Inca Empire area that natives called "the navel of the world." My heart raced with anticipation.

The red-and-white fuselage leveled off above the cloud cover that looked like a huge overstuffed mattress. Sunlight danced from one snow-capped peak to another as our plane sped over the Andes. Then the air became clear, and the clouds disappeared. Below, I saw deep valleys of terraced green fields climbing up steep mountainsides. I dreamed of my exciting life in this new, exotic country, my imagination soaring with the altitude of the plane.

The voice of a female Peace Corps volunteer in the front of the plane broke my reverie. The woman talked too loud to the point of becoming obnoxious. No doubt she'd drunk too many Pisco Sours, a popular alcoholic drink. Thank heavens she wasn't part of my group.

"Sharon, pipe down," her male seatmate said, holding the woman's arms as she attempted to stand.

"Let go of me," Sharon shouted to the arm holder, slurring her words and struggling to get out of his grip. "You go sit across over there. I don't want you to sit by me."

Occasional laughter from those around Sharon encouraged her bad manners. After another drink she finally sat down and her volume lowered a bit. But her chattering continued. Volunteers from my group cringed and crouched down in their seats, not wanting to be identified with this "ugly American."

I returned to my view from the window. Ribbons of rivers ran by villages that dotted deep green valleys. I could see fields of yellow in the few flat areas between mountains. The majesty of the country unfolding below captivated me. We flew low over a sea of reddish-tan tiled roofs broken by threads of streets running up and down steep hills. We had arrived in Cusco.

The plane landed and taxied to a stop. We walked down the stairs into the thin air of Cusco's twelve-thousand-foot altitude. The air, smells, quaint airport, the people—how different. Even in Mexico I'd never seen anyone like the short, narrow-eyed men with high cheek bones crowding around us offering to carry our suitcases.

Taxis, arranged by the Cusco regional director's secretary, whisked us along a paved thoroughfare to our hotel. The people sauntering along the sidewalks struck me as a strange mix. Some wore western clothes with shiny leather shoes, but many were barefoot and wore what looked to be hand-woven hats, skirts, and trousers.

Our small group settled into a hotel on the main street, Avenida Sol. I set off with two other female volunteers to explore the city before our scheduled two o'clock orientation meeting. We ignored warnings that we should first adjust to the high altitude. That turned out well enough. The difficulty breathing slowed me down so I could take in my surroundings.

Lima had resembled all large cities I'd seen—high concrete buildings towering overhead and darting taxis with blaring horns hurrying along nondescript streets. Cusco, built on hills like my home area of San Francisco, looked more rustic than any place I'd ever been to. It was everything Lima wasn't—compact, sunny, surrounded by mountains and filled with exotic architecture and people. Having been raised in the quiet of the Montana country-side and the calm of a California suburb, I found Cusco neither quiet nor calm. The only smell I recognized was the familiar earthy odor of soil. I found the strangeness of my new country captivating.

Avenida Sol, a crowded four-lane thoroughfare and main business area, teemed with polluting trucks and honking Volks-wagen beetles. The Avenida, one of the city's few paved roads, ran two miles from the airport to the Plaza de Armas in the center of town. There, two Spanish-style churches built on foundations of huge limestone boulders loomed over the main plaza on adjacent sides. Incans had built the impenetrable walls in the thirteenth century. The builders had fit the stones together so tightly, without mortar or use of metal tools, a pin couldn't be lodged between them. Four centuries later, invading Spaniards used the boulder walls as foundations for their churches and other buildings. Each time Cusco had a major earthquake registering over 7.0, the churches fell but the walls stayed upright. Strong foundations built by sturdy people.

Scores of small, leather-skinned men of Incan ancestry ran up and down the cobblestone streets carrying huge bundles. They carted market merchandise, food, or wood on their bent backs. The women wore several calf-length skirts, one on top of another, made of bright blue, black, or red homespun wool. One-inch bands in all colors of the rainbow trimmed their outfits. Matching waist-length jackets with white buttons ran down their lapels and made for a pretty, yet unique, type of suit. My eyes widened in amazement.

Each man and woman wore one of a variety of hats. Which hat they wore, I learned, indicated the town they came from. The men wore knicker-type britches in neutral colors ranging from gray to black that contrasted with the colorful ponchos thrown over their shoulders. If they weren't barefoot, the natives wore sandals made from recycled tires. I had come to the right country for a unique experience.

An Aztec warrior statue stood atop the fountain in the center of the Plaza de Armas—a mix-up by the French vendor. A statue of an Inca warrior existed somewhere in Mexico. The statue was as out of place as I felt.

At the afternoon meeting, the regional director and our boss, Mr. Cavendish, said he hadn't been aware there would be a new group of volunteers needing placements, so he had none ready. No one seemed concerned. Peace Corps volunteers had to be flexible. And I too could wait for a permanent assignment in this exotic world.

Finding a Place

One by one other volunteers departed to live in their assigned towns. Rick, assigned to a small Quechua-speaking community, said the townspeople ignored him, probably because he didn't speak their language. His hut had a dirt floor and thatched roof with mice running across both. But his room overlooked a green valley surrounded by 16,000-foot snow-capped peaks, which I thought breathtaking. At least he had an assignment. I still awaited my chance, my opportunity, my placement.

Colleagues Karen, Marilyn, and Skeeter asked to be placed together. They ended up in Compone in a house on the Pampa de Anta, steps from the Cusco-Lima road. Their two-story, dirt-floor house had no water, so they carried what they needed from a nearby stream. Unlike Rick, the women seemed to like their place. Maybe because they hadn't been greeted by many rodents. And still I waited.

The second week in Cusco, the regional director informed me that I would be placed in Acomayo with Sharon. Whenever I asked other volunteers about her, a look of pity came over their faces. If they commented at all they said something like, "If she takes a liking to you, there won't be much trouble. But if she doesn't, then you'd better transfer." Others thought her to be bossy and lazy and someone who had trouble adjusting to Peace Corps life. Then I recalled seeing Sharon on the plane from Lima to Cusco, where she had displayed drunken, loud behavior. I'd been relieved she wasn't part of my group. I didn't want to be placed with her.

While awaiting my destiny with or without Sharon, I gradually became acquainted with Marie. Like me, she had no assignment. She'd trained in my group at Cornell but had run around with "The Bobbseys," a tight-knit clique, so I hadn't gotten to know her well. Now we were the last two without assignments, so we spent more time with each other, often eating together.

I liked this tall, slim, southern belle from Georgia. My new hazel-eyed friend spoke fluent Spanish, because up to the age of twelve, she'd lived near Guadalajara, Mexico, where her father had managed a textile plant. Marie had belonged to a college sorority, which may have been why her medium-length auburn hair was always well-coifed. She took more care of her appearance than I did. I'd been raised in rural Montana and educated in the casual San Francisco Bay Area. To my mind, women needed little makeup to trudge down Peru's dusty roads. I seldom even wore lipstick. Compared to Marie, I looked like a country bumpkin. Still we hit it off and wanted to be placed together.

Mr. Cavendish initially said Marie would be assigned to Chacán along with several others, including her ex-boyfriend. She didn't like her proposed placement any better than I liked mine with Sharon. At lunch one day we ran into a couple of volunteers who, in February, would be coming to the end of their assignments teaching preschool in Quillabamba.

"Let's ask Mr. C," I said, "if we can take their place."

Marie nodded. We thought we had backgrounds that made us ideal replacements for the teachers. We approached the director. He didn't agree. He said eight volunteers in Quillabamba were enough to meet that town's needs. Mr. Cavendish maintained his decision that I work in either Acomayo with Sharon or in Accha, a town beyond Acomayo that had requested volunteers. He instructed me to drive out to see the towns with Norm, a veteran Peace Corps volunteer. Marie decided to look over the sites with me in case we could be placed together. We left the next morning.

The beat-up Peace Corps jeep wound through dusty towns and up steep mountains for five hours. The brakes smoked from overheating and the gas tank leaked. Norm plugged the leak with bubblegum. We finally arrived in Acomayo and stopped at Sharon's. She recommended we set off immediately if we wanted to see Accha in the daylight. So we drove for another hour to the town of Pilpinto, where the road ended. There we happened upon a priest who lived in Accha. He said we should go up the mountain to the community the next morning. He'd have horses sent down for us. We returned to spend the night in Acomayo with Sharon.

Over a dinner of baking powder biscuits and Spam with cheese, Sharon told us tales of how men in the town misunderstood her having drinks with them. Even the married mayor assumed she wanted sex. Once, the mayor said he needed Sharon's assistance in finding some person. With that pretext, one evening after they'd both had a few drinks, she and the mayor walked along Acomayo's river. With no provocation, the mayor accosted her. She screamed and got away but was so drunk she fell in the river twice and bruised her legs. That same night, after her ordeal, two of her new male friends knocked on her door, also drunk. She became hysterical and cried so hard that they left. Sharon's world of drama overwhelmed me. I hadn't come to Peru to live with a wild American whose reputation would tarnish mine.

Marie, Norm, and I arose at 5:30 the next morning so we could meet our horses in Pilpinto at seven. Neither men nor horses awaited us. So we walked up the path until 8:45, when we saw the priest and three horses coming toward us. The animals were thin, small, and slow, but had four working legs. They didn't collapse when we climbed onto their bare backs. The dirt path became so narrow that only one scraggly horse could pass through at a time. Our legs brushed the sides of the cliffs. My horse struggled up the steep incline ahead of Marie's.

"How do you think we'll get our bedsprings up here?" I shouted back to Marie.

"With great difficulty," Marie yelled to me. "Maybe we should rethink this."

Ferns waved along the sides, and bushes with small pink roses greeted us as we continued our climb. Our tedious ride took us to a plateau just below a mountain. There, expansive green fields of vegetation spread out on a wide, fertile plain. We were wowed at the magnificent Andean snowcaps glistening in the sun. We rode across rushing streams of pristine water that ran from the mountains. We stopped to let the horses drink while we admired the blue and white flowers in nearby fields. I recalled my early journey to find the source of water in Ismay and smiled. Back then, I could never have imagined a place as beautiful as this.

After three hours winding around mountains and fording streams, little Accha opened out in front of us. The town's few adobe buildings looked like miniatures on the large, flat, green pampa. All else appeared small compared to the high Andes. Now to attend to the business of settling here.

We set about finding the village leaders. Norm asked around until we located those in charge. They, in turn, told us about a vacant house we could rent. Inquiries revealed that the town needed a steady source of poultry. So we developed a plan to live on the second floor of the rented building and raise chickens on the first level's dirt floor. We located water and bathroom facilities two blocks away from our future flat. Not too bad.

A friendly family invited us for a meal of *chicharrónes*, seasoned and fried chunks of pork, with potatoes and corn. The two big dogs wandering around our table helped us eat the undercooked meat that we offered them when no one was looking. Then the discussion caught my attention. The locals said that during the winter rains, the path to the main road became an impassable river that took much longer than the usual three hours to navigate. In addition, only one truck a week left from the road at Pilpinto to a town called Acos. And one truck departed daily from Acos for Acomayo. The town seemed too isolated and maybe not the place we should live.

On the three-hour walk back down to the road to Pilpinto, Marie and I discussed our concerns. The inconsistent transportation would be worrisome. How could we get to a doctor if we had an appendicitis attack or some major injury or illness? For sure we'd need horses for transportation. Both of us longed for a place to live and work. We'd give Accha a try.

Hotels had been our home for the past three weeks, and we wanted a town and home of our own. First, however, we needed the director's permission to be stationed together. Marie and I arrived at the Peace Corps office at six, the morning after we returned from our exploratory trip. Mr. Cavendish rushed into his office at 7:15.

"I have to leave right away," he said, glancing at us while he gathered papers from his desk. "My train for Puno leaves in fifteen minutes."

"Marie and I would like to be placed together," I said, ignoring his impatience.

"I'm late already," Mr. Cavendish said, not hearing me as he dashed from the oversized wooden desk to the metal filing cabinet. "I have to check on volunteers in Puno."

"We saw Accha," Marie said, following our director with her voice, "and we could raise chickens there for the community."

"That's fine," Mr. Cavendish said, looking for something, "You two can be stationed there together."

"We'd be nine hours away from a doctor, not the required seven," I said, pleased we could be placed together but concerned about distances. "There's just a dirt trail up the mountain. No road."

The director didn't react. Apparently, he had no time to discuss transportation to Accha. We'd pestered our boss for half a month about a place in which to do our community development work. Now he seemed tired of us. He'd have six hours on the train to think about the Puno volunteers, but couldn't give us a few minutes. Mr. C's lack of interest in our fate disappointed me.

"We'll need horses." I said in my most urgent voice, "to get to the nearest road three hours away."

Mr. C stopped gathering papers and looked up. His furrowed brow made me think he might be having second thoughts about assigning us to such a remote area. We'd certainly caught his attention.

"Horses are out of the question," the director said. "The Peace Corps has jeeps, not livestock."

With that, he hurried off to check on other, more important volunteers. Marie and I resigned ourselves to hiking up and down the mountains of Accha on foot. But then, as we began our preparations for living there, a handsome man from paradise came to our rescue.

Saved

An exhaust-spewing city bus transported Marie and me from the Peace Corps office to the Cusco home of the woman who owned the Accha apartment. Bargaining secured us a rental price of fifty *soles* for the second-floor living space and fifty for the ground-level dirt floor room—a total, affordable six dollars a month.

We set about gathering the items we'd need to furnish our new home. Among the dwindling provisions at the Peace Corps warehouse we found silverware, beds, sheets, a small table and chairs, and a few saucepans—leftovers from volunteers who'd finished their commitments. The rest would have to be purchased with our $100-a-month stipend.

In a hardware store on Avenida Sol we purchased a blue pail and basin for carrying water and washing dishes. Now to find equipment for cooking our meals. A copper-colored portable stove and oven set caught our eye in the window of an appliance store. But it cost forty-one dollars—nearly half of our month's pay. We imagined ourselves baking cookies in the oven and bought it.

Our next concern—how to wash our clothes. Washing machines cost too much and wouldn't work in towns with no electricity. Some natives pounded their clothes clean with rocks along streams—a fine method for them but not for us. A pretty pink plastic tub was our solution. I'd used a corrugated metal washboard before we bought a washing machine in Montana. But I hadn't seen any washboards in Cusco's hardware stores. An artistic colleague came to our aid and drew a diagram of a washboard. We took the sketch to a woodshop. The carpenter said he'd have the board ready in a week.

The next morning found us at the *mercado*, the open-air marketplace, bargaining for a set of blue-trimmed enamel plates and cups. Tins of tuna fish and sardines and boxes of crackers went into our cart at the grocery store. Matching turquoise felt hats we bought would protect our skin from aging prematurely in the hot sun and high altitude. After all, we said laughing, competing for the man of our dreams back to the U.S. would still require pretty complexions.

Norm, our Peace Corps chauffeur, offered to transport our household goods and us to Accha whenever we wanted to go. And we wanted to go now that we finally had an assignment.

Two days before Marie's twenty-second birthday on October 29, I cornered the manager of the Cuzco Restaurant and ordered a birthday cake. The evening of Marie's special day, after we'd finished our quinoa, potato, and beef lunch at the restaurant, the birthday song came over the loudspeaker in English. Everyone in the place joined in to sing "Happy Birthday" with Spanish accents. Marie's eyes registered surprise, then more surprise, when the manager brought out a large chocolate cake encased in chocolate frosting. I hurried to place the twenty-two small candles I'd purchased in the pink and white roses adorning the top. The server lit the candles and Marie tucked her hair behind her ears. She mustered as much air as she could at twelve-thousand-feet and blew out her birthday candles. I hoped she'd wished for success in our Peruvian town.

That evening we ate dinner in our favorite restaurant with Norm. He mentioned that he'd run into a Señor Eguiluz from a town over the mountains called Abancay. For two years, Norm said, Señor Eguiluz, who worked with the Food for Peace program, had been requesting Peace Corps volunteers to work with him on several projects, including teaching at a nursery school. That caught our attention. Norm said he'd introduce us if he ran into the man.

That night Marie and I had a frank discussion. Our enthusiasm for living in Accha waned the more we thought about its isolated location. Norm's information about this new place seemed to hold a greater promise of success and safety than Accha. Furthermore, we had doubts about living and working in Accha with so little commitment from the director. Now we wanted to find out more from Señor Eguiluz about his town.

The next morning, we went to track him down. Norm said Señor Eguiluz might be at the local Food for Peace office. We stood talking to a secretary in that agency asking about Señor Eguiluz's whereabouts, when a slim, smartly dressed man with a cravat neck scarf bounded up the steps.

"There's the man," the secretary said pointing to the light-skinned, tall gentleman. "That's who you're looking for."

We introduced ourselves and enthusiastically shook hands with Señor Eguiluz. He ushered us into an office. He bent over an architectural drawing and pointed to the five kindergartens he planned to build in his town of Abancay. His dark wavy hair fell over his sparkling brown eyes. I was impressed with Señor Eguiluz's enthusiasm. Then he invited us for tea to talk about his plans and his town.

Andean Countryside

Over light refreshments our host informed us that Abancay was located eight-hours west of Cusco and had a population of 10,000. It sat at an altitude of 7,800 feet—four thousand feet lower than Cusco. Below one of the mountains, Ampay, lay a pristine, snow-fed lake. Abancay's location in a beautiful valley surrounded by fifteen-thousand-foot Andes mountain peaks, gave it a mild climate. The warm temperature of the valley made for an abundance of flowers and vegetation that grew all year around. And the best part—buses ran regularly to Lima and to Cusco. And Abancay, the capital of the Apurimac province, had paved streets. This place sounded like a Shangri-La.

Señor Eguiluz invited us for lunch at a restaurant at the end of town on a hill overlooking Cusco's university. The meat he ordered for us tasted delicious.

"It's called *anticuchos*—a typical Cusco dish," he said. "That's marinated bull's heart cooked on skewers over hot coals."

We blanched at the thought of what we'd eaten. Yet the spices made the dish delicious. The local delicacies could suit our palates.

Abancay sounded like a more welcoming town than any we'd yet considered. Should we change our minds again and ask Mr. Cavendish to approve an assignment in Abancay? Maybe Mr. C sent us to Accha to get us out of his hair. He seemed increasingly irritated with each suggestion we made.

"I'm leaving for Puno tomorrow," Señor Eguiluz said, getting up to leave. "I'll check with you two when I return."

"We may not be here then," Marie said, looking our host in the eye. "Mr. Cavendish assigned us to Accha."

Marie and I needed a strategy to talk our director out of the assignment in Accha. Then, a fellow volunteer told us that orders had come from the head office in Lima that all volunteers must have places to live by the following Saturday. The urgency might help our case. Mr. Cavendish had five days to firm up where we would go.

On Monday, November 2, Marie and I arrived in the Peace Corps office at 8:30 a.m. Mr. Cavendish, back from Puno, waltzed in at 11:30 to see us waiting.

"Why don't you come back," he said in a pleasant tone, "at two this afternoon."

We left, disgruntled at being dismissed again, but we had no alternative. Mr. Cavendish remained our boss.

A surprise awaited us when we sat down in the Peace Corps office at two. Señor Eguiluz had postponed his trip to Puno. Instead, he'd cornered Mr. Cavendish and spent two hours discussing his desire to have us assigned to Abancay. Norm, our chauffeur, had added a good word in favor of the newest assignment.

Mr. C said that Norm could drive us out on Wednesday to see if Abancay would be a suitable place for volunteers. The town sounded wonderful. No need to see it to know this new place would be better than Accha. We would move there sight unseen. We canceled the apartment in the remote village. When our scrub board was ready, we were too, and left Cusco for our new home—Abancay.

Abancay

Norm steered the green Peace Corps truck full of our household goods up the red dirt road out of Cusco. We stopped twenty-two miles east of the city in Compone to see fellow Peace Corps volunteers from our group—Karen, Marilyn, and Skeeter. Our colleagues showed us around their newly rented house. The dirt floor felt damp and emitted a musty smell. Water for tea, hauled from the nearby creek, boiled on the kerosene burner called a primus. I hoped we would find more upscale lodgings in Abancay.

Leaving Compone, we crossed the chilly Pampa de Anta at 12,000 feet. Inca descendants here raised barley, quinoa, and potatoes on communal land. Two hours after leaving Compone, our vehicle arrived at a wooden bridge stretched across the Apurimac River. Norm stopped the truck and we got out to stretch our legs. Our driver pointed to two stone structures on opposite cliffs above the river.

"Those carved boulders are what's left of the Incan suspension bridge written about in the novel, *The Bridge of San Luis Rey*," Norm said.

I looked at him in amazement. In college I'd read the story by Thornton Wilder about the braided rope bridge above the Apurimac River that gave way and plunged five travelers to their deaths. The uprights hadn't supported the ends of a bridge in decades. How weird and wonderful to be looking at the remnants of the actual passageway. I imagined walking high above the steep gorge on woven grass—and felt dizzy.

The truck chugged on. I rolled down the dusty window and peered five thousand feet below at the rushing Apurimac River. My stomach fluttered. Now I had a reason for dizziness. The dirt road reminded me of those in southeastern Montana, where I grew up. Except this road hugged mountainsides not hillsides. Here abandoned vehicles perched precariously on inclines—too risky to be removed.

Just then, a truck came barreling toward us. I screamed. Norm pulled the pickup close to the unfenced edge of the narrow road. The truck passed inches from us. The pungent smell of hogs drifted with dust into our vehicle. Still shaking from the close call, I peered down the cliff. We hadn't fallen off the side of the mountain—this time. What was I risking my neck for? I knew. I loved adventure, new experiences, and helping others.

Our truck struggled along twists and turns high above the river for miles. At one thirty-degree bend, where one mountain ended and another one began, a sign in front of a narrow four-plank bridge made us stop. Marie translated the writing on the sign:

CAUTION! PASSENGERS MUST EXIT
VEHICLE AND WALK ACROSS

Before us a ten-foot-long bridge spanned a stream that flowed to the Apurimac River thousands of feet below. The absence of side rails reminded me of the bridge in front of the

Ismay school. I got out and stepped carefully onto the thick planks. My body tingled in fear. No one spoke. Only the sound of the stream tumbling down to the river could be heard. I held my breath afraid to look down and tiptoed across. Once on the other side, I breathed again.

Marie hurried across the chasm in concerned silence. Then, we waved our arms to direct Norm as he slowly maneuvered the truck across the narrow, sideless bridge. How many more harrowing places could there be on our way to Shangri-La?

Five hours into the journey we encountered a series of flat meadows laid out among rolling hills. Cows with their ribs showing and fluffy beige-colored alpacas grazed on the grass. Tan thatched-roof huts dotted green fields. Beside most of the adobe shelters lay blue tarps covered with yellow corn set out to dry in the sun. White flags waved outside some houses along the roadside. Norm said the flags signaled that *chicha*, the local liquor made from fermented corn, and Inca Cola, a bubble-gum-flavored soft drink, were sold there. We didn't stop for either refreshment.

After six hours of travel, we crested the final mountain to see a miniature Abancay appear seven thousand feet below us. We descended the mountain along scores of switchback curves for two more hours. Near the base, our truck entered the town. A surge of warm air greeted us.

Just as Señor Eguiluz had promised, Abancay's valley floor boasted a pleasing California-like climate. High mountains enclosed the town on three sides like a giant cocoon. A road ran through Abancay and down the valley toward Peru's capital, Lima, thirty hours away. We passed a bridge over the rushing Pachachaca River and saw natives catching freshwater trout. Bushes and grass interspersed by fields of barley, corn, and quinoa covered much of the mountainsides above the town. We'd have plenty to eat here.

Our truck purred as it drove onto Abancay's smooth, concrete streets. Norm steered the pickup to the center of town. The main plaza overflowed with tall palm trees, cup-shaped white lilies on slim green stalks, and yellow daisy-like flowers on fat leafy bushes. Tiny pink roses peeked from under dark verdant foliage. True to Señor Eguiluz's description, we'd arrived in Shangri-La.

Two-story buildings of adobe bordered the wide streets. Parallel rows of new-looking roadways crisscrossed the town. Apparently, the governmental money allotted for the capital of a province, had been well spent. Streets and sidewalks had few cracks or debris—just some missing manhole covers. I found these thoroughfares more attractive than the mud path to Accha or Cusco's streets that often smelled of urine. That night we slept in the tourist hotel. The picturesque surroundings convinced me I was dreaming.

The day after our arrival, Señor Eguiluz walked us two blocks up Diaz Barcenas Street to Apurimac Province's Department of Education. The big wooden doors to the offices stood flush with the public sidewalk in front. Our friend introduced us to the two directors of the Ministry of Education, Señors Chávez and Landeo. Both measured about my five-foot-two-inch height but were twice my width. The suits and ties they wore made them look like two square boxes accented with blue striped ribbon-ties. They seemed impressed that two American girls had come to work in their town and maybe in their department.

The two directors and Señor Eguiluz discussed what our jobs would be. No one mentioned a plan for the five kindergartens our host had mentioned. The three men decided we should help the Department of Education as teachers, when needed. In between, we could accompany our host to distribute powdered milk and butter from the U.S. Food for Peace Program. Señor Eguiluz would drive us to outlying towns where we would demonstrate how to mix the milk with potable water. But first, we needed to locate living facilities.

"No problem," Señor Landeo responded when we said we'd need a place to live. He took us through the long, wide entryway and up a set of six broad concrete stairs to the rear of the Education Ministry offices. Sets of stairs going in two directions led to two tin-roofed buildings on opposite sides of a dirt yard. We were introduced to the agency's caretaker, a tall, thin, quiet man named Agapito, his wife, and two pre-school-aged children. The family lived in the long adobe house on the left. Their dwelling had few windows and a dirt floor. The smaller plastered cement-block storeroom on the right could be ours, the education minister said, once the caretaker removed the few supplies it housed. The twelve-by-fifteen-foot hut had windows and a concrete floor. Marie and I looked at one another surprised. How could we be so lucky as to find an acceptable place to live so quickly—and at no charge? We gratefully accepted the housing offer. Now we wouldn't have to go through the stress of looking for an affordable apartment.

When cleaned out, the former storeroom looked like a jail cell with two barless windows. The little bungalow seemed too small to hold our pickup-load of household goods. Yet behind the thick wooden doors of the education offices and the long corridor, we'd be well protected from curious outsiders. It would do just fine.

Pink and red zinnias bloomed alongside an avocado tree in a small walled plot at the front of our tiny abode. At the rear boundary of the property ran an eight-foot-high adobe wall that formed one side of a four-by-six-foot basin. To our delight, the mini swimming pool sported a water faucet. The pool structure contained no water, but if we climbed over its four-foot wall to the inside, we might wash clothes there with our new washboard. And we'd have running water from the faucet. No carrying water from a creek, like our colleagues in Compone.

Our Home

The window on one side of our room overlooked the roof of the Education Department's offices. Adjacent to our front door, facing our flower garden stood a six-by-seven-foot porch enclosed on three sides by plastered brick walls. The open-air room with a roof and a window made a perfect semi-outdoor cooking area and expanded our living space. The new oven and kerosene burners could vent on the outside and not intrude on our living area. The glances between us said, *We can make this place work.*

Employees of the Education Department, who labored from nine to five in the offices below, used the bathrooms off the stairway below our yard. Those living on the grounds, like us, had access to the toilet facilities. One stall had a cold-water shower. A second booth contained a hole in the floor we'd have to squat over. But a third cubicle featured a western-style toilet that flushed. Marie smiled at me. I flashed back my contentment. No chamber pots or squatting in fields for us.

Education Department personnel informed us that electricity came on in the evenings. Running water, toilet facilities, and electricity—luxuries many volunteers didn't have. The next nineteen months here could be very pleasant.

"Getting our bedsprings up the stairs," I said to Marie as we lifted the single-sized bedframes through the entryway and up the steps, "is sure easier than fitting them between the cliffs going to Accha."

The small table, four chairs and the standard Peace Corps library of classic paperback books crowded the room. Placing the beds at a 90-degree angle against two adjoining walls gave us the most useable space. We bought and painted three four-foot-long pine boards and stacked them on scavenged bricks—and we had a set of kitchen shelves. A black-and-white plastic curtain strung around the structure hid our dishes. Now, where to hang our clothes.

A departing couple near Cusco sold us an open closet where we hung the clothes we didn't keep in our under-bed trunks. We fashioned a curtain we made of beige material around the open wardrobe and placed the five-foot-high closet at the head of one of the beds. This gave our bedroom some privacy and separated our sleeping and eating areas. Over our two windows we hung heavy red cotton rectangles with vertical Inca-design stripes of yellow, orange and blue, purchased in a local market. The vivid colors livened up our little hovel.

Preparing our meals didn't resemble cooking at home. If we wanted a salad, we went to the open-air food market in the early morning and bargained for lettuce and tomatoes. Then, the lettuce leaves had to be soaked in water containing dissolved iodine tablets for twenty minutes—as recommended in the Peace Corps handbook. After drying off the iodine water and adding the tomatoes, the salad tasted delicious. Water for drinking needed to be boiled for twenty minutes and cooled. We also heated water on the kerosene burners for washing dishes or clothes. Rather than take cold showers in the Education Department's facilities, we purchased a big metal tub and filled it with water we heated for warm baths. Our primitive living conditions felt like a combination of playing house and camping.

We used primus burners, fueled by kerosene, as our stove. They functioned in the way that stateside kerosene camping lamps worked, with compressed air and a priming pan. We'd pump air into the small primus tank, using the stem on the side until a fine spray came out small holes at the top. A match often wasn't hot enough to light the vapor, so we poured, then lit, denatured alcohol in the shallow reservoir surrounding the kerosene spigot. Between the flaming alcohol and the kerosene spray we usually managed a flame.

One of the first days in our outdoor kitchen, Marie encouraged a primus to come to life by igniting the alcohol she'd put in the ring under the opening that emitted the fuel. Flames blew up, singeing Marie's hair. Then, the container of alcohol in her hand caught fire. With a scream, she threw the burning object into the yard. It landed on a pile of dry leaves and flames shot into the air.

Yelling "Fuego!" "Fire!" we threw dirt on the flames and extinguished the fire. Shaking at our close call, we boiled water and sat down for a cup of tea. We congratulated ourselves on how fortunate we'd been to not burn down the Education Department's offices. Cooking in our outdoor kitchen was just another adventure.

Buying food could be a challenge. Shoppers had to arrive at the open-air marketplace before seven a.m. to obtain edible meat and produce. Barely awake, Marie or I bargained for the leanest cuts of meat with the fewest flies for making hamburger. We ground the beef using a friend's meat grinder. I turned the crank and beef that looked like hamburger oozed out. But when cooked, the hamburgers didn't taste like those we knew. A friend advised us to buy meat with fat on it to get flavor. The fatty meat tasted better, but not like the hamburgers in the States.

Baking biscuits in our pretty new oven took an hour. The temperature rose at a snail's pace and didn't stay at a consistent baking level like our ovens at home. We thought the high altitude might have something to do with our baking woes. With instructions from the cookbook I'd brought, *The Joy of Cooking,* we researched baking at high altitudes. Still no luck with the oven. We analyzed everything. But nothing worked. Fed up, we switched to using the kind of unattractive, boxy black oven set atop two primuses that other volunteers used. The ugly setup cost a tenth the price we'd paid for our copper-colored oven but worked ten times better. We used the disappointing new oven as an expensive breadbox.

Bricks of sweet chocolate bars, chopped into bits supplied the main ingredient for chocolate chip cookies. Our ugly oven

Bargaining at the Market

baked them just right. When offered our specialty, friends and neighbors said they had never tasted such a delicious dessert.

We longed for hot dogs and found some canned ones at a corner store. The cost put a dent in our food budget, but the wiener-like *salchichas* were more sanitary and easier to make than hamburgers. After a few months of eating the canned hot dogs regularly, we accumulated a great many empty cans. We didn't want to look like rich Americans by throwing them in the trash. So each time we emptied one, we washed it and put the can in a box in the outdoor cooking area.

One day, the caretaker next-door asked if he could have the round metal cylinders that filled the box. We handed them over, embarrassed at the extravagance so many cans represented. The caretaker used our cans to put a new roof on his house. We cut back on buying food in cans.

Work

Within two weeks we'd converted the storeroom behind the Education Department's offices into a cozy home. Marie and I had just finished a breakfast of cinnamon-and-sugar biscuits, baked in our ugly oven, when Señor Chávez knocked at our door.

"You're needed to take over a class in town," he said to us both, sounding like an administrator. "The fifth-grade teacher is sick."

I'd never taught anything but one-hour catechism classes back in California and didn't feel capable to teach an entire fifth grade in Spanish. We knew nothing about the curriculum in Peruvian schools. Marie had taken education courses in college but didn't think her knowledge would apply here. Nevertheless, we couldn't refuse our generous hosts. I grabbed the battery-powered record player I'd brought from the States and a couple of the children's books and phonograph records in Spanish I'd purchased in Mexico City.

When we arrived at the middle-class school, the principal directed us to a first-grade classroom. We looked at one another relieved. My record that taught the alphabet would be more appropriate for first graders than fifth graders. Neither lesson plans nor instructions of what to do with the twenty-odd boisterous children sat on the teacher's desk. On the phonograph I started the LP of Cri-Cri, a Mexican composer and singer of children's songs. The music caught the students' attention.

Under our instructions, the students marched and sang along to "The March of the Vowels." The storybooks that I'd carried with me kept most of the six-year-olds occupied until dismissal time. With the long day finally over, Marie and I came home, punched on Marie's tape recorder filled with the Beatles music, and wilted in our chairs.

The two of us evaluated the day and agreed. We didn't want the education directors to dictate all our work. Cornell had trained us in rural community development to improve the lives of Peru's indigenous population, not those of middle-class students in Abancay. We should work among the poorer citizens of Peru.

The next day, after a night's rest, we felt more confident. We checked in with Mr. Chávez to see if he wanted us to return to the first-grade classroom.

"Marie, you will begin teaching math tomorrow at a local school," he said as if he were our boss, "and Evelyn, you can work with the nutrition program in the smaller places outside town."

"Our training is in rural community development," I said to Director Chávez. "We want to work in a poor area."

The portly director stared at the ground, deep in thought. Then he looked at us and said, "Well, there's a first-grade class without a teacher in the poor section of town a mile from here. They'll need a substitute tomorrow."

"I'd like to try teaching there," I said.

The following morning, carrying my trusty phonograph, records, and books, I walked the mile to my assigned school in the area called Villa Gloria. The twenty boys and girls in the first-grade class varied in size and ranged in ages from six to ten. I learned that the older pupils were required to wait to begin school until their families could spare them as workers in the corn and potato fields. All had rough facial patches—chapped cheeks, caused by wind and strong sunshine at high altitudes. Their threadbare blue-and-khaki uniforms looked as if they hadn't been washed for weeks. I wondered if their bare feet got cold on the room's dirt floor.

Most students spoke their native language, Quechua. I brought out my Cri-Cri records. The students stared at the plastic disc turning around and around. Twenty pairs of black, almond-shaped eyes grew wide. Smiles appeared on their faces. I guessed they'd never before seen a record player.

I directed the students to troop around the room to the beat of the "March of the Vowels." At first, they didn't understand. But one of the boys translated my Spanish into Quechua, and the class began stomping around the packed-earth floor in time to the music. When the record finished, I taught them the names of the fingers using songs in Spanish that the Puerto Rican children had taught me. I ended the day reading children's stories in Spanish that I'd purchased in Mexico. The students clapped to show their delight at the colored pictures. I walked the mile home more satisfied with my accomplishments than I'd felt two days before.

Señor Chávez said he didn't need us every day to teach in the Apurimac Department's schools. We'd wait several months before being given a more permanent assignment. In the meantime, we continued to settle into our new home.

One day, not long after our arrival in Abancay, a slender, curly-haired, dark-eyed fifteen-year-old named Alfonso appeared in our yard. He introduced himself as a relative of the caretaker, Agapito, and said he'd come to live with the family. Alfonso had a gleam in his eye and a chip on his shoulder. He took an immediate interest in us and spent more time in the yard between our houses than necessary. He observed as we washed our hair under the faucet in the mini-pool. He scrutinized us laundering our clothes. He seemed to take a special interest in the garments we hung on the clothesline between our houses.

If we weren't home as soon as our clothes dried, we'd find a pile of neatly folded laundry, including underwear, on the wall by our door, compliments of Alfonso. I believed this an improper invasion of privacy. But Alfonso defended his actions saying he had to take our clothes off the line as soon as they dried so dust wouldn't dirty them.

When another relative, about the same age as Alfonso, joined the family for a time, the two male teens caused us double trouble. From the sly looks they gave us, I guessed that maybe they ogled our nightgowns, bras, and panties that'd been hung out to dry. But I could do nothing. We had no other way to dry our laundry and Agapito's family had a right to the common area between our houses. Our clothesline intruded on their yard. Marie and I took to staying out of the area between our houses as much as possible when the two boys were around.

Once, when Alfonso hadn't seen us outside for a few hours, he came knocking at our door. I prepared to give him a piece of my mind, but he stood there offering me three fat avocados. I accepted them, thinking that his gift didn't make up for his inappropriate behaviors. The next day, when he knocked and offered more avocados, I refused them, saying I still had some left from the day before.

"Well," Alfonso huffed, "I guess I shouldn't bother you with *Peruvian* avocados. Oh, and we've seen you ladies undress at night. We peek through your curtains."

Anger and my limited vocabulary of Spanish swearwords prohibited me from giving any retort. Blushing, I slammed the door on the brash young man. He would later be more helpful. But for now, he was an insolent and pesky teenager.

Señor Eguiluz returned from his one-week trip to the countryside, where he delivered American powdered milk and butter in cans with the Food for Peace program. Marie and I felt relieved he hadn't requested that we accompany him because we'd come to perform real community development, not mix food. We hoped he would rescue us from a future of substitute teaching in a system for which we were ill prepared and didn't think were needed.

Our sponsor located us where we'd gone with Señor Chávez to observe yet another set of classes—at the local boys' high school. We weren't any more eager to teach there than we'd been to instruct the students in the prosperous elementary school.

That evening Marie and I decided not to work in the Food for Peace program or as teachers in Abancay's middle-class schools. Since our training at Cornell University had been in rural community development, our work should involve helping the poorer people in the rural areas obtain access to education, medical services, and basic life necessities. Stirring powdered milk into water and reading to unruly, well-off students didn't appear to achieve our goal of helping the indigenous people become contributing citizens of their country. We were hopeful, perhaps naively so, that we could expand the skills of the less-educated population of Peru.

When we broached the subject with the education directors and Señor Eguiluz, they came up with a solution more to our liking. We could live and work in Suncho, a town being built for the indigenous population an hour away from Abancay. Our hosts said plans were to build a school, homes, and a medical dispensary in the new town.

We visited the prospective community and saw two adobe walls of a school and flags that marked out a town-sized grid in a flat area below a mountain. The education officials said they would soon finish the school and numerous houses, using the labor of the people who would live there.

The future residents now lived on the cold mountaintop where they grew and preserved potatoes. Local Abancay officials believed that the indigenous Quechua-speaking community would come down from their mountaintop to live near the road with the buildings completed and educational and medical services begun. If these Incan descendants moved closer to civilization, they could have water and other basic services for their children—and contribute to Peruvian society. Marie and I would at last be participating in the development of a community. Our hosts agreed that first we needed to acquire some medical skills for working in the distant town.

Señor Eguiluz arranged for Marie and me to be trained in basic medical procedures at the local hospital. Since rural people in the Andes spoke Quechua, I needed to learn the language. Marie, already fluent in Spanish, had studied Quechua at Cornell so knew more of the language than I did.

Alfonso spoke Quechua, so I asked him to teach me some phrases. Maybe it would bring out his intellectual side. Though awkward at first, I was as eager to learn as Alfonso was proud to teach me, and my knowledge progressed. He wrote down phrases in my *cuaderno* (notebook) and I faithfully practiced the Inca greeting, "Ama suwa, ama llulla, ama q'ella," meaning, "Don't steal, don't lie, don't be lazy." The language sounded like items it portrayed. "Mayu" sounded like a flowing river. "Urpi" sounded like a bird chirping. Quechua was a beautiful language, and Alfonso proudly showed off his language-teaching talents.

When we'd first moved to Abancay, I let Marie do most of the talking in conversations with townspeople because of her Spanish language fluency. One day, a nice-looking young man was introduced to us.

"Why doesn't Evelyn speak Spanish?" he said to Marie, "Is it that she's not as intelligent as you?"

I understood his Spanish perfectly and from that moment on, rattled off my Spanish, no matter how many mistakes and mispronunciations I made.

Marie Feeding a Llama

First Holidays

I bounced off the plastic seat of the Tagli bus. Another pothole. Dust from the dirt road to Cusco drifted in through a crack in the window where I sat next to Marie. This was our first trip away from Abancay, where we'd lived for the past month. We were two birds let loose from our cage. Marie, an elegant hazel-eyed Spanish-speaking parrot. Me, a blue-eyed parakeet trying to communicate, but mostly just flapping my newly discovered wings. Once freed, there was no limit to how far we could fly.

I watched fine silt drift down and settle on Marie's hair as the sun gleamed in from outside. Several Quechua-speaking indigenous women entered our bus at the first stop. Judging from the bursting bundles they carried, they were on their way to sell home-grown produce at a Saturday market in one of the upcoming towns.

We two birds had an eight-hour ride to hatch travel plans for the upcoming weekend. The Peace Corps regional office, where we were due on Tuesday for more immunizations, and the city's grocery stores, would be closed on Sunday. Why not use the time to see Machu Picchu, the "Lost City of the Incas" outside Cusco?

Guidebooks listed it as a wonder of the ancient world. I'd seen the Incas' engineering skills in the limestone boulder walls in Cusco and wanted to see more.

Hiram Bingham, an English explorer, helped by local natives, had discovered the Incan citadel in 1911. Marie and I would do the same in 1964. We had time. Our training at Abancay's municipal hospital, to prepare us for work in Suncho, would not begin for another nine days.

After our Sunday visit to Machu Picchu, we could continue on to the jungle town of Quillabamba, where fellow volunteer, Larry, had been placed. Then we would return on Tuesday to Cusco to see the Peace Corps doctor. We could remain in Cusco a few days after our immunizations to have Thanksgiving dinner with other volunteers.

❤⟨❤⟩❤

I shivered in Cusco's crisp morning air and pulled my new alpaca sweater tight. Bright blue polyester slacks kept my lower half warm, but only Peruvian alpaca wool could heat my upper half in the thin, cold air. Before we caught the 7:20 a.m. train to Machu Picchu, I had to attend 5:00 a.m. Sunday mass at one of the big Spanish churches on Cusco's main plaza. Marie, an Episcopalian not bound by Catholic rules, would meet me at the train depot after mass.

Indigenous workers scurried across the main plaza on their way to the marketplace. Their strong backs carried huge bundles of alpaca wool blankets, rugs, sweaters, and hats to sell to the tourists. Eggs, onions, carrots, avocados, and seasonal produce destined for the food market passed by in baskets slung across muscular arms or balanced above Indian women's thick black braids. The aroma of freshly brewed coffee wafted from hole-in-the-wall stalls along Cusco's main artery, Avenida Sol. Bells rang out from tall Spanish-style church towers announcing the start of church services.

A few of the passing entrepreneurs dangled live upside-down chickens from their wrists and stepped into the cathedral to offer a quick prayer before continuing on to their market spaces. Animals in the church didn't seem out of place here. A painting inside showed *The Last Supper* with Jesus and the twelve apostles having a meal of *cuy*—a local delicacy of herb-flavored guinea pig.

At the railway station, Marie's head bobbed above the crowd of natives waiting to board. When I reached her we went to purchase tickets on the local train, not the more expensive one for tourists. Trains were one of the few things that arrived and left on time in Peru. We hopped aboard and settled onto a couple of scratched blue vinyl seats. Three toots of the whistle and the train began to move. The diesel engine labored forward, then backward, to pull, then push, the six passenger cars along the zigzagging rails up the side of the mountain and out of the city. Close to the top, burning oil replaced the musty smell of red clay soil. Smoke billowed outside the window of our car. I voiced concern to the man checking our tickets.

"Just a dirty carburetor," the man said.

I wondered why someone hadn't cleaned the carburetor. The smoke dissipated. The view from the window improved as the train lumbered along.

Miles of beige grass spread out across an immense pampa replacing the reddish-gray adobe buildings of Cusco. For an hour we followed the lush green banks of the gurgling, then gushing, Urubamba River. We arrived close to our destination three hours after we departed.

A yellow bus waited to take us up the mountain to Machu Picchu at the Aguas Calientes station. We hurried aboard. Soon we were zigzagging up the side of a steep mountain on the gravel road. The fifteen sharp switchbacks jerked our bodies left, then right with each thirty-degree turn. Marie laughed as she fell across my lap. I giggled and pushed her back.

Switchbacks to Machu Picchu

Solemnity returned when we exited the bus. There before us at 8,000 feet, stood the place Incan nobles had come for religious ceremonies over five hundred years before. I stopped on the crest of the mountain a few yards past a cream-colored hotel, spellbound. Spread out for five miles below were hundreds of stone steps and buildings. Gray stone walls surrounded terrace after terrace of lime-green grass. Behind the structures stood tall, forest-green mountains. Their sharp peaks poked through white clouds. Cliffs on three sides dropped straight down fifteen hundred feet to the Urubamba River. A bright blue sky with wisps of white clouds swirled above us. I felt within reach of heaven.

Marie and I hurried off to explore before the sites became crowded with tourists. The huge stone walls and buildings fit together without mortar—the same masonry techniques used for the impressive walls in Cusco. We trotted up and down the varying levels of stone houses, marveling at the workmanship. Here sat an altar, there, a solar clock. A sophisticated irrigation system of aqueducts crossed the terraces. We ducked through trapezoid-shaped doorways, careful not to bump our heads. The builders must have been shorter than us.

At the far side of the ruins, a steep trail led to Huayna Picchu, a pointed mountain towering 1,200 feet above where we stood. It called to us to climb it. We picked our way up the narrow dirt path, trying not to look down until we reached the top lest we be overtaken by vertigo. This higher peak was where the priests and virgins began each day— appropriate for us two virgins.

Heavy blue-gray clouds from the nearby tropical rain forest floated below us. I saw the perfect background to snap a photograph of Marie with my Instamatic camera. She looked regal sitting on the precipice in her red-and-black alpaca sweater. Quiet beauty surrounded us. We hated to leave. But the only afternoon train to Quillabamba would depart soon.

Back on the bus, we plunged down the hairpin curves and scurried onto the train. The engine chugged for an hour through a tropical jungle thick with vine-covered trees. At the end of the line we boarded a bus that sped along an unpaved road for another hour to Quillabamba. The bus deposited us at our destination at dusk.

Marie found a reasonably priced hotel and we checked in and washed the sweat and dust from our sunburned bodies. Then we sauntered over to the town square, where we found Leah, one of the female Peace Corps volunteers. She told us that Larry, who'd trained with us at Cornell and in Puerto Rico, had gone to a nearby soda fountain. I wondered how he liked his new home. We found our tall, blonde friend sitting with a group of companions.

"What are you two doing here?" Larry said, little surprise registering in his blue eyes.

"We had a couple of extra days in Cusco." I said. "Marie and I thought we'd see where you got placed."

"Some locals told me two new *gringas* were in town," Larry said, with a slight smile. "From their descriptions, I figured it had to be you two." I wondered how we'd been described.

The three of us exchanged the latest gossip about others in our training group. Larry invited us to see his place. His apartment was bigger than our room in Abancay. And he had indoor plumbing. Two turkeys strutted around the common yard of the apartment complex. Larry said he was fattening them up for the Quillabamba volunteers' Thanksgiving dinner.

"Hey, you two," Larry said, in a serious tone, "tomorrow morning is a requiem mass commemorating the one-year anniversary of President Kennedy's death. Want to go to it with me?"

"Sure," I said, surprised that this foreign country would be honoring my beloved president.

"What time?" asked Marie.

"Seven o'clock," Larry said, "I'll come by your hotel to get you."

◇·◇·◇·◇

The mass touched me. I recalled the shock I'd felt a year ago when the president had been assassinated. Now, on November 23, 1964, I worked in the very organization President Kennedy had initiated and felt proud. I tucked the funeral card with a photo of our handsome dead president into my purse.

After breakfast, Larry turned us over to Leah for a tour of the town. Wide streets led into Quillabamba's mango tree-filled main plaza. Both the plaza and the local hospital were bigger than those of Abancay. Leah showed us the maternity ward where she assisted. From there she ushered us to where another volunteer taught in a nursery school. The school looked well equipped with books and educational toys. The town's marketplace and tennis courts appeared in better shape than Abancay's smelly *mercado* and cracked clay courts.

The noontime humidity sapped my energy. I could see Marie fading too. I understood why people in these parts took siestas.

"I'm glad we were placed in the cool mountains," Marie said, under her breath.

"Me too," I said.

Back at the ice cream shop, the regional Peace Corps physician surprised us. Marie and I had expected to see him for the latest round of tests and immunizations the next day in Cusco, not here in Quillabamba.

"Come see me," the doctor said, "I'll be over at my hotel."

"I bet he's having a party," I said to Marie when the doctor left.

"Ready for Pisco Sours in urine sample cups," I said to the doctor when we entered his hotel room.

"Roll up your sleeves," the doctor said. "No liquor shots, just plague shots and TB skin tests to finish off the slate of immunizations you began when you entered the country."

"What a dirty trick," I said, and pulled up my shirtsleeve.

❖❖❖❖

Marie and I were at the Quillabamba depot at 4:30 a.m. on Tuesday to catch the first bus to Cusco. We bid farewell to the jungle town in the cool of the morning and arrived in Cusco in time for lunch. After dropping our gear off at our hotel, we stopped at the Peace Corps office to request permission to go to Lima at Christmas. We got right in to see the regional director, Mr. Cavendish. The blonde, slim, director sat behind a big oak desk that dwarfed his 5'10" height.

"And how was your recent trip?" the director asked, with piercing gray eyes and a stern face.

"We loved Machu Picchu," Marie said, smiling.

"Quillabamba was humid," I chimed in, "but cleaner and more modern than I expected." I wanted to get right to the purpose of our visit and kept talking.

"We'd like to go to Lima," I said, ready for another adventure, "around Christmas." The director cast a serious look in our direction.

"You've had your vacation," he snapped. "Volunteers are not to leave their assignments unless authorized to do so. You two took off for Machu Picchu and Quillabamba without my permission."

Mr. Cavendish didn't return our friendly smiles. Marie looked at me in disbelief. The doctor, or one of the Quillabamba volunteers, must have mentioned our trip. There had been no reason to keep it secret. We merely killed a couple of days when nothing in Cusco was open. Before we could respond, Mr. Cavendish continued.

"Volunteers are not allowed a vacation until they've been in their assignment for three months. You two have been in Abancay for less than two months. Ordinarily, you'd be docked pay. This time I'll overlook that if you submit a vacation request for the time you spent in Machu Picchu and Quillabamba."

"But," Marie said, "we didn't know spending a Sunday seeing sites around the area was against the rules."

"We were coming to Cusco," I said, "for immunizations, and we just took a little side trip on a Sunday when everything was shut."

"The matter is closed," Mr. Cavendish said and ushered us out of his office.

How could this be? All our Peace Corps friends would be in Lima at Christmas. We'd already planned what we'd wear. I'd spent hours sewing a slim skirt and vest out of expensive red alpaca wool. I'd trimmed it with fuzzy white alpaca fur. Marie would wear the black organza cocktail dress she brought from the States. A friend, Darcy, had offered us a ride to Lima in his truck. We'd set up everything. This reversal of fortune was devastating.

Christmas meant gathering together with like-minded friends. We all looked forward to seeing one another. Being together, we could catch up on happenings in our group. Some crazy Peace Corps rule we'd never been told, or that was made up just for us, dictated that we'd have to stay home in our little Abancay nest, grounded. Our wings had been clipped.

Over the Andes

Mr. Cavendish had reprimanded Marie and me for visiting Machu Picchu and Quillabamba and turned down our oral request to go to Lima at Christmas. We didn't dare ask him for permission to stay in Cusco for the Peace Corps Thanksgiving Day dinner. He might tell us to head right back to Abancay. Then we'd be cooped up in our little town for both turkey day and Christmas.

In two months of living in Abancay, we hadn't gotten to know many of its residents well. And those we did know were headed to Lima at Christmas. Now we'd be the only Peace Corps members from our training group not attending the December festivities in Lima. Holidays were the hardest times of the year to be away from fellow Americans.

We reveled with Peruvians on their many holidays, but they didn't celebrate Thanksgiving or the Fourth of July. With time, Marie and I could make friends and introduce Peruvians to our special days. For now though, we just wanted to spend our first Thanksgiving in Cusco with our colleagues. We decided to remain in town and commemorate the American holiday without our director's permission.

What would our fellow Peace Corpsmen find in the country of yucca and cherimoya fruit to replicate the sweet potatoes and cranberries? And what about the pumpkin pie? We'd seen no canned pumpkin on grocery store shelves here. But Peace Corps volunteers usually found creative ways to overcome obstacles—especially if food or drinks were involved.

Somewhere, our colleagues found a turkey and an oven large enough to cook it in. The dressing tasted just like the stuffing Mama made. The mashed potatoes, gravy, Jell-O salad, and cauliflower couldn't have been more delicious. For dessert, someone had made banana bread and a raspberry pie. We returned to Abancay with full stomachs but despondent hearts.

Mr. Cavendish had declared us grounded, but Marie and I yearned to spend Christmas with our colleagues. Determined to get to Lima at the end of December, we filled out and sent in the required forms requesting eight days' vacation at Christmas. After receiving no response, we wrote a letter.

"We are two girls working in an isolated community," our letter read, "who need to be with companions over Christmas. We're sorry if we violated rules we knew nothing about."

When no word of our request had come by the morning of December 20, we called the director's office. The Peace Corps secretary advised us to forget about going anywhere. Our request forms and letter, she reported, were on Mr. Cavendish's desk with a note that said, "These girls have had their vacation." Then the impossible happened.

That afternoon, ignoring the secretary's advice, we phoned the Peace Corps office again and to our surprise, reached the director himself. We crossed our fingers as we listened. His voice sounded less harsh than we'd become accustomed to.

"Do you think you deserve to go?" he sounded like he was in a good mood. How unusual.

"We're sorry about leaving our site without your permission," we said in our most repentant voices. "We've been working hard in the local hospital and need a break with other volunteers—all of whom will be in Lima for Christmas."

"Well then, okay." Mr. C said.

And that was that. Our persistence had paid off. We located Darcy, the brown-haired friend who'd offered us a ride, to say we'd love to accompany him to Lima. I baked a batch of chocolate chip cookies, made cheese sandwiches and packed boiled eggs and oranges so we wouldn't starve on the thirty-hour ride.

On December 22, Darcy picked us up in his truck at 4:30 p.m. and we headed to Lima. Marie sat next to our driver friend by choice. She found him attractive. Several hours later, the truck climbed in darkness out of the temperate valley and we struck out across the flat *altiplano*.

A full moon illuminated the passing landscape. The Andes appeared magical and otherworldly. Millions of stars twinkled in the clear nighttime sky. A large object sparkled high above and moved too slowly to be an airplane. The three of us agreed—it must be a flying saucer. Then I slept, dreaming I too flew above Peru. Marie dozed on Darcy's shoulder.

The next morning we passed guanacos, alpacas, and the occasional vicuña—all relatives of the camel. They grazed on tough yellow grass, the only visible vegetation. I'd never seen such desolate terrain, even in dry Eastern Montana. Andean condors, with ten-foot wingspans, coasted on air currents high above the 17,000-foot mountain peaks. We were the only ones in this mysterious wonder world.

When we stopped for gas, Darcy made a bed for us in the back of the truck. Marie and I laughed with delight as we changed into our bathing suits in the bathroom. We wanted to get a tan. We lay on our backs in the truck bed looking up at the clear blue sky, enjoying the agreeable warm weather. It felt good to stretch out.

Five hundred miles along the bumpy inland road from Abancay to Lima, we arrived at the trip's halfway point. Marie and I moved to the front and the truck chugged up a hill near the town of Nazca. As we descended, I looked at the flat land below and gasped.

Spread out over miles on an arid plateau lay an array of huge mythical figures and designs drawn in the dirt. Darcy said early natives had made the figures across a stretch of 280 square miles around 500 A.D. by removing reddish pebbles that uncovered gray ground underneath. The hundreds of animal drawings and geometric figures remained intact because it never rains in that area. I could make out drawings of a monkey, a hummingbird and a spider. Darcy said the figures measured around 600 feet across. He told us that no one knew precisely how the ancients managed to configure such large representations, called "The Nazca Lines," without plotting them from the sky. Perhaps UFOs had guided the artists from outer space.

The ride became more interesting and smoother once we left the plains and turned north onto the paved Pan American Highway at Pisco. We were delighted to see the blue of the Pacific Ocean. The Pisco Sour, Peace Corps volunteers' favorite drink, was named after this city where grapes for the liquor grew. The cocktail combined the sweet and sour tastes I liked.

A dune of brown sand stretched alongside the highway. The white sands on top made the long brown bank look like a string of low snowcapped hills. The asphalt road would continue up to Alaska, but we had to travel only another 150 miles to Lima. We arrived dusty and grimy at our hotel in the capital at 10:30 p.m. of the second day. Our first order of business—warm showers to wash the soil from our pores.

After a good night's sleep and getting our hair done in the hotel's salon, we were ready to party. Friends had given us the name of the restaurant where the volunteers would meet for Christmas Eve dinner. Our hotel mirror showed two stunning, tanned young women. Our new outfits brought the city out of us two country girls.

An expensive taxi took us to the restaurant. We passed Christmas trees with colorful lights in the plazas and spotted a Santa, much like in our home country. But street vendors sold multicolored *retablos* that showed three-dimensional nativity scenes with llamas and alpacas instead of our familiar donkeys and sheep. Not wanting to arrive late, we didn't stop to purchase the handcrafted folk art.

When we reached the restaurant, no lights illuminated the building's inside. We stood before it, unbelieving. It was closed. We found a phone booth and called our friends' apartments, then we called our hotel for messages. No one had left any word of where the festivities had been moved. Disappointment hung over us like the thick clouds covering Lima.

Hunger pangs hit. We gave up trying to find our partying fellow volunteers and walked toward our hotel in our heels looking for any open eatery. We found none. After hours of searching, we arrived back at our lodging in disheveled outfits, tired and famished. The hotel restaurant readied to close, but the headwaiter took pity and let us purchase two chicken sandwiches to go.

On Christmas Eve 1964, Marie and I sat on our hotel beds, coifed in our wilting salon hairdos, adorned in our now drooping city clothes, and ate chicken sandwiches. Our ordeal in getting to Lima hadn't turned out the way we'd planned. We weren't with friends, just one another. So we wished each other a "Feliz Navidad," and went to bed.

Unexpected

W hat? No bus to Cusco? I couldn't believe it. Notice had come via the mail to report for more immunizations and to collect our February paychecks. Marie and I had lived in Abancay for three months and twice caught the eight a.m. Tagli Lines bus to Cusco. Both times the town's main commercial transportation left an hour late and for eight hours we breathed exhaust fumes and bounced on hard seats. But buses remained the most reliable way to get to the regional Peace Corps office. We'd purchased tickets on Tuesday. Now, a day later—no bus.

"The bus from Cusco to Abancay broke down on its way here yesterday," the Tagli Lines ticket seller said. She looked at me and sighed. "They had to haul it back to Cusco, so there's no bus today. You could go in tomorrow on the bus that'll arrive here from Cusco this evening."

Without so much as an "I'm sorry," the woman refunded our two dollars. The company had two old buses so we shouldn't have been surprised about one breaking down. But we were packed and ready to leave today. We gathered our bags and trudged off to find another way to our destination.

If we stood at the corner of Abancay's main thoroughfare, we might catch a ride going east to Cusco. I knew others hitched rides in private vehicles, and we could give that a try. A red pickup stopped in front of us. The woman on the passenger side rolled down her window.

"Are you headed to Cusco?" I asked.

"Yes," she said, "Do you need a ride?"

"*Si,*" I answered, "*Hay espacio*? Is there room?"

"Yes," she said, "but we first have to get gas. We'll pick you up afterwards."

They sped off. We waited. Twenty minutes later, a green truck with wooden slats lumbered by. The mustachioed driver bent across passengers in the front seat and hollered out the window.

"Hey," he said, "You gals lookin' for a ride to Cusco?"

"Yes," we said in unison. The red pickup had not returned. What if its occupants had forgotten us or found other passengers? We threw our bags into the back of the truck, walked to the front, and opened the door. There, almost filling the seat, sat a woman with her elementary-aged son. I squeezed in and Marie followed. Just then we noticed the red pickup return. I made a quick calculation. There would be more room in the newer model pickup than in the truck.

After conferring, we decided to take the faster and more comfortable pickup. Marie told the truck driver we'd changed our minds and asked him to take our luggage out from the truck's bed. He refused. We had committed to go with him for three dollars, he barked. I didn't want a fight, but we had chosen the red pickup first. It had arrived, so we would go in the pickup. I got out and glanced between the wooden slats of the truck at our hostage bags. Marie would have to get our suitcases released while I dashed and sat in the pickup's front seat.

Marie argued with the truck driver. Meanwhile, a little Indian woman, who also wanted to ride in the red pickup, began pulling me off my seat. Amidst the pandemonium the pickup driver ordered the Indian woman and me out of his vehicle and motioned for me to wait at a corner farther down the road. I got out.

Marie had finally extricated our luggage by climbing into the back of the truck and lifting out our bags. She jumped down and joined me. Suitcases in hand, we headed to the next corner. The vehicle we wanted awaited us. Relieved, we opened the door, ready to climb in when the concerned driver stopped us.

"I don't have a chauffeur's license," the driver said through missing front teeth and peering around his female companion, "so I'm not supposed to transport passengers for pay." We were crestfallen. "But," he continued, "I can take you now because you met me down the road."

I couldn't see where getting on at this piece of road was any different than boarding at the previous block, but apparently Abancay had a regulation that we didn't know about. We settled in next to the couple and headed toward Cusco. Our trip hadn't started well. We'd been jerked around even before hitting the mountain switchbacks.

By 10 a.m. the pickup had climbed out of Abancay's valley. Our dark-haired driver and his skinny girlfriend huddled together behind the steering wheel, leaving a comfortable space for Marie and me. Though cool toward us, our chauffeurs appeared very friendly with one another. The girlfriend asked about our work. We responded politely, saying we hadn't yet settled into anything definite, which was true. Every so often, the driver spoke Quechua to his girlfriend, then gave a lustful laugh. We couldn't understand what the two said, but we guessed their talk was about sex. Marie and I spoke in English, so the driver and his girlfriend wouldn't know what we said. Mostly, we talked about what we might be charged for this trip.

The ride along the Apurimac river and around the mountains was smoother than on the bus. We picked up speed crossing the pampas and arrived in Cusco in five and one-half hours—three hours faster than the bus. The couple dropped us off in front of our inexpensive hotel at 3:30 p.m. and refused to take any pay for the journey. Surprised and pleased, we thanked them, and they drove off.

An hour later, I picked up my February paycheck at the Peace Corps office. Marie and I submitted a request asking that the Peace Corps pay for our hotel during our stay because we'd come to Cusco for required immunizations. If reimbursed, we'd spend less of our hard-earned compensation. We always looked for ways to save money.

The Peace Corps regional director responded saying that since we didn't pay rent for our place in Abancay, we shouldn't complain about paying for our hotel. He denied our request. His response disappointed us. How unfair to be penalized for securing free housing. But we could appeal our case to no one.

Our disappointment lifted as we left the office and ran into three Cusco Peace Corps volunteers on the street. They planned a party for Saturday night and invited Marie and me.

I had important errands to run. At the bank, I obtained a check in dollars and mailed it off to *Time* magazine for a subscription. I wanted to keep in touch with U.S. happenings—especially the escalation of fighting in Vietnam. At the drugstore, I purchased milk of magnesia, calamine lotion, and more insect repellant. At the El Chinito grocery store, I found good chocolate, tuna fish, peanut butter, and pudding mixes, items not available in Abancay's stores. Within hours of receiving it, I'd already spent nearly half my monthly earnings. My remaining forty-five dollars could go into my savings account when Marie paid me for her half of the groceries—if she had any *soles* left after buying alpaca sweaters at the tourist shop.

On Friday, Marie and I met at the U.S. Agency for International Development office to request a library for our town. Then we went to the Peruvian agricultural agency, SIPA, *Sistema de Información de Productos de Apoyo*, to see about financial assistance to help local farmers raise chickens in Abancay. Personnel at both agencies said we'd have to wait for our applications to be processed. That was okay. In the interim, we'd find other useful endeavors.

Back at the Peace Corps office the doctor gave us two vaccinations, one for plague and another against rabies. He told us to return the next day for two more. We could always count on getting stuck by the Peace Corps doctor.

On the way back to our shabby hotel, we decided to check out the shop in Cusco's newest tourist hotel, the Savoy. A couple speaking English entered with us. I asked them if they came from the U.S. They said they'd traveled from Illinois with another couple and their university-aged son. They wanted to know all about our living conditions. Talking to these kind Midwesterners reminded me of people from my homeland. When we mentioned that we had just a shower in our cheap hotel, they said we should take baths in their hotel room's tub. They'd be on a tour that afternoon and we could have the place to ourselves. In addition to the use of their room, they invited us to dinner when they returned. We accepted everything. We bathed in luxury, had our hair done at a salon, then dressed for dinner.

The friendliness of our compatriots didn't end with paying for a great meal at the luxurious hotel. They suggested we give them letters for our parents, which they would mail upon their return to the states in a few days. That beat the three weeks it took

for letters to get to my parents in California. One of the couples said they would call our folks to tell them we looked healthy.
Others' compassion was the best antidote for feeling homesick.
The only way we had to demonstrate our appreciation was to invite
the cordial Americans to Saturday's party. The congenial couples
looked uneasy and didn't say they'd come but they didn't outright
decline our invitation.

◇◦◇◦◇◦◇

Marie and I were eating lunch Saturday noon at the Roma restaurant when in walked Señor Adolfo Eguiluz, the Peruvian who
had invited us to live and work in Abancay. He joined our table
where we'd ordered plates of *lomo saltado,* our favorite beef-
tomato-potato dish. He said he'd come to Cusco to pick up his
twenty-year-old son from the university. Marie and I looked at one
another, mouths agape. We couldn't believe the thirty-five-year
old Señor Eguiluz had a son only fifteen years younger.

For the first three months we'd lived in Abancay, Livia and
Adolfo Eguiluz had invited us often to their home for meals. In
all that time, no one, not even their two young children, had mentioned an absent member of their family. My mind flashed on
movie scenes where a handsome, eligible man enters the picture
and the movie takes a romantic twist. My musing came to a halt
when I realized the son was over two years younger than me. A
mere child compared to my sophisticated age of twenty-two. We
invited Señor Eguiluz to that night's party.

Our Minnesota friends weren't at their hotel when we went
to collect them. But Adolfo came to the party smelling of Old
Spice and with his dark hair slicked back. He looked a little over-
dressed in his maroon cravat and dressy pants. Peace Corps guys
just wore jeans and t-shirts.

A Peace Corps buddy from out of town brought delicious champagne, which he sprayed all over the room in celebration of something. We drank what was left. It tickled my throat all the way down.

Someone put, "Louie, Louie," on the phonograph, and Wayne, a volunteer with the group trained to develop cooperatives, asked me to dance. After, we talked until my voice was hoarse. Everyone knew that Wayne had a steady girl assigned to a city on the coast. I'd convinced myself that we had a purely intellectual attraction when Wayne's friend, John, walked by.

"You might as well give up on bedding her, Wayne," John said. "She's a Christian."

Neither Wayne nor I responded. At first I was taken aback, then proud. I preferred to be thought of as "holy" rather than having the reputation of being easy—like all the women in the U.S. movies shown in local theaters and some of the Peace Corps girls. From the beginning of our stay, Marie and I had been careful not to get labeled "sexually available." We wanted men to treat us with respect. Pure when I arrived, I vowed to remain that way until I left.

Besides plain Cokes, someone made rum-and-Cokes and Pisco Sours. I hadn't drunk much liquor during the four years I'd attended my all-women's Catholic college. Now I made up for that drought. Drinking and dancing to "Hard Day's Night" and "Twist and Shout" by the Beatles dulled the soreness in my arms from four immunizations and the pain in my blistered feet from dancing.

At two in the morning, Wayne walked Marie and me back to our economical hotel. The entry door was locked. We rang the bell repeatedly to rouse the night clerk, but he never came. Then Wayne made an unusual proposal. He and John had an extra double bed in their room at a higher-class hotel. Marie and I looked at one another. It was against our principles, but we couldn't sleep in the street. No other solution existed but to spend what was left of the night in Wayne and John's hotel room where he said John was probably already asleep.

The next morning John looked shocked to wake up in his bed and find Marie and me in the bed across from him. But he had no time for smart remarks. He and Wayne had to catch the 6:00 a.m. bus back to their work site out of town.

The hotel people looked surprised when Marie and I came out of the guys' room at 9:00 a.m. At our cheap hotel we raised Cain about not being able to get in the night before. Our complaining stopped when the manager promised us a discount.

❖ ❖ ❖ ❖

We traveled back to Abancay six days after we'd worried about getting to Cusco. A repaired Tagli bus rumbled along as I slept, dreaming of dancing at the party. Besides supplies and happy feelings, we carried 13 cc of gamma globulin, an anti-hepatitis serum. The nuns at the hospital would inject the solution into our backsides in two weeks. At least on this trip we didn't have the pain of bouncing on sore bottoms in a bus for eight hours. Eight hours—when mechanical breakdowns or landslides didn't slow us. For now, we had full cupboards and bank accounts. We could look forward to meeting Antonio, Señor Eguiluz's college-aged stepson.

Beginning

The Eguiluzes invited Marie and me to lunch at their home almost daily for the next weeks. I sat across from Livia Eguiluz's son, Antonio, whom she said was almost twenty-two, not twenty. Between conversations about the latest political events in Peru, I admired Antonio's thick, wavy jet-black hair, broad shoulders, and slim waist. He stood a few inches taller than Marie but towered a head above me. I caught him sneaking sly glances at me during meals from the first course of soup through dessert. I couldn't deny our mutual attraction.

After a week of our flirting, an inner force urged me to take matters into my hands to become better acquainted with this attractive college student. We would never get to know each other by sitting at lunch surrounded by his family. We needed to be alone somewhere. I toyed with ways to talk privately with Antonio. Several meals later, I got up my nerve and scribbled a note.

"Brigida," I whispered to the hired girl when she set the bowl of hot lentil soup before me, "give this message to Antonio after I leave." She smiled, nodded, and put the piece of paper in her apron pocket. The note read: "Meet me at the grove of trees on the cliff above the swimming pool this afternoon at three."

Regrets swirled in my head the moment the note left my hand. Taking the initiative might be perceived as too aggressive. Maybe I shouldn't be so impulsive and daring as to suggest a clandestine meeting. On the other hand, I could be impetuous when I wanted something—or thought I wanted something.

Antonio had paid attention to both Marie and me since we'd met him. At first I thought of him as a kind of brother, like Marie did. He teased us equally when he walked us home. But he seemed to glance at and joke more with me. I sensed Antonio's attraction to me from the beginning. Why then didn't *he* suggest a move from friendship to the next level? He seemed more timid to pursue me than I was to learn about him. He could have sent me a note.

A bit before three, I walked to the edge of town dressed in the red and pink Inca-print sundress I'd just finished sewing. Perspiration beaded on my forehead, and not because of the warm afternoon. I stood beneath one of the tall pine trees, nervous. How could I be so bold? Maybe I shouldn't be here. But the looks Antonio and I had exchanged during meals signaled allure. I'd never before felt such a strong yearning for a deeper connection than with this handsome young Peruvian.

The sounds of happy chatter and laughter floated up the cliffside. Young people swam in the pool far below. I leaned against a tree and looked down at the joyful scene. Panic welled up inside me. I could run down the road and join the swimmers or even turn around and go home. Maybe my note lay forgotten in Brigida's pocket. If Antonio did read it, would he think me too brash? I heard rustling in the grass coming toward me.

"Boo!" Antonio said in a teasing tone as he poked his head around the tree where I stood. "I got the note. What did you want to see me about?"

"Oh," I said, my cheeks burning and probably matching the color of my sundress, "I just wanted to get to know you away from the others."

He smiled and looked pleased. I relaxed a little and my agitation calmed. A warm glow stirred inside me.

"What more did you want to know about me?" he said, his brown eyes full of mischief.

He put his arm around my waist and pulled me down onto the grass. I gasped at his boldness and strong arm. What feelings had I unleashed in him and in myself? I might be playing with fire. Still, his presence comforted me. I loved the feel of our bodies next to one another.

"I don't think I can stay long enough to hear about *all* your hopes and dreams," I said, quivering in the heat and not looking at him. "And, I don't want anyone to get the wrong idea."

"What idea would that be?" he said with a twinkle in his eye. I didn't answer.

We talked for an hour, sitting side by side on the cushion of grass. Antonio hesitated when I asked about his early life. With occasional stops to squeeze my shoulders, he explained a bit about his past. Until he was thirteen, he and his mother had lived with her parents either in Cusco or in his maternal grandparents' hacienda below Machu Picchu. He may have been born in the town below the mountain of Machu Picchu, but he had never visited the famous ruins above the hacienda. He lived with cousins while attending the best high school in Cusco. Summers, he and a gaggle of cousins helped his grandparents harvest sugar cane and other crops on their hacienda. I loved gazing at Antonio's ample lips as he spoke about his life.

Antonio didn't like studying economics. His stepfather, who'd married Antonio's mother nine years before, selected that course of study for him. Antonio liked science and wanted to study physics, but his stepfather paid the bills. He had come home this summer to experience being part of his nuclear family for the first time. His biological father had left Peru many years ago to live in the United States, and except for an occasional letter, had never been part of his life. I didn't insist on details. I didn't want to pry into an area he seemed unenthusiastic to share.

We had much in common. I, too, had grown up around crops and animals in a rural area and lived away from home during my high school years. Both of us were the first-born children in our families. Though we came from countries on dissimilar continents and spoke different languages, we possessed similar values. Our love of nature and empathy for those less fortunate connected us. Talking under the trees, I saw the type of man I could care about and who might care for me. We related at a more personal level than when we sat at the Eguiluz' meal table.

Most evenings after our first rendezvous, Antonio invited me to stroll around Abancay with him. I was interested to know what he thought and felt about everything. We didn't always understand one another. He talked faster than I could follow with my basic Spanish. His large vocabulary made his ideas too complex for me to grasp in their entirety. Yet my Spanish improved dramatically with each conversation and Antonio's corrections of my grammar.

My affection for him grew with each outing, but I couldn't show it. I had to be careful not to provoke town gossip. The American movies that played at Abancay's El Nilo Theater gave the impression that most American women were eager to jump into bed with any man who glanced their way. Marie and I didn't want to reinforce that view with our behavior. We were the first women from the States many locals had ever seen. Resident males often said that they'd be happy to provide companionship if we were lonesome, since we were so far from home. We became adept at changing the topic when men wanted to discuss their desire to bed us.

We had to be super vigilant of our reputations in our small town. We dressed modestly and outwardly ignored the sexual advances from hormonal men. Inside the walls of our house, however, we complained to one another that we walked a fine line between sexual provocation and innocence. We gained a wholesome reputation in Abancay by ignoring sexually tinged remarks sent our way by the men we encountered.

One friend, whose parents had died, had a brother who didn't allow her to accompany us to the movies. He checked to make certain her clothing didn't appear suggestive, though she couldn't totally hide her curvy figure. Her brother allowed our friend to leave the house only to work in the family's fabric store. Maybe the brother had the right idea because another unmarried woman was pregnant with the baby of a friend of ours. The male friend paid more attention to us than he did to her—and he didn't appear inclined to marry the mother of his child.

However, both Marie and I enjoyed talking to the local men more than to the women. The men had read more books, been more places, and knew more about the world, so we enjoyed their more stimulating conversations. The women, confined to their homes, had a narrower range of experiences and interests. Except for our teacher girlfriends who were single, many women in Abancay appeared to be pawns of their boyfriends or husbands. Domestic issues might interest most of the town's females, but food preparation, childcare, and who was dating whom didn't always interest us. Our educational opportunities and financial independence encouraged us to think beyond domestic issues— prospects these women didn't yet have. I'd known such women where I'd grown up in Ismay, Montana. But I wanted to be like the strong, not the submissive women I knew there.

Strong Women

In the 1950s most Ismay girls were destined to marry a local rancher by age eighteen, cook for scores of hired men, and raise a brood of little ranch hands. To me, boys seemed too much trouble to ever marry one. Besides, my parents had other goals for their four daughters. Daddy wanted his children to obtain university degrees. For him, our futures held college, not horses and husbands.

Mama looked at higher education from a different perspective. She had taken a year of business classes and worked as a secretary for three years before marrying Daddy. But she had little time to use her education with five children born one after another within the first eleven years of marriage. Seven days a week from dawn to dusk she cooked, cleaned, and washed clothes, often carrying water from an outdoor well. Her harried days left her little time to enjoy her children. She seemed happiest when sewing on her Singer treadle machine. Though I admired my mother's work ethic and frugality, I didn't want a life whose value appeared to come from having a clean house and well-fed children. Mom pushed us to earn good grades and college degrees for practical reasons.

"If you girls ever have to support yourselves," she said, "a college education will come in handy."

I wanted enough education so I could be like Mrs. Hoem and not like Winnie. I admired Evelynn Hoem, my tall, blonde, brown-eyed eighth-grade teacher. I felt sorry for diminutive Winnie, a rancher's wife for whom I worked now and then as a hired girl. Both had husbands not worth a damn, but one was happy while the other suffered the humiliation of being dependent on a mean man.

Mrs. Hoem didn't depend on her husband to support her or make her decisions. She had a mind and functioned independently, in part because her husband was away hauling cattle for long periods. Winnie had no college education or employable skills and, therefore, few options. She had only what her husband said she could have. Winnie was destined to do whatever others, mostly her husband and sons, demanded of her. Mrs. Hoem's path would be better for me. She was a role model, and Winnie, a warning.

Mrs. Hoem had an interesting career that allowed her to live in a world of learning and books. She decided where she would work and live. She arranged her life to suit herself and that of her two children. The outcome made her a dynamic woman who seemed happy without her husband around. I liked that. Independence and adventure would be in my future too.

Winnie's husband yelled for her to fix him a meal whenever he wanted food. Winnie complied, her lips tight and unsmiling. She pleaded with her young sons to be quiet so their noise wouldn't bother their father. The kids rarely obeyed her, and Winnie's thin body shrank under the threat of her overbearing husband. She vacillated between choices, unsure what would please others. Her

uncertainty made her appear nervous. Her effort to make everyone happy seemed to leave everyone unsatisfied.

When driving her car, Winnie demonstrated her uncertainty. She stepped on the gas pedal of her big Buick and it lunged
forward. Uneasy about her speed, two seconds later she released
the accelerator. The car slowed in response. For the entire sixty-
two-mile drive from her ranch to Miles City, Winnie's three small
boys and I propelled forward, then lurched backward—like riding
a bucking bronco. By the time we got to the kids' doctor appointments, Winnie's driving had worn us out.

"I need two husbands," Winnie lamented, shrugging her
bony shoulders and scowling. "One to support me and one to
have fun with."

Evelynn Hoem had backbone, so provided her own support
and fun. Teaching gave her the self-confidence to deal with
whatever she faced, including the rowdy boys in my eighth-grade
classroom. Displaying a kind but firm manner she got those boys
to do what she told them. I admired my teacher so much that I
changed the way I wrote the *E* in my signature to look like how
she wrote hers.

I also admired Fernande Garber, my mother's Belgian-born
best friend. She displayed Mrs. Hoem's same confident nature and
more. I worked at Garber's sheep ranch as a hired girl weekends
and a summer during my high school years—and I loved the job
and Fernande. She was fascinating and fun.

Fernande had lived in a far-away country, Belgium, which
I'd never heard of. She'd survived war-torn Europe and arrived in
the U.S. at age nineteen with ten dollars in her pocket. She met her
husband, Gene Garber, in Sheridan, Wyoming, where she worked
as a maid and nanny. After Gene and Fernande married, they
moved to a ranch outside Ismay. The couple became my parents'
best friends, and Fernande became an important role model for

me. She had a determined attitude that had helped her overcome much adversity in the first decades of her life.

Fernande had had little food in Belgium during WWII, so she hadn't learned to cook. Yet in Montana, she became skilled at cooking along with the challenge of ranch life. She could feed crews of thirty men at a time during lambing, shearing, branding and haying seasons. Summers, she canned vegetables from her large garden. She carved beef, lamb, and pig carcasses with skill and could butcher one-hundred-twenty chickens in a day. She adapted and triumphed over adversity.

Gene Garber claimed to know the best solutions to most local and world problems and also wanted his meals ready when he came in from the fields. Despite her husband's strong opinions and demands, and unlike Winnie, Fernande couldn't be intimidated. She was an equal partner with her husband. She participated in conversations and storytelling and stood her ground with Gene and the hired men—even when she misunderstood American expressions.

"Fernande, you're pulling my leg," one of the hired men, Vern, said at dinner one evening after my employer had recounted a lively story.

"Why Vern," Fernande said, her face becoming red, "I'm not even touching your leg."

Fernande wouldn't do three things. She wouldn't ride a horse because she didn't trust them. She wouldn't drive a tractor because she couldn't see herself driving anything more powerful than her Chevy station wagon. And she wouldn't milk cows because she wanted her husband at home each evening for dinner with her children. If the men had to come home to milk the dairy cows, they couldn't stay in the fields past mealtime. She was adamant on the subject of family dinner together.

Often Fernande cooked the meat for the ranch's working crews while I stood beside her peeling potatoes as she described a land far beyond Ismay. I never tired of hearing Fernande's stories of her childhood or how she improved her life. Her foreign-looking silver and copper vases and the French lace doilies I lifted to dust under fascinated me as much as her tales of survival. Fernande liked beautiful things. Her high standards of home decor, cleanliness, and caring set an example for me that fed my curiosity about art, people, and foreign places.

From the ages of eleven to fifteen I worked summers for twenty-five dollars a month as a hired girl on the ranches of four different families. But I enjoyed working for Fernande Garber the most. In a gentle voice she asked me to set the dishes for supper or put her latest toddler on the potty. Fernande seemed less demanding and more empathetic than the other women I worked for. Maybe her attitude stemmed from having been a nanny and maid ten years before.

Fernande Garber and Evelynn Hoem set a standard that fired my determination to have an interesting and independent life. Antonio seemed like the kind of man who, as a husband, wouldn't try to dominate me.

Falling

Antonio also proved the most discreet of our friends. He didn't hang out with the young men of Abancay so no nasty rumors circulated about our growing friendship. Several rainy evenings he invited me for tea or ice cream in a downtown shop where, at first, people's stares made me uncomfortable. Locals seemed to view me as a novelty because I'd become friends with one of their own. When I expressed my unease of being stared at, Antonio had me sit with my back to people entering the ice cream shop. That way I could enjoy his company and ignore patrons' curious gazes.

One evening before dusk, we passed a bicycle shop. Antonio stopped.

"You want to ride bikes?" he asked.

"Sure, why not?" I said.

Off we went, riding up and down Abancay's smooth concrete streets laughing until we reached the muddy road that led to the hospital. There, we had to ford a running stream. Antonio made it across, but I hesitated. The current was strong. He took me by the hand, helped me jump across, and then picked up my bike and brought it to me. I couldn't recall when anyone had ever treated me with such consideration. I felt special.

Often, we sat on one of the white benches beneath the palm trees in the main plaza and talked as the sun slipped behind the mountains. Antonio regaled me with tales of his life when he hunted small game, farmed with his grandfather, or played soccer. I comprehended half of what he told me. He became most animated recounting the history of the Incas in Peru. He proudly announced that he'd descended from that indigenous culture. His light skin and his mother contradicted his pronouncement, but no doubt he had some Indian blood, as did 80 percent of Peru's population.

One evening we encountered a wizened old blind man below the church steps in the main plaza. The man bent over his cane and seemed confused about which way to go. Antonio spoke to him in Quechua, then led the man up the stairs and set him on the sidewalk to continue on his way. My friend's kindness impressed me, and a bolt of affection surged through my body. I couldn't comprehend these strange new stirrings. When not with Antonio, I thought of him. Work no longer was a top priority. My emotions swirled in turmoil. I had no appetite and had a hard time sleeping.

When Antonio returned to his college classes in Cusco in mid-March, my feelings alternated between loss and relief. My appetite and full nights of sleep returned. Then I was summoned to Cusco for a dental checkup.

A dentist in Cusco had performed a root canal on my front tooth two months earlier—the aftermath of damaging my teeth in an impulsive attempt in college to jump over a tennis net and falling flat on my face. Now the dentist reported that, depending on what he viewed in new x-rays, he might have to cut my gum open. I tried not to think about it.

In Cusco I distracted myself by watching the hordes of university students walking down Avenida Sol at the beginning of the new school year. Hundreds of young people my age filled the sidewalks. I scanned the crowds hoping to see Antonio's mop of wavy black hair bouncing above the throngs.

When the dentist said I'd healed fine and my treatment was finished, I prepared to return to Abancay. I celebrated my good fortune by visiting a fabric store and purchasing green tweed wool to sew a new outfit. Then I had my hair cut at my favorite salon. The short hairdo turned out better than expected. I hoped Antonio would like it too, if I ran into him.

Before I left Cusco I needed to stop at the El Chinito grocery store, the only place that sold the American-type foods that Marie and I depended upon. I rounded the corner after leaving the store and saw a familiar slim body coming toward me. I was delighted to see Antonio.

"I just finished signing up for my classes," he said giving me a quick hug. "But I have to get back to Abancay. I got a phone call that my mother is ill. The baby is due soon."

"Oh, I'm sorry your mother isn't well," I said, tossing my new hairdo. "The dentist said I'm finished with him so I need to get back home too."

"I'd better buy my bus ticket for tomorrow," he said.

He seemed not to hear that I'd be returning too, or notice my haircut. I waited for him to suggest we travel together on the Tagli bus the next day. But he stared into the distance, anxious to be on his way. He gave me a peck on the cheek goodbye and went off in the direction of the bus depot. I'd never seen him so preoccupied and wondered how ill his mother might be.

I'd only recently learned that she was expecting. The notice about the baby occurred in the same matter-of-fact way that Señor Eguiluz had informed Marie and me of Antonio's existence. We'd been caught off guard again when Livia mentioned at a recent lunch that her fourth child was due in April. Neither Marie nor I had noticed her pregnancy in the past four months even though we'd seen Livia almost daily. I hoped her pregnancy problems weren't serious.

After Antonio left me, I returned to the fabric store to buy some flannel to make a layette for the newest Eguiluz. When I reached the bus depot later, the ticket seller said there were no seats available for the next day's trip to Abancay. I looked down the list of passengers and didn't see Antonio's name. He must not have gotten a ticket either.

At lunch a Peace Corps colleague said he'd encountered a lawyer who would be driving to Abancay the next day. I chanced upon the attorney as I left the Cuzco Restaurant. I asked if he had room in his car for Antonio and me. He did. I hurried off and miraculously encountered Antonio on the Plaza. I informed him that I'd found a ride for us back to Abancay. He seemed relieved and pleased.

We left Cusco at 4 p.m., with Antonio and me squashed into the back seat of a Volkswagen beetle. Antonio knew the lawyer. They were members of the same political party. We arrived at the Pampa de Anta plains an hour later as the sun dipped below the Andes. The light of a full moon sparkled off the snow on the 16,000-foot mountain peaks. A river of moon glow bathed the countryside. The beauty of the night filled me.

The men's talk of politics ceased, and Antonio's hand reached for mine. I didn't resist. My body tingled. We held hands, exchanging few words for the next five hours. I was in heaven.

We arrived in Abancay in the evening. The lawyer dropped us off in front of the big wooden doors to the education department behind which I lived. We stood in the darkness, reluctant to say goodnight.

"Will you be my *enamorada*?" Antonio said. He bent down and kissed me.

I thrilled to his full lips on mine. But I felt troubled. I didn't know exactly what being an *enamorada* meant. I knew it entailed some form of commitment. I liked Antonio a lot and missed him when we were separated. Since I didn't plan to live my life in Peru, however, I couldn't promise to be his girlfriend. I didn't want to give him the false hope of a future life together in Peru. And, I had other conflicts.

Other guys besides Antonio circled around me. Like Julio, the intern physician brother of our best friends, Zoila and Zulma. My feelings for Julio weren't as deep as for Antonio, but I did enjoy the kind, entertaining young man and didn't want to offend his sisters by ignoring their brother. If being Antonio's *enamorada* meant going steady, then I wasn't sure I wanted to be exclusive.

"Let's just be good *amigos,*" I said.

"But I love you," he said, "and want us to be together."

"I love being with you too," I said, "but I'm not ready to commit to anything."

Antonio persisted. His words and actions seemed sincere. Not like many of the Latin guys who'd asked me to marry them before but really only wanted to bed me. But what did being an *enamorada* entail? I worried it meant having sex with him. That was out of the question. I was a chaste, devout, Catholic girl.

Antonio held me in another warm embrace and kissed me again. My skin warmed to his touch. I reconsidered my long-held religious beliefs. I liked Antonio's quiet, attentive ways. I guessed it wouldn't hurt to agree. I did love being with him.

"*Sí,*" I said. "I'll be your *enamorada.*"

Antonio kissed me one last time before he hurried down the street to his ailing mother. My heart seemed to echo inside the hallway as I floated up the stairs to my house. What had I just agreed to? We had no future together. Antonio had said he could offer me nothing but himself. Maybe that would be enough for the time being. I determined to enjoy what existed now and not focus on what could not be in the future. I'd enjoy Antonio when we could be together, which happened off and on during the next months when he came to Abancay, or I went to Cusco. But I had to remember why I'd come to Peru. My main focus needed to be on training for a move from our town out to the countryside.

Preparing

Marie and I had been granted our wish to use our community development training in an area poorer than Abancay. Our Department of Education hosts had suggested we move to Suncho, a town under construction an hour away. An adobe house could soon be built for us near the one-room school just completed there. Governmental officials in both Lima and Abancay agreed that the Indians in the area should come down from the mountaintops where they grew and preserved potatoes. By moving closer to a school and a road, agency personnel said the indigenous potato growers could participate in Peruvian life. Marie and I reveled in the belief that we could assist poor people in the province who were in most need of help.

In order to provide health care to the isolated population, we would need medical training. So Señor Eguiluz arranged for us to intern at Abancay's German-built hospital staffed by German nuns and Peruvian doctors. Local statistics we collected in a government-sponsored survey in the small surrounding towns disclosed that half the children born died before age five.

The idea of us working in the countryside with people in greater need seemed more meaningful than reading stories to rowdy middle-class students.

◇·◇·◇·◇

The gleaming two-story, white cement-block hospital stood out among the adobe dirt-colored houses on the outskirts of Abancay. Inside the facility, new stools, chrome-trimmed tables, and medical instruments reflected on the polished blue tile floors. The place smelled of disinfectant. I looked forward to spending my days in the cleanest place in town.

Until now, my only contact with a hospital had been at age twelve when I occupied a room at Holy Rosary Hospital in Miles City, Montana. For the month of December 1954, my pediatrician attempted to determine if my flulike symptoms meant I had rheumatic fever. Except for the occasional pain of blood tests and spinal taps, which remained inconclusive, I had enjoyed my stay. During the day I read books, and each evening I listened to comedians Bob and Ray on the radio. I had never considered entering the medical profession since I didn't like seeing others' pain. Now, ten years after my initial hospital experience, Marie and I were working in the Abancay hospital clinic. Daily, from December through April, we learned about the ailments and injuries in this part of the world.

On the first morning I pushed the plunger of a syringe through its tube until water squirted out the tip. With a hypodermic needle in one hand and an orange in the other, I jabbed the fruit's tough skin, one, two, three times. Injecting produce was practice for the day I'd puncture patients' arms and backsides. Oranges couldn't feel the pain.

I wasn't so confident, however, when I had to give a shot to real people. If they flinched, I hesitated to inflict more discomfort.

I bent two needles trying to pierce the leathery backside of a thin little indigenous man. When the needle finally went in, it hit a bone and the man winced. So did I. Only after I'd given scores of injections, did I stop empathizing with patients' pains. I progressed to where I could stab the two-inch arm of a sick child with a three-inch needle without it coming out the other side and without feeling squeamish.

I understood the benefit to any hurt I might cause with a needle prick when ailing children perked up after a shot of penicillin. Besides, I'd had plenty of experience getting jabbed with needles from my early life in the hospital. Even now, the Peace Corps doctor inoculated me almost monthly against the plague, hepatitis, or some other potential affliction.

Every morning we arrived at the clinic to find local and out-of-town indigenous people lined up looking for relief from a myriad of ailments both large and small. Babes in arms played with their mothers' long black braids. Runny-nosed toddlers clung to their plump caretakers' multicolored skirts. Children arrived from the countryside with mosquito bites that blanketed every spot on their legs. We swabbed red Mercurochrome on their mosquito bites and bee stings, infected from being scratched with dirty fingernails. Afterwards, the kids looked like they belonged to a strange species of spotted red people.

Battered women came in with bruises and black eyes, the targets of drunken husbands. We applied bags of ice and treated the women's physical lacerations. Soothing their damaged emotions proved harder. We could only listen to their tales of woe. I'd experienced my father verbally abusing my mother, but he never laid a hand on her in anger. At age ten, when I spent the night at an aunt's, I'd heard her husband beat her. The violence paralyzed me with fear. I assumed the women in the Apurimac Province, like in North Dakota, thought they had little choice but to remain with their abusive men. I could never remain with a man who mistreated me like that.

A stocky man came in with teeth marks in what remained of his ear. A member of the opposing soccer team had bitten off the outer portion. The ear could not be reattached. The doctor could only treat the remainder of the appendage against infection.

A bullfighter limped in holding his gored right side. The nurses on duty wound gauze and tape around his midsection. We saw the matador back in the bullfighting ring a week later. Tough but reckless people, I mused, like where I grew up.

Nothing could help the man with the cut in his arm that had gone untreated for weeks. Gangrene had set in. All the doctor could do was amputate the limb. I wondered how well the farmer would be able to work in the fields with only one arm. I had compassion for these little bare-footed men who drank as hard as they worked. They had to survive a life spent tilling the soil at high altitudes to grow enough food for their families.

Marie and I treated scores of severe puncture wounds each week. The open sandals the laborers made from discarded tires gave no protection from the long, sharp cactus spines that lurked in the cornfields. Men came to the clinic when they could hardly walk. I'd helped treat cactus injuries previously in Mexico, so I wasn't surprised by the damage the sharp needles could do.

One man had a foot swollen to the size of a ham. We removed the cactus needle and soaked the sore foot to remove the layers of dirt. I watched a nurse drain pus from the abscess, disinfect the wound, and bandage the limb. Then, like the bullfighter, the man hobbled right back to the place where he'd been injured in the first place. The farmer had the help of a crude wooden crutch he leaned on in the fields where he eked out a living. The ball of coca leaves he stuck in his cheek would boost his energy and dull his pain.

Buses rounding hairpin curves too fast plunged off mountain roads. Trucks ran into cars on narrow two-lane thoroughfares. New patients arrived at our hospital with punctured lungs and broken feet, legs, and arms. The vehicle crashes, like the wife beatings, were often the result of drinking *chicha*, homemade beer made from fermented corn. Excessive alcohol consumption brought the hospital considerable business. No matter the cause of the calamity, the doctors and nurses treated everyone with dedication.

In the operating theater, we witnessed the doctors remove uteruses and appendixes from abdomens, and growths of all sizes from legs, arms, and skulls. Each cut and stream of blood made me cringe. I admired the physicians' surgical skills but remained mystified at how nonchalant they acted when performing serious procedures. They joked and laughed when they removed a tumor, even if blood squirted all over and the patient needed another shot of painkiller. I didn't see anything funny about what happened. Even though the doctors kidded around in the operating room, they could also be deadly serious. And they taught me more about the human body and its vulnerability than I wished to know.

I wanted to know how to deliver a baby because we might be called upon to be midwives in Suncho when we moved there. The opportunity arose a month into our training. The first woman we saw looked relaxed and asked us our names. Before she went into the delivery room, she requested we give her a list of American names. The baby slipped out the way I'd seen in a movie in high school biology class. Before we had time to write down any names, the woman named the girl Evelyn. I liked my name and felt happy that now someone in Abancay would share it.

A pretty sixteen-year-old girl had difficulty giving birth to a nine-pound boy and was in labor for an entire day. For six hours we cooled her forehead, held her hand, and listened to her moan in the delivery room. No man had come with her to the hospital. Perhaps it was her beauty that had put her in such a difficult situation—unmarried and about to give birth. I felt sorry for her and swore I'd never let myself be in that position.

However, at age twenty-two I knew less than the pretty teenager about how she'd gotten pregnant. My knowledge of sex had come from three confusing sources: phonograph records the priests played in summer catechism classes that explained male–female differences; illustrations in my parents' big medical book, viewed with a flashlight from under my blanket; and a movie in high school of a birth. Though I had an idea about how women got pregnant, I'd never been told how to prevent it. Now, however, I only needed to know about birthing babies, not preventing them.

One time, the afterbirth didn't expel from a woman's womb after she delivered her fifteenth baby. She bled and bled and her blood pressure dropped to a dangerous level. I stood by as the crisis worsened and she continued to hemorrhage. Nothing seemed to stop the bleeding. What would happen to her fifteen children if she died? Dr. Delgado had had only three hours of sleep, but he worked tirelessly to stop the woman's blood loss. When he finally got it under control, he gave her a transfusion of his own blood. He saved her life, and her brood of children would have a mother.

Another time Dr. Alvarez delivered a baby who didn't breathe after coming out of the birth canal. As the newborn struggled to get enough oxygen, the doctor sucked phlegm from the baby's lungs. He kept at the procedure until the baby's color went from blue to pink.

After Marie and I saw the pain of labor and knew what could go wrong, we agreed we'd think twice before ever getting pregnant. Our fears were reinforced when a nurse showed us recently born Siamese twins, joined at the breast and preserved in a big jar of formaldehyde. I gasped with revulsion. The vision of those twins haunted me for days.

One January day I watched Dr. Alvarez conduct a pelvic exam. Over time I'd become less self-conscious when viewing patients' private parts alongside the young doctors, though I still remained uncomfortable in the situation. To my surprise, Marie entered the examining room, a look of concern on her face.

"The Education Department received a message for us from the Peace Corps office." she whispered. "They say an important call came in from Mr. Cavendish."

The urgency gave me an excuse to leave the awkward exam. Something must be seriously wrong. Peace Corps Regional Director Cavendish had never phoned us before. Likely he never thought of us except to point out our violation of his unknown policies.

"Maybe we are in trouble for taking a week to return to Abancay from Lima after Christmas," I speculated as I hung up my white coat in the nurse's room. "He probably wants to dock our pay or take more vacation time from us." Monitoring our vacation time seemed more important to him than any work we did.

"Or maybe something has happened to someone at home," Marie said, alarmed.

We waited at Abancay's central telephone office for our boss to call back. He didn't. After one and a half hours, we rang the Peace Corps secretary.

"Call back at 3:30," she said, "when Mr. Cavendish will be here."

"I'll be coming out to Abancay," Mr. C said when we finally reached him.

Was that the urgent message? He had announced his imminent arrival in Abancay four times before and never appeared. We wondered if this time he would really show up. In two and a half months, he hadn't seen where we lived, even though his job required assessing each volunteer's worksite.

"I'm sending out two new volunteers, Al and Ken," Mr. C continued. "They're agriculturalists. I'll be out next week to check on them."

Once we knew we weren't in trouble and that no one at home had died, we liked the idea of new talent joining us. Volunteers with some specialization that the community needed would be a real plus. Local farmers could use outside expertise to help improve the yield of their wheat, corn, and quinoa crops. The guys could also work at raising healthy chickens at the state agricultural farm on the outskirts of Abancay.

Al and Ken, recent college graduates, arrived by bus two days later. Al was six feet tall, with the build of a football player. He had brown eyes and a crew cut, and he had been an English major in college. Ken was thin, three inches shorter than Al, with baby-fine light brown hair and thick glasses that covered his blue eyes. He looked like an accountant but had recently graduated from the University of Wisconsin with a degree in political science. Ken and Al's college majors were even less useful in Peru than Marie's and mine.

It turned out that Ken and Al had been given only a few weeks of training in agriculture in Mexico. They said they weren't competent to provide new knowledge to the local farmers. Neither spoke much Spanish. Both refused to raise chickens. Our hopes evaporated. And Mr. C didn't visit Abancay as promised.

Señor Eguiluz helped the two new volunteers find a place to live. He located an apartment for them, larger than ours, but one that required paying rent. In the beginning, we liked having other Americans share our town. Al and Ken were more polite than the male volunteers who'd been in the country for a while. We thanked them when they brought our checks and mail from Cusco. We enjoyed it when they pulled out chairs for us and paid for our dinners at the main restaurant in town. They hadn't heard about the Peace Corps rule of always going Dutch, and we didn't educate them.

Ken offered to build us a set of shelves or anything else we needed. But he often voiced concern about our health and welfare. Didn't he realize that we had been getting along fine before he arrived? Once he voiced alarm at seeing me walk barefoot on our concrete floor.

"You'd better get some shoes on," he said, furrowing his brow. "You might get worms."

"We keep our floors clean," I said, laughing. "We just have a mouse we can't get rid of."

"I don't think the wall behind your place is high enough to keep the local men from climbing over it," Ken said scanning our impenetrable back wall.

"That adobe wall is eight feet high and two feet thick," I said. "and we haven't had any trouble with anyone crawling over it yet."

In some ways his anxiety about our welfare was sweet. We returned his favors by giving him our home-baked chocolate chip cookies.

Even after several months, neither Ken nor Al expressed himself very well in Spanish. They had no ideas about what projects they might do. Their lack of expertise and initiative frustrated me. I began to suspect maybe they'd joined the Peace Corps as a way out of fighting in Vietnam. Regardless, I believed they could contribute more here than there.

Our hopes faded as it became clear that the guys would not do much to help our adopted community. Al began to drink heavily and create chaos in the town bars. Some of the local drinkers welcomed Al's generosity when he paid for their drinks and said he'd give his possessions to them. Though usually

Ken's Catch of the Day

Ken in the Countryside

tolerant and respectful of Americans, several locals finally asked Señor Eguiluz to remove the drunken Al from their premises. We didn't want Al's actions to tarnish our reputations in our town but weren't sure what to do.

Ken caused less trouble. He spent most his time traveling around the area and fishing with a fiberglass pole he had brought from Wisconsin. He didn't catch any fish until he switched to a sugar cane pole like the natives used. Then he pulled dozens of trout from the river. When he wasn't traveling or catching, cleaning, and cooking trout for us, Ken suffered from stomach problems. Rather than accompany us to parties and socialize with our many friends, he stayed home and read books. Our frequent meals and discussions kept Ken from quitting and returning early to the States. We hadn't expected the new volunteers to be such problems. They barely survived while we thrived. And now we'd made plans to live in an even poorer, more isolated community.

Suncho

My alarm rang at 5 a.m. I hit the button to turn it off so I wouldn't awaken Marie. She had decided not to take the trip, but Ken and I would go with Señor Landeo, the Education Director, to see if our house in Suncho was ready after two months of waiting. I wanted to sleep a little longer, but I had to attend Sunday morning mass because I'd made a bargain with God. I'd promised the Almighty I'd go to mass daily for three months if Mr. Cavendish gave us permission to join our friends at Christmas. We'd gone to Lima, so I'd been on my knees at the Virgen del Rosario Cathedral every morning since January. In the morning darkness, I procrastinated. Considering how the Lima trip had turned out, I regretted having made the deal.

Fifteen minutes later, the bedsprings strained against their metal frame and I sat up. I grudgingly put my bare feet on the cold concrete floor. In the dim light of dawn, I dressed in my green print blouse, reversible wrap-around skirt and black tights. Peace Corps instructors had said that female volunteers made a better impression on officials if we wore dresses. I had always worn dresses at Holy Names so was used to them.

I tiptoed down the stairs and slid back the metal bolt on the heavy wooden door of the Education Department offices. The cool morning air slapped my face as I slipped out and hurried under dim streetlights to the cathedral. When I arrived at the five-thirty mass, it had almost finished. Rats! I ran to attend the seven o'clock service at the Carmelite convent. The singing of the cloistered sisters hidden behind a screen soothed me until the mass concluded at eight, and I began rushing again.

I joined Ken for a hurried steak-and-egg breakfast at the Apurimac Restaurant. Ken insisted on paying for my meal—after he borrowed fifty *soles* from me. In ten minutes back home, I slapped together a couple of peanut butter and jelly sandwiches and threw them and a can of fruit into a paper bag. I never wanted to be without some familiar food.

Señor Landeo picked Ken and me up at nine in his station wagon already loaded with the Landeo children and his pretty dark-haired wife. We drove through a light rain for an hour until we entered the road to Suncho.

Flowers, grass, and bamboo were woven into the wire fences along the entrance to the town. Their red, green, and yellow colors brightened up the roadside. I'd never seen decorated fences before. Where I lived in Montana, we'd never beautified our barbed wire fences. Barbed wire barriers existed to keep the cattle off the roads, not to be admired. Mrs. Landeo explained that the enclosures had been garlanded to impress the Peruvian Minister of Development, who would arrive soon to inspect the progress in Suncho.

Suncho hadn't changed much since I'd first seen it three months before. The façade of a church and one completed schoolroom stood as the only structures. Not a single block of the adobe house promised to Marie and me by March had been set in place. Tall wild grass waved in the breeze where houses were supposed to be. Rock fences surrounded a few mounds of dirt. We couldn't

Layout of Suncho

tell which mound stood as a marker for our house. Ken and Señor Landeo set about measuring lots with some local men. I went back to the car and napped with Mrs. Landeo.

Beeping horns from a caravan of vehicles awakened us a short time later. Mrs. Landeo said the Peruvian minister had arrived. I hoped the decorated entryway impressed him because surely he wouldn't like the lack of completed structures in our future town. I watched the country's head of development check the planning documents for Suncho. Then he strode over to the mounds of dirt to inspect the work so far. He didn't look at all disgruntled.

The indigenous people who the government expected to populate the town were absent. Apparently, they continued to live at the top of the mountain in Huayrapampa. It looked like the farmers preferred to remain with their potato crops high above where we stood. They were at the bottom of the class structure. Most likely, they couldn't take time off from growing and preserving their crops to greet a government official, who lived far above their subsistence level. I wanted to meet the potato-growers and asked the education director if Ken and I could ride horses up to where they lived. Señor Landeo said it would take two hours up and back, and he had to return to Abancay before then. He instructed everyone to head for the lunch table, where women from somewhere nearby had set out a spread of noodles and papaya.

I tasted a mouthful of native food. Most of the meals Livia Eguiluz prepared tasted delicious. But food in the countryside wasn't as tasty or nutritious as her meals. Today, I preferred the familiar food I'd packed, and in the disorganization of the setting, no one noticed when I headed to a hill by the river. Ken came too. The peanut butter and jelly sandwiches hit the spot, along with canned peaches we ate with a stick. I'd neglected to pack spoons. Meanwhile, local mosquitoes bit through my tights to lunch on my legs.

After eating, the men measured the velocity of the river, and the children ran up and down the mounds of dirt. I didn't want to do either. I returned to talk with Mrs. Landeo.

"Was it easy," I said, "giving birth to so many children?"

"It was fine," she said, "up until the last one. I had trouble. What about you? I imagine you'll want children someday."

"I don't know," I said, remembering the woman in the hospital who had almost died in childbirth. "I'm afraid, now that I've seen how painful it would be. Though I am eager to deliver babies of the families who will soon live here."

"Oh, didn't you know?" she said. "There probably won't be any families here until July. Right now, everybody's busy growing potatoes up on the mountain-top in Huayrapampa."

Everyone seemed pleased with the day's work. They congratulated one another with handshakes and hugs. Cases of beer appeared from somewhere, and each man had at least two bottles. Loud laughter filled the vehicle as we traveled the road home. I couldn't join in the frivolity. I felt disappointed that our mission to help develop the new town of Suncho wouldn't begin until July, if ever.

Potato Caper

The moisture that fell during the night of March 25, 1965, had been unexpected because the rainy season in the Andean Mountain area of Peru usually ended by February. But the morning dawned dry and warm in Abancay. The cloudless day meant my clothes would dry. I snatched the galvanized steel bucket from the porch and headed to fill it from the nearby faucet in the big water basin.

"After laundry duty," Marie shouted from inside our small cinderblock home, "let's hike up the side of one of the mountains."

"Good idea," I said, turning on the faucet. "We can pack some cheese sandwiches, apples and cookies and have a picnic."

I filled the bucket with water, still frigid from its origins— the melting snows of the 16,000-foot Mt. Ampay that towered above Abancay. Cold liquid sloshed on my skirt as I carried the pail to our open-air side room cooking area. I lit one of the kerosene primus burners and set the container of water on top of the flame.

When the water was warm, I dumped it into the plastic tub that sat on the knee-high adobe wall surrounding our small front yard. ACE soap granules rained down from the packet in my hand to form bubbles in the water. I grabbed the scrub board and began washing gray mud out of my reversible brown skirt.

I was plunging the skirt in and out of the sudsy wash water when Regional Education Director, Señor Chávez, and Ken came through the Education Department offices below and up the stairs to our yard. The roly-poly director with thinning black hair looked official in the gray suit he always wore. Chávez's girth dwarfed my blonde colleague. Ken's jeans hung loose on his thin frame. He'd tightened his belt another notch after his latest bout of dysentery.

Señor Chávez looked quizzically at me, the *gringa* washerwoman. I figured he must hire an indigenous *mamacita* to wash his family's clothes. He probably wondered why I hadn't done the same.

"Hey," Ken said. "Are you still planning to go to the *campesino* farmers' meeting?"

"No one told me anything about an Indian gathering," I said, thinking someone may have invited me in Spanish and I'd not understood.

"We're leaving in half an hour," Señor Chávez said, turning to go. Ken followed.

"Oh, we'll be ready," Marie shouted to their backs.

I hurried to rinse and hang up my wet clothes, and then we went outside expecting to see Señor Chávez's green Chevy drive up along our sidewalk. An hour passed. I hated the way locals treated time—like we had plenty of it to waste.

Around noon, a pickup came bouncing down the street and stopped in front of us. Inside sat a man whom we'd seen but didn't know. He had a big grin on his face and mischievous brown eyes.

"Hop in," the man said in Spanish through the open window, "I'm Señor Aguilar, a lawyer friend of Señor Chávez." He leaned over to open the passenger door. "He asked me to come by and get you," the young man said. "A bunch of us officials are going to see what trouble the *campesinos* are stirring up."

I was surprised the director would send a stranger to get us. I hoped he knew the way to the site and would tell us more about the meeting's agenda. Marie got into the pickup first.

"Thanks for giving us a ride," she said. I got in beside her and closed the door. Our new acquaintance bent his lean body across both our laps as he locked our door.

"The official meeting is thirty-six kilometers down the road," he said. He slid his nondriving arm along the seat behind Marie. "But we could find somewhere more secluded for just the three of us to go."

Maybe I'd misunderstood his flirtatious statement in Spanish. Marie looked over at me and rolled her eyes. I hadn't misinterpreted his intentions. Here was another Peruvian man who saw us as a couple of females to be conquered. I felt happy not to be the one sitting close to this aggressive guy.

We settled in for the uncomfortable twenty-two-mile ride—and not just because of the potholes. We'd have to endure whatever Señor Aguilar chose to dish out during the hour-long drive. Neither of us liked the lawyer's innuendos, though we were used to suggestive remarks from Peruvian men. Their off-color comments made us feel like sex objects. They often acted the same way when local young women accompanied us, but then seemed less vocal and insistent and were easier to ignore. Maybe they thought we had less family protection so were easier game.

"We usually take a bus or walk where we need to go," I said, ignoring Señor Aguilar's invitation. I had no attraction to this guy in the way he seemed to want.

"How about we park in those trees and enjoy the scenery?" the driver said, trying another approach.

Marie scooted closer to me. She disliked forward-acting men as much as I did. I hugged the door. Time to change the topic.

"What's the *campesino* meeting about?" I said.

"There was some incident at a hacienda," Señor Aguilar said. His leer changed to concern. I relaxed. "A group of indigenous people, who work for the woman landowner, had some trouble with her and asked the town officials to intercede."

After another forty-five minutes of chitchat, the truck slowed down. We saw several men stopped by the side of the road. Apparently, we'd arrived at the meeting place. The lawyer parked his pickup next to a cornfield on the side of a hill. People had gathered in two groups—the city officials in a huddle along the roadside and the indigenous residents sitting and standing on the hillside.

The heads of many of the local organizations had come. Those I recognized were the chief of the Food for Peace Program, two directors of the Regional Education Office, Ken, Agrarian Reform officials, investigators, lawyers, and the Guardia Civil regional police. I counted more than twenty-five armed, uniformed police officers. So much armament made me nervous.

Most of the city men wore their khaki Sunday best. The Education Department officials, as always, sported suits and ties. The seventy or so indigenous residents all wore hats. The men's fedoras ranged from faded gray to faded black. Round, black or beige felt hats topped the long black braids of the indigenous women. The ever-present headgear shaded their skin from the sun's damaging rays at the 10,000- to 16,000-foot altitude where they lived and farmed. I relished this time out in nature in glorious weather—but not the sunburn we'd probably get because Marie and I had neglected to bring hats.

The women's hat colors contrasted with their bright ankle-length, hand-woven red wool skirts, with bands of white trim along the hems. On their feet a few of the men sported dusty leather oxfords, while others wore the familiar sandals made from old tires. But most of the men and women walked on the thick field grass and gravel in bare feet. I could see why we treated so many foot wounds at the hospital where Marie and I worked.

Señor Aguilar left the pickup and approached the group of officials and Ken. Marie and I watched. After conferring with the others, the lawyer gathered together a small group of indigenous men. He seemed in charge of getting the details. To do that, the men had to climb through a cornfield up to a potato field at the top of the hill. Marie and I had exited our vehicle but weren't invited. None of the red-skirted women went either. Apparently, females couldn't be included when examining potato fields.

The Indian women glanced at us as they scurried back and forth between the houses across the road. They set a table with white enamel plates, cups, and food. We'd learned the Quechua language greeting of the indigenous people, "Allillanchu," and used it. The women smiled back. A pack of scruffy-looking dogs sniffed around the food. I ducked inside the pickup whenever a dog growled near me. I'd been afraid of all canines—except my dog Teddy—since childhood. In my youth in Ismay, Montana, dogs had snarled at me, and a German shepherd almost ate me alive when I was in high school. Dogs seemed to sense my fear of them.

The men returned after half an hour, and Señor Aguilar told us what he'd learned. The indigenous farmers who lived near the hacienda had gotten permission from the owner to plant some potatoes for themselves in the field up the hill. When the potatoes matured, the woman owner of the hacienda, the *dueña,* changed her mind and decided she wanted not just the agreed-upon portion but all the potatoes for herself.

The previous day, the *dueña* had armed herself and gone to the potato patch where the Indians were working. Then she forced the workers to dig up "her" potatoes—at gunpoint. When she stuck a shotgun in the stomach of one worker, the man's wife grabbed the firearm and other Indians wrested a second gun away from her. The *dueña* turned to run back to her house and fell. No one pursued her as she picked herself up and ran across the field to her house.

I wanted to admire the *dueña's* assertiveness, which I'd not often witnessed in married women here. But she hadn't been protecting her property. Instead, she'd tried to steal from those who had much less of everything than she had. She shouldn't try to cheat the workers from food she'd agreed they could raise on her land.

The Indians had strapped the guns they'd confiscated to a fence post at the edge of the nearby field. I hadn't noticed the arms before, but now I could see a long rifle and a smaller firearm on a nearby post. This excursion had become exciting, not quite the sightseeing outing I expected.

The officials, preparing for trouble, must have arranged for the high number of guards. When the sentries weren't lounging in the Indians' cornfields, they swaggered around, threatening the people with their pistols by raising their firearms if someone didn't clear a path for them. The show of force, meant to intimidate the Indians, made me angry. The number of armed guards present seemed uncalled for.

Around three in the afternoon, the Indian women served us what they had cooked in their huts on kerosene gas burners and outside in nearby adobe ovens. We had a choice of pork, chicken, or the local delicacy, herbed guinea pig called *cuy*. Side dishes included potatoes and corn, and the drink was lots of *aguardiente*— the homemade fermented and distilled sugar cane liquor. I downed a polite thimbleful of the alcohol. It burned my throat.

The tiny eyes of the herbed, roasted *cuy* looked up at me from my plate. It smelled of oregano and cumin. I sank my teeth into the middle rib area of the small animal careful to not make eye contact with my food. The spicy flavors surprised me. When we finished our meal, the women took the dishes and leftover food back to their homes. This Peruvian food was tasty and plentiful. People were always feeding us no matter how little they had for themselves.

The meeting finally got underway at 4 p.m., with fewer than one-third of the original hundred *campesinos*. Most of the natives, who had waited to participate since 9 a.m., had given up and returned home. I suspected they needed to prepare for the next day's work in the fields.

Everyone spoke in Quechua. I didn't understand much of the conversation, so couldn't tell if the gathering ended with an agreement. Our lawyer friend gave us his analysis on the drive back to Abancay. His more serious demeanor made him more tolerable.

"Although three hundred indigenous families live in the area," he said, "they have no schools. They're supposed to get paid six *soles*, or twenty-five cents a day, but often get nothing."

"So that's one reason they can barely survive," I said. "And without education, they can't influence the government, if they even know they have a government."

"*Sí*," Señor Aguilar said. "Too bad they are all spread out and not organized."

I liked our lawyer friend better when he explained current events and stopped coming on to us. Seeing some of the problems these people faced motivated me to work in rural community development after finishing my training in the hospital. I had a new understanding of the plight of indigenous Peruvians. But so far, today I had eaten a *cuy*, gotten sunburned, and managed to avoid any dog bites. Not great accomplishments. And I'd begun to lose hope that the potato issue would be solved anytime soon— like so many things in Peru.

To work with these Incan descendants, I needed to learn their language. Not likely. Fluency in Spanish continued to be my goal. I had made progress speaking that language in the six months since I'd arrived. But what could I accomplish in the year I had left?

◅◦◅◦◅◦◅◦

When I arrived at the hospital the next morning, I noticed a portly woman waiting for Doctor Delgado. I greeted the woman and her husband as I walked past them and went into the cloakroom to put on my white medical coat. Inside, Marie and a nurse friend, Elsa, discussed yesterday's adventure.

"The lady, the *dueña* owner of the hacienda," Elsa said in a hushed tone, "is the woman sitting out in the waiting room."

"What's she here for?" I asked, astonished at the coincidence.

"She said she'd gone up to a field on her hacienda to see how the potato digging was going," Elsa said. "The Indians had called her by a name of endearment, *mamacita*—and then attacked her. She said they must have been planning it all along."

"That's not what the *campesinos* said yesterday," Marie said. I, too, doubted the woman's story from what I knew of the incident.

"It turns out the woman is expecting a baby," Elsa said sympathetically, "and as the result of her fall, she may lose it."

I found it difficult to feel sorry for the *dueña*. The Indians seemed more sincere and honest, with less to gain. The unfairness of situations like this potato caper demonstrated how the gap between rich and poor created injustices that no one seemed able to bridge, least of all me. But I'd keep looking for ways to have a meaningful impact in this mysterious and wonderful country.

Finding a Purpose

From mid-January to March 1965, Antonio stayed in Abancay off and on during his college's summer hiatus, and we walked and talked most evenings. In April, Antonio's mother almost died giving birth to her fourth child. Antonio left his studies to stay by his mother's side night and day for a month until she recovered. During that time my admiration for him increased. Anyone so devoted to his mother certainly would treat a wife well. But I hadn't thought ahead.

"Could you live in Peru married to me?" he said as we sat in Abancay's central plaza. He held my hand as he spoke.

I had imagined myself married to such an attentive and loving man, but not in Peru. Antonio had never mentioned how he would support a family here or anywhere if we did marry. I was skeptical of a long-term relationship with him.

"I plan to do more traveling," I said, hesitating. I felt uneasy about being too honest. I didn't want my lack of commitment to end such a pleasurable relationship. I resisted falling totally in love with Antonio because I didn't plan to settle down soon. And when I did, most likely it wouldn't be in Peru.

"The longer our courtship goes on," Antonio said, in a sad tone, "the deeper we'll fall in love."

I'd been questioning our relationship too, so wasn't surprised by his comment.

Breaking up in the first stages of infatuation would be easier than when deeper feelings developed. Better to separate now, since a life together looked unlikely, if not impossible.

"We aren't ready for a permanent relationship," I agreed, my heart sinking. "You have no means of support and I really don't think I could live forever in Peru. I'd miss my family too much. We can continue as friends, though." Antonio frowned.

He dropped me off early in front of the Education Department doors to my house. After a quick peck on my cheek, he headed home. The next morning Antonio left on the bus for Cusco.

Over the next month the streets appeared dark and bleak as I walked them alone. The townspeople smiled when greeting me, but they seemed like strangers. Every slender young man with a shock of black hair made me think of Antonio. Everyone but me seemed to enjoy Abancay's sunny fall days.

At the Eguiluzes over lunch, Marie conversed and laughed with the family. I remained silent. She put on her usual makeup and wore attractive, clean clothes. No makeup brightened my face, and, I didn't care if I wore a shabby dress. Antonio wasn't there to appreciate my appearance, so I had no reason to look appealing. Even sadder, I might never again have a reason to look attractive for him since we'd ended our *enamorados* status.

When I peered into the big brown eyes of Antonio's new baby brother, Antonio's eyes stared back. Nostalgia overcame me if I spied a dirty ashtray where my ex had crushed out his cigarette. No one in the family said they missed Antonio, and I didn't let on how deeply I cared for him. I couldn't understand how others could be happy. I didn't want to darken everyone else's mood or appear emotionally weak, so I talked only to Marie about my longing for Antonio. She liked Antonio as a friend and agreed with me that a future with him seemed unlikely.

We concluded our training at the hospital when it became clear that plans for living in Suncho wouldn't happen anytime soon. Marie and I looked for other ways to be useful. We still had over a year to accomplish something. That's when two projects came our way.

Local engineers we'd met from SIPA, the Peruvian department of agriculture, suggested we start a 4-H-type girls' club, like volunteers had done in Cusco and other areas of Peru. They could introduce us to residents of a farm community two miles up the mountain called Tamburco. We liked the idea of shaping future young women to be leaders in the poor, indigenous community and decided to organize a girls' club there. Maybe I could diminish Antonio's pull on my heart by concentrating on work.

I had belonged to the Busy Bees 4-H club in Montana, where I'd learned how to set a proper table, prepare nutritional food, and give demonstrations. If we started a club here, we could train the girls in Tamburco how to run a meeting and become community leaders. Our presence in this poor area might just make a positive difference.

Twenty-five girls, ages twelve to sixteen, met with us after hours in their school. They voted for officers and decided on "Club Micaela Bastidas" as the group's name. Micaela Bastidas had lived in the Abancay area with her husband, Tupac Amaru II. The two indigenous heroes were martyred in Peru's fight for independence from Spain in the late 1700s. A lovely white statue of Micaela stood on a major plaza on Abancay's main street. The members had come up with an inspirational name for their club.

The girls next voted to collect dues of one *sol*, or four cents, a month. The money would provide a sense of club ownership and contribute toward the purchase of needed cooking and sewing supplies they didn't furnish. Together we decided to hold club meetings every Monday afternoon, except on holidays, or when the schools went on strike. The first gatherings implemented democracy well. Baking, not so well.

Girls who had volunteered to bring ingredients we needed to make banana bread didn't come through with their items. Marie and I couldn't always carry our cooking equipment the two miles uphill to Tamburco. When our oven weighed too much for us to transport, we asked acquaintances with vehicles for help. The agricultural agency or the Food for Peace chauffeur often came to our rescue. Training the girls of Tamburco to become independent and resourceful young women like us proved challenging and frustrating.

The second project came about when the Education Department directors requested that Marie and I teach weekly physical education classes a mile up the mountainside in the semi agrarian suburb of Villa Gloria. We had more than a few problems.

I hadn't taught an entire class before. Now, on a winter afternoon, seventy boys and fifty girls of assorted sizes confronted us. One hundred twenty pairs of brown and black eyes stared at me. The same number of feet moved restlessly. The students appeared eager to exchange the hard dirt floor of their adobe schoolrooms for the softer soil of the soccer field. Marie and I weren't certain we were up to the task.

Peace Corps training in Puerto Rico had provided us with a curriculum of games designed to develop ball-handling skills. Catching and throwing balls served as lead-ups to the more organized sports of volleyball and baseball. From day one we recognized we were not in the States. Every student we threw a ball to tried to field it using only his or her feet. They were used to playing soccer. And, the number of students was far greater than would be in a stateside class.

The boys had on khaki-colored uniforms that ranged from well-worn to threadbare. The girls wore blue-checked jumpers topped by white aprons that showed what they'd had for breakfast—and other meals of the past week. The students had walked several kilometers from their dirt-floored homes on the mountainside to the school. Many didn't wear shoes. The bottoms of the boys' feet had skin as thick as the soles of my tennis shoes. The families in this area didn't make sufficient income from selling corn, eggs, and other foodstuffs to buy footwear for all their children.

The pupils' little noses had various shades of mucus running from them. Their respiratory problems stemmed from houses that had no heat other than the smoky fires for cooking. Few of the youngsters used handkerchiefs, if they even had them. Beatrice, a girl with uncombed hair, looked up at me with soulful eyes. My heart melted. I took a wad of tissues from my pocket and wiped green snot from under her nose. My heart went out to our new charges.

Marie and I each took a group of sixty students and started them on games to build ball-handling skills like we'd been shown in our training. Using our best Spanish, we directed the pack to divide into two groups. No one moved. They started to mill about and we lost them. Why weren't they paying attention to our commands? An older boy began translating our instructions into the regional language of Quechua and we understood our problem.

"These kids," Marie said, "speak only Quechua."

"I think you're right," I said. "You took Quechua during Peace Corps training at Cornell, didn't you?"

"Yes," Marie said, "but I'm not fluent enough to order them around."

I didn't speak either Spanish or Quechua fluently, so I couldn't help give instructions they'd understand. We'd gotten our wish to teach in an impoverished school. Teaching here would be more difficult than what we'd experienced in the more affluent

Abancay schools. We hadn't expected to be assigned to students who spoke little Spanish. Eventually, we got directions across by using simple Spanish, the translation skills of the few bilingual students, and hand and arm motions. The class seemed longer than the one-and-a-half hours on the school schedule. We went home to ask our neighbors to teach us useful Quechua phrases.

One day I taught my young charges dodge ball. They loved it. But classrooms of older boys, dismissed earlier, disrupted the game by throwing the ball too hard. I found discipline difficult to maintain. I felt helpless and a bit resentful. Local residents who spoke Quechua would do a better job than we could.

I wondered why the Peruvian teachers in the nearby schoolrooms weren't teaching PE. The answer came when I looked at the regular teachers. All were overweight and considerably older than Marie and me. Being young and agile, we had enough stamina to teach PE—and we provided free labor to the school district. Even if we two American girls had less experience, we appeared better suited to teach physical education classes than the native veteran teachers.

The second week, a more reasonably sized group of thirty shoeless six-year-old boys appeared for my class. Marie taught the same number of girls. I led my group in a series of calisthenics. A few students imitated jumping jacks and running in place. Then I recalled a racing game I'd loved to play in Montana called "Three Deep" and taught it to my pupils. One little boy in a ragged shirt zipped around the circle chuckling. All the students caught on quickly and enjoyed running around the circle to beat their opponents —until they lost interest. Half an hour from dismissal time they all began to wander off. I needed to get their attention.

"Anyone who doesn't want to play," I shouted in desperation, "can just leave!"

Apparently, they understood my Spanish. They all left for home. I stood on the field speechless. Then I, too, left in disgust.

Marie and I complained as we walked the mile back to Abancay. Why had we insisted on teaching in such an impoverished school? We knew why. We were meeting an unfilled need in the community and felt useful. And for me, working served as an antidote for the melancholy consuming me from Antonio's absence.

Succeeding weeks, we practiced catching and serving volleyballs. We had to hit the white vinyl sphere over an imaginary net because we had no real one. I came home evenings with stiff joints, not used to the strenuous activity it took to corral so many active students. But I no longer tossed and turned, yearning for Antonio each night. Sleep came as soon as my head hit the pillow. I dreamed of tossing balls. I exchanged my aching heart for aching muscles.

One day I struggled to divide my class into two soccer teams when a young man appeared. He offered to help. His orders in Quechua achieved my objective quicker than I ever had. I handed him our ball to begin the match. He took it, then gave me a surprised look.

"This ball will get ruined," he said as he returned the only ball I had. "This is a volleyball, not a soccer ball."

I felt my face turn warm with embarrassment. I used the equipment given me. My students usually kicked around wadded up rags for soccer balls. At least I had an actual ball—even if it was the wrong kind. I thanked the nice young man for his assistance. Thereafter, I vowed to find the correct ball for each sport I taught—if I could.

We tried to engage our fellow Peace Corpsmen Ken and Al in our work. Al took over my boys' PE class a few times. The male students loved having a big, strong man teach them ball-handling skills. But he didn't continue helping. The girls in our 4-H club loved teaching Ken to dance the marinera, a costal dance of Peru. But after his first visit, Ken didn't return to the club's weekly meetings. The guys viewed us as capable females who didn't need their assistance. They were right about me. From an early age I'd had challenging jobs.

Working on Ranches

Twelve miles from Ismay at Polluck's sheep and cattle ranch, a rooster's crow woke me at 6 a.m. as it did every day the summer I was eleven. I splashed water on my face from the enamel bowl on the nightstand. No indoor plumbing here like at our house in Ismay. The cold liquid smacked me into reality. Another day caring for the Polluck's two little girls and helping with household duties. From morning to night, I worked as a hired girl, doing what others needed, not what I wanted.

I pulled on my blue jeans, saddle shoes, and plaid cotton blouse ready for another day. Sunlight streamed through my second-story window. In daylight, a trip downstairs to the outhouse would be safe. I wouldn't walk the path to the outdoor toilet at night. I feared a skunk, a badger, or some other wild animal might lurk in the dark waiting to pounce. If I had to pee, I used the empty baked bean can hidden under my bed. This morning the can was full. I opened the window and tossed the liquid through the screen, too embarrassed to carry it downstairs to the outhouse. The earth below drank in the yellow fluid. The patch of grass beneath my window was the greenest around.

I hurried downstairs. John Polluck had gotten up early to light the wood logs he'd placed in the bowels of the stove the night before. The black cast-iron cooking range along one wall of the large kitchen, warmed the room. I set about stirring up a batch of buttermilk pancakes from a powder mix. Then Edna Polluck fried eggs, bacon, and pancakes on the warmed griddle, which she did every morning. The big breakfast gave us fuel for the day's work. Bits of pancake not eaten by the girls landed on the floor. The slurp-slurp sound of the family's dog meant the dropped food had found an eager appetite. Then it was time to plan the day.

"As soon as the dishes are cleared and washed," Mrs. Polluck said, her plump figure hurrying out to gather the eggs, "you can do the ironing."

"The dishes will have to wait," I said, placing the heavy flatiron where the griddle had been, "until the water in the stove is warmer."

With the water in the stove's side reservoir hot, I removed what I needed to two basins in the sink. I washed, rinsed, and drained the cups and plates, then checked the temperature of the flat iron. I removed a succession of damp cowboy shirts, denim jeans, and little girls' cotton blouses from the ironing basket and pressed out the wrinkles. Oh, how much easier life would be with running water and an electric iron like at home.

At lunchtime, I served the family sandwiches and sliced apples. Then more dishes to wash before I put the little girls down for their naps. After lunch, Mr. and Mrs. Polluck saddled up their horses. I remained alone with the two little sleeping girls—the time of day I dreaded. The butterflies in my stomach ran races the minute the Pollucks mounted their palominos and galloped over the hill out of sight.

What if the girls got sick? What would I do if a wild animal came near the house? At age eleven, I was responsible and competent, but I couldn't fight off wild animals. Where could we hide if a big thunderstorm arose and lightning bolts hit all over the place? The Pollucks might get caught by a gully washer or be struck by lightning and not return. How would I notify anyone? At home I could spin the handle on the side of our big, wooden wall phone in the kitchen hallway to reach help. No such modern communication device here. I worried about sickness, rain, and lightning for two hours.

What to do to get through my fears? I turned on the battery-powered radio and got busy. On my hands and knees, I scrubbed away the pancake syrup the dog hadn't licked off the floor. I swished the rag over the linoleum back and forth in time to the music. A pleasure I'd never before known engulfed my body and awakened my senses. The rock 'n' roll beat of Elvis singing "Hound Dog" comforted me. The butterflies in my stomach quieted when his deep, velvety tones crooned, "That's All Right Baby." His soothing, sexy baritone washed across my body to melt my heart and stir my soul. I felt cared for by a strong, masculine presence.

When the hypnotic beat of the music stopped, the spell broke and life again filled with responsibilities. Tears welled in my eyes from imagined and real fears. I tried to see my work as an opportunity to earn good pay. But now I realize I was too young for some of these responsibilities.

I worked for the Pollucks, the Baldwins, and other ranchers— all nice people. But most of our interactions were directives about work. I wanted summer fun, companionship, and to be at home reading books, practicing the piano, or playing with friends. I missed sleeping in my own bed and riding my bike. I yearned to hear the voices of my three younger sisters and my rascally little brother. I didn't like the sadness I felt.

My parents and siblings drove out to see me Wednesday nights to help ward off my homesickness. With their midweek visit, I could make it to Sunday. After a day at home, the routines of work, fear, and loneliness began again on Monday.

For three long summers my duties included doing whatever the woman of the house needed me to do. If the Mr. needed another person to haul hay or brand and castrate calves, the Mrs. would go out to the field and I'd take over in the house. Sometimes I watched the children outside so they didn't fall into a well or the outhouse holes. I cooked for scores of field hands. I lived up to my mother's strong work ethic. Yet the work was hard, and the time away from fun and family took a toll.

Mama paid a penny for brushing each step leading upstairs, a dime for cleaning the silverware drawer, and a quarter for sweeping all thirteen rooms of our house. She said working on ranches was an opportunity to earn money that she'd never had at my age. True, I could earn more money working for ranchers' wives than Mama could pay, so my savings accumulated fast. I survived the summer when I was eleven, and the next, and the next, earning five dollars a week. But the isolation frightened me, and the grind of long workdays wore me down.

The desire to be home wasn't worth the twenty-five dollars I earned in a month—especially when I spent a total month's wages on a sweater set and a pair of jeans. So I plotted to work for myself. I looked for opportunities to have my own businesses. That way I could control my work hours.

Several summers, I piled my brother's red Radio Flyer wagon high with fresh produce and pulled it from neighbor to neighbor. I sold tomatoes, cucumbers, and corn that I helped to grow in my family's one-acre garden. Other families who didn't raise their own vegetables purchased all I had. I'd arrive back home with an empty wagon and a pocketful of money. This feeling of success led me to find other products and places to market my goods.

My best friend Maxine and I made fudge, divinity candy,

and popcorn, and sold the refreshments at the annual rodeo in the stockyards down by Ismay's grain elevators. Our homemade sweets disappeared into the mouths of hungry rodeo viewers, performing horse racers, and trick-and wild-bull riders. Rarely did we see a cowboy competitor get bucked off his horse. We were too busy hawking our wares.

In the fall, my feet pedaled up and down on our treadle Singer sewing machine as I sewed dozens of potholders from left-over fabric scraps. Then I went door to door to the thirty or so households in Ismay selling my masterpieces. Eventually, word of my attractive products became well known. Housewives came to me. Most homes had at least two of my brightly colored fat squares to protect their hands when taking fresh bread from Ismay's ovens. Again, my efforts proved successful.

In winter, I sold Christmas cards. Families looked at my sample book from the card company in early November and selected one or more of the cheerful designs. The woman of the house then gave me a 10 percent deposit. I mailed a money order to the Christmas card company and weeks later a carton of colorful cards arrived at the Ismay post office. With each delivery, the neighbor paid me the balance due. I sent off another money order to the company, minus my 15 percent profit, and smiled at the growing figures recorded in my savings book.

I saved enough money to buy a long-desired bicycle, which I ordered from the Sears, Roebuck and Company catalog. The beautiful green-and-silver bike with unique curved handlebars arrived and I proudly rode it to school. My pride and joy was barely a month old when, without asking my permission, Gavin, a schoolyard bully, grabbed the bike and rode it around the play-ground. He drove so fast turning dangerous corners that he broke the handlebars—and my heart. My treasured new transportation, the product of my labors, lay wounded and helpless. I hated Gavin.

He'd disrespected my hard-earned property and didn't offer to pay for the damage he'd caused. And no one made him.

I paid for replacement handlebars, seething with fury at having to use money I earned to correct someone else's wrong-doing. I resented the fact that no one disciplined Gavin. Boys seemed to get away with their wrongdoings. Not fair. I had to use my money for Gavin's carelessness instead of spending it on what I preferred—clothes. My clothing budget often equaled my earnings.

Mama usually sewed identical dresses for my sisters and me, like the ones with the tiny apple design and ribbon bows in the back. We three girls looked like a set of different-sized triplets. But Mama's flour-sack dresses embarrassed a sophisticated preteen like me. So as my savings-book balance increased, I purchased more stylish and attractive clothes. I ordered a pink gathered skirt from Sears, Roebuck and Company for $4.50 and pink shoes to match from the Alden's catalog. When the shoes arrived, they measured smaller than my size five feet. I wore them anyway and suffered in silence.

I loved the rolling hills of the countryside where I lived and worked, but like my trip up the hill to find the source of the water, I now yearned to see what was beyond the hills. I knew how to be entrepreneurial and could make my own money on my own terms. I would not spend my life cooking, scrubbing and watching over little future farmers in Montana—or Peru, I hoped.

Back and Forth

Marie and I waited for our friend Darcy outside our place on a warm day in June 1965. Today we would hitch a ride with him to Cusco for our required annual physicals with the Peace Corps doctor. I also needed the doctor to check out the sharp pain I felt in my ribs whenever I coughed. The trip in Darcy's two-door, open-air jeep over the bumpy one-hundred-twenty miles would be smoother than by bus and take five hours as opposed to eight.

As promised, Darcy drove up on the dot of 11:30. We appreciated this Peruvian's unusual punctuality. His red, canvas-topped auto lacked window glass, but that didn't matter on such a sunny day. We were happy to catch a ride with someone we knew, especially Darcy. Since our trip with him to Lima at Christmas, he and Marie had become fond of one another.

Darcy slipped out of his vehicle with the smoothness of a soccer player. He grabbed our bags and lodged them between the back seat and the spare tire bolted onto the tailgate. The noonday sun highlighted his thinning light-brown hair and the crinkles around his brown eyes. His physique was that of a young man, but his face looked older than his twenty-eight years. Supervising road construction in the altiplano had wrinkled his forehead and freckled his skin. Sun exposure in the thin mountain air tended to make people look older than they were.

My hurting twenty-two-year-old body settled into the back seat of the jeep. I wanted to get going for many reasons. I could rest and rejuvenate in Cusco, and I might see Antonio, who was still attending classes at the university.

When he'd left Abancay, we'd agreed to continue as friends, not *enamorados*. That hadn't worked for me. My mind reasoned I could forget him but my heart disagreed. Now that I had to travel to Cusco, I hoped he'd be eager to see me.

Marie got into the front passenger seat next to Darcy. Though fond of our driver, Marie had no desire to become as attached to him as I was to Antonio. She didn't plan to settle in Peru any more than I did. Darcy didn't seem like the settling-down type anyway. He hunted, drank, and dabbled in black magic. His five-room house contained the largest collection of long-playing records that Marie and I had ever seen. He often traveled out of town to whichever road he was working on. We'd heard rumors that he had his pick of any number of attractive women between Cusco and Abancay and maybe all the way to Lima. He said we were good company. The feeling was mutual.

Darcy had just started the car when Señor Eguiluz came running up and thrust an envelope of money into Marie's hands. He asked her to deliver the cash to Antonio. My heart beat a little faster. The money would be a legitimate reason to contact my former boyfriend, and I wouldn't look too needy if we took it to him.

The three of us sang Peruvian tunes we'd heard on Darcy's LP's as we sped toward Cusco. Singing and conversation distracted me from my aching side and hurting heart. We stopped for lunch at the trip's halfway point in Limatambo at 2 p.m.

"I'm too tired to drive," Darcy said, slurping up the last of his corn soup. "Could one of you take over?"

"I don't know how to drive a stick shift," Marie said.

"I guess I could," I said, trying to forget my aching side.

I hadn't driven a car since I'd left the States over seven months ago, but I'd learned to drive cars with stick shifts on Montana's dirt roads. I could handle the jeep's five gears—if I didn't move my ribcage too much. Darcy stretched out in the back seat for a nap.

"Driving these unending curvy mountain roads," he said, yawning, "tires me out."

The car started, and right away I stepped on the brake instead of the clutch. The jeep died. Embarrassed, I started the engine again, and we took off. I barely had the strength to maneuver around the thirty-degree curves. No power steering in this vehicle. Sitting in the back seat during the first half of the trip, I'd only felt discomfort when the jeep hit a pothole. Now, each time I wrestled the wheel to make a sharp turn, the pain in my side flared up with a burning sensation. I persevered despite the pain.

The Apurimac River lay half a mile below us. I shook my head in disbelief at how far above it we drove. My clammy hands tightened on the controls, but I kept my foot pressed on the gas pedal. We were making good time with me behind the wheel.

Then, as the jeep rounded a curve, I heard a loud 'pop' from the right side. We rocked back and forth. I held onto the steering wheel with all the strength my sore ribcage allowed. My foot slammed hard on the brakes. Marie grabbed the dashboard and screamed. I veered the jeep away from the cliff and toward the mountainside. We slid to a stop. Darcy woke up.

"What the—" he said, sitting up.

"All of a sudden the car started swerving all over," I said, my voice wavering. "I couldn't control it. Something is broken."

"We could have died," Marie said, getting out, holding on to the side of the jeep, her legs shaking.

Marie and I walked to the side of the wounded vehicle. The jeep had a flat right front tire. Darcy, still sleepy, yawned and climbed out to look. He took the spare off the rear of the leaning vehicle, then set the jack underneath. Marie and I looked for bushes to squat behind. The Fantas we'd had for lunch had been scared right out of us.

With the spare on, I resumed driving. I felt secure—until we rounded another curve. The jeep jerked violently from side to side trying to shake us out. Marie and I banged against the flimsy doors. For a second time Marie's nails dug into the dashboard. I imagined plummeting off the ribbon of road straight down 3,000 feet into the Apurimac River. There were no fences or other barriers to slow a vehicle's tumble down the steep embankment. Even if I survived the descent, I'd end up in the rushing river. And I didn't swim well. I could see the headlines in the *Oakland Tribune*, "Local Peace Corps Volunteer Plunges off Mountain and Drowns in Andes Accident." I clenched my teeth and stared straight ahead. Could it be another flat? Maybe I shouldn't be driving. I tightened my grip on the steering wheel and pressed hard on the brakes. We stopped.

Again, Marie and I got out to inspect. More alert now, Darcy got down to check. No flat, but the entire front side wobbled. The tire he'd just changed was nearly off its hub. He hadn't sufficiently tightened the nuts. We could have been killed. Lesson—never allow a sleepy person to change a tire.

◦·◦·◦·◦

The next morning Marie and I stopped at the Peace Corps doctor's office. Fellow volunteer, Bill, emerged from the examining room. He'd been healthy during our training at Cornell and in Puerto Rico. Now he looked pale and weak.

"I've had pneumonia for two weeks," Bill said, in a barely audible voice. "I'm going back to bed."

No sooner had Bill left than another male volunteer rushed into the waiting room. He looked bad. The doctor ushered him in ahead of us. Our compatriot emerged half an hour later.

"I have pneumonia," he said, his voice shaking. His face was as pale as his blonde hair.

Both volunteers lived in Cusco, which had cold nights and no heat in most houses. In Abancay's mild climate, we didn't need heaters and rarely had more than a sniffle—except for my last bout. How could so many of these volunteers, so strong when they'd first arrived, now be so frail?

"I guess," Marie said, looking at me, "volunteers here have as many respiratory problems as the locals."

"Yeah," I said, "but we have doctors to treat us." I thought of the runny-nosed children in our PE classes.

Two hours after we'd arrived, my turn came for a physical exam. I didn't escape a serious diagnosis. I, too, had lung issues. My cough had broken a rib. The doctor said my cold had turned into bronchitis. He gave me antibiotics.

◦·◦·◦·◦

I cried myself to sleep the second night in town, sobbing quietly, careful of my hurting rib and not to awaken Marie. If Antonio really cared he would want to find me, if only to get his money. He must know by now that we had it. Antonio and I may have broken off our *enamorado* relationship but we could still see one another. If only I could forget him.

After lunch on day three in Cusco I couldn't stand the longing inside me and convinced Marie that we should deliver Antonio's money. We set off to find the address on the envelope. I could do nothing for my aching rib, but I could do something about my aching heart.

Antonio lived with a cousin, her husband, and children in a large apartment complex near the university. Several people in the vicinity had to direct us to the three-story building. We climbed the stairs to the second story. My heart raced with the anticipation of seeing Antonio again. How would he react when he saw me? I hesitated as we neared the apartment door.

Marie knocked and Antonio opened the door. My face flushed and my knees went weak. Antonio's thick wavy black hair and wide shoulders set my hormones ablaze. He greeted Marie warmly and gave her a big hug. I waited for him to say something to me. He didn't. He glanced my way with cold brown eyes and an angry expression. I could hardly breathe. My welcoming smile faded. Tears of bitter disappointment filled my eyes.

Marie handed Antonio the envelope with the money. He thanked her and said he couldn't invite her in because the family was eating lunch. In a brief conversation, they agreed he would come to the Cuzco Café later that evening. My heart beat in my throat with a fright I didn't understand. Tears flowed so I couldn't see the stairs in front of me as I descended. Marie looked like she understood my pain but said nothing. What was going on? I hated the upsets of this emotional world that I didn't comprehend and couldn't control. I preferred the physical pain of my broken rib to these feelings of inner turmoil.

At dinner Marie and I sat with several other volunteers in the Cuzco Café when Antonio breezed in. I stopped eating my fried pork dish mid-bite. Antonio acted as though he didn't see me. Then, he issued a blanket invitation to the Elvis Presley movie, *Fun in Acapulco,* looking at Marie and the others, but not at me. I loved Elvis's singing and stifled the urge to say, "Take me." No one accepted Antonio's invitation. He shrugged off their response.

After we finished our meal, Antonio walked Marie and me back to our hotel, talking only with my roommate. When we reached our lodging, Marie said goodnight and headed toward the elevator. I moved to enter the building after her but Antonio grabbed my arm and pulled me back outside.

"Why," he said, "are you being so cold toward me?"

In the glimmer of the streetlight he looked stern. My feelings were bruised more than my rib. I didn't understand.

"What?" I said, astounded at his statement, and pulled away. "You've been ignoring me. You didn't even invite me to the movie."

Antonio's interpretation of the day's events dumbfounded me. He had ignored *me*, not the other way around. He must have wanted to punish me for our breakup a month ago.

"You are too sensitive," he said, gently pulling me back. "And stubborn too."

Stunned by his words, I couldn't respond. Why wasn't he showing me he cared? But raw emotions of anger and hurt would spill out if I spoke. I didn't want that, so I said nothing.

"It seems," he said, "as though I am the only person who loves in this relationship. It would be better if we completely ended it."

His words confused me. I thought we had ended our close relationship. I didn't believe his statement of love after the way he had treated me today. He'd hurt my pride and crushed my feelings. In my eagerness to see him, I had not counted on his back-and-forth rapid change of heart. First, he ignored me, then blamed the coolness between us on me. Then he said he loved me. But his actions showed otherwise. I couldn't trust what he said were his feelings, and I could no longer be sure of mine. Switch-backing emotions knocked me one way, then the other. I loosened Antonio's hold on me and ran upstairs.

I buried my face in my pillow to quiet my sobs. For another night I cried myself to sleep. I wanted this seesaw romance to end—until I didn't. I couldn't be with him or without him. We were like two magnets with attraction poles that changed from day to day. Now we were repelling one another.

⚬·⚬·⚬·⚬

Marie didn't want to leave Cusco yet, but I did. I put the word out through the Peace Corps grapevine and among the agency people we knew that I needed a ride back to Abancay—the sooner the better. Returning home might calm my emotional hurt. But after a night's sleep, I felt less emotionally vulnerable and decided to try and patch up my friendship with Antonio. If I could talk to him, maybe we could continue as friends.

I'd heard Antonio mention to Marie that he wished to return to Abancay for the weekend to see his mother. She had been hospitalized again after giving birth to a baby boy two months earlier. I set about looking for a ride back to Abancay for us. I hoped a ride together would give me a chance to speak with him and mend our friendship.

A flirty engineer from SIPA offered a ride in the depart-ment pickup for the next day. He would be transporting 2,000 five-hour-old chicks to the agency's Granja farm in Abancay. He said he wanted only me in the pickup with him. I wanted to get back home, but something told me I shouldn't go alone with this wolf. Peace Corps young women were used to being viewed as sex objects by Peruvian men, but Marie and I demanded respect. We preferred to interact with them by having intellectual discussions and nonsexual fun. We tried hard not to give Peruvian guys sexually provocative signals.

I had no romantic interest in any of these older, balding men, especially this SIPA engineer who Marie said had once propositioned her. Thinking of Antonio, I asked the SIPA man if he could take a second passenger. When he said no, only me, I declined his offer.

Fate intervened early the next afternoon. The SIPA engineer found me to say he had reconsidered. He could fit one person besides me in his vehicle. He'd leave in an hour. I ran to catch a taxi to where Antonio lived. He was eating lunch, but when I told him I'd found him a ride to Abancay, he grabbed his jacket and said he was ready to go. We caught a bus to the hotel. Then Antonio and Marie hurried to help me pack. Preparations to travel had taken an hour. I figured I could count on the SIPA engineer to still be at the agency. Most everyone here was on "*hora Peruana*," at least an hour later than the time they specified.

Antonio carried my suitcase and we rushed to the SIPA office. No sign of the engineer, but his pickup, full of cartons of chirping little chicks, sat in front of the agency.

"Oh great," I said to Antonio, regaining my breath after our run. "Now we'll have to spend five hours listening to constant chirping."

"The peeping of chicks," Antonio said, "is one of the most beautiful sounds in the world."

His brown eyes sparkled and he smiled. He looked at me with the warmth he'd shown before when we were special to one another. Our magnetic poles attracted one another once more. He leaned over and gently kissed me. His actions spoke louder than any words of explanation. A glow went through me. We were back in sync.

We waited by the SIPA truck, and Antonio talked of politics, spelling out the pros and cons of Peru's recent nationalization of its petroleum industry. I listened with interest. When at last the SIPA engineer arrived, I introduced them. They looked at one another with recognition. The engineer said he and Antonio's stepfather were good friends. He had no hesitation about Antonio coming along. But then our chauffeur added so many boxes of supplies on the seat around us that I practically had to sit in Antonio's lap. I didn't mind.

Before long, Mr. SIPA realized his two passengers were in a relationship and he went looking elsewhere for female attention. As he drove from the agency, he stared so intently at a girl on the sidewalk that he rammed the truck into a concrete barrier. Then, leaving town, he "accidentally" rolled the pickup back at a stoplight and hit a car full of girls. He ran to apologize to them, but the traffic light turned green and they sped around us. Touché, I thought. Serves him right. Antonio didn't seem to notice. He occupied himself with my comfort and my hurting rib. I snuggled up against him. Antonio didn't pursue females like most other Peruvian men I knew. Now he cared about me, and I was content.

This trip reminded me of the first one Antonio and I had taken together five months earlier squeezed into the back seat of a Volkswagen bug. Like then, Antonio discreetly put his arm around me when the driver had his eyes on the road. Each time the engineer stepped out of the pickup to check on the chicks, Antonio embraced me. He knew I feared to show my affection for him in front of others lest small-town rumors ruin my pristine reputation. I didn't want the males circling about to think I invited just any guy's attentions. They'd think it was open season for capturing *gringas*. The ache in my heart and my rib disappeared.

When we arrived at the Granja outside Abancay, we released the two thousand little balls of yellow fluff. The tiny chicks ran into their prepared pen. Heat lamps swung overhead to keep the newborns warm. Antonio and I helped count the hatchlings. He marveled at the incessant, beautiful peeping sounds.

"How beautiful they are," he said over and over as the chicks scurried around their new home. I loved how gently Antonio treated the little fowls. He made me feel like one of those newborn chicks—warm from his caring. Maybe his and my pairing could work, though I didn't know how.

A Choice

Now, in July, Antonio's classes were suspended again. I didn't care about the reason, only that Antonio had spent a day on the bus traveling to be with his family and me. Antonio's university in Cusco went on strike, a week at a time, almost monthly. Each time, he and I greeted one another with warm embraces. Antonio visited Abancay almost as much as he studied in Cusco. At the end of his first unexpected visit, we acknowledged the futility of any permanent future together, and we held off any physical contact as long as we could. That proved futile.

Antonio didn't know how long his classes would be adjourned this time. I took advantage of his free time and invited him to help me with the girls' club and the PE classes. Marie had stayed over in Cusco, leaving me with our commitments. I could have managed everything alone, but I loved being with Antonio.

We walked the two miles uphill to Tamburco carrying a kerosene primus burner and assorted metal cooking pans. The after-school gathering of the 4-H- girls' club met in a classroom. The room smelled dank and musty, like most of the classrooms in the poorer towns on the outskirts of Abancay. I wished the government heads would bring the Tamburco and Villa Gloria schools up to the standards of those in Abancay, capital of the Apurimac Province. The capital's schools had glass windows that let in sunlight. The sun warmed the concrete floors. On the mountainside where farmers lived, the schools had few openings in their thick adobe walls, so the dirt floors were cold.

Marie had written the script that Paulina, the newly elected president of the girls' club, read to call the meeting to order. The new leader's long black braids swished back and forth. The black-eyed president surveyed the thirteen similar-looking adolescent club members in attendance this Monday. The girls' bright-colored dresses contrasted with the drab brown of the rough wooden tables they sat at. Today, the girls would choose the club's colors. Another chance to practice democracy.

I suggested Paulina present several colors and take a hand vote to see how many favored each color. Antonio interrupted to propose that each club member state aloud the two colors she preferred. Fine with me. I liked my companion's involvement. Using his method, the girls selected green and white, the colors used internationally for 4-H clubs and appropriate for the cloverleaf badges we would make the following week. We moved on to the fun part of meeting, making potato pancakes—a good dish for a country that grows 3,800 types of potatoes.

To my chagrin, none of the girls had the ingredient she'd previously volunteered to bring. In fact, no one even remembered what she'd committed to the week before. I frowned in disapproval. Now what could we do?

Antonio interceded. Without a word of judgment, he told one girl to run and get kerosene for the primus, another to find potatoes and a third to borrow some eggs, oil, and flour from women in the nearby homes. Working together, we divided the girls into teams—one group to peel the potatoes, another to grate them, and one to stir in the egg mixture. Then we fried the pancakes and sampled them. The girls had never eaten a dish like this and voiced their approval. Afterwards, everyone helped clean up and each girl took a leftover potato pancake for her family. Two pancakes remained for me. Another successful meeting. I was finally performing a worthwhile function—teaching young indigenous women how to organize to get things done.

Antonio carried the burner and bowls down the hill for me. We arrived back at my house as the sun set. I invited my able assistant in for a potato pancake supper even though, without Marie, it might look improper to anyone who saw us alone. I didn't care. I loved being with this handsome, considerate, and helpful man.

I prepared a salad and Antonio's favorite, crystal dressing. He measured the vinegar, sugar, salt, and dry mustard into a saucepan and lit the primus. After the mixture boiled one minute, I added oil. Antonio loved the dressing so much he said he would put it on rice.

"If I lived with you the rest of my life," Antonio said as we sat down to eat, "I'd be *tan grande como asi*! I'd be this big." He spread his arms out as far as they'd reach. We laughed.

"We'll grow old and fat together," I said in Spanish, warmed by the thought of cooking for him forever. I headed toward the burners outside to fix water for tea.

"And where" he said, pulling me over to sit on his knee, "will we spend our vacations?"

"Well," I said knowing we traveled well together, "we could go to Germany, Italy, and China, try out their food and bring home the recipes of what we liked." Antonio laughed.

Just then the room went dark. The electricity had failed. I found a candle, which Antonio placed in an old wine bottle.

We dined on our salad and potato pancakes by candlelight. A romantic ending to a perfect day.

Antonio had offered to help me with my PE class of thirty, six-to-ten-year-old boys, at Villa Gloria when he could. I asked him to come the next afternoon. He said he'd be there if his mother didn't need him. He wasn't at the soccer field when I arrived and, for a while, I thought he might be observing me from a cliff above. Imagining his presence made the shambles of a class bearable.

I had shouted, attempting to bring order to boys who ran around like a herd of alpacas, until I had little voice left. I needed help with the chaos—someone who the noisy students could hear and obey. I croaked my way through the last instruction, disappointed that Antonio hadn't joined me. A boy whined in Quechua, but I couldn't understand him. I didn't know what made him cry. Unannounced, Antonio arrived.

After listening to the crying youngster, my boyfriend said the boy's problem had something to do with a stolen notebook. He spoke gently in Quechua to the little guy. Both pupil and rescuer laughed. I understood the part where Antonio referred to me as the *gringacha,* an affectionate term for *gringa* in Quechua. The incident gave me an idea.

Maybe Antonio could teach Quechua to Peace Corps volunteers destined for Peru. He would have a job and we could be in one another's lives in the States. When I suggested my idea to Antonio, his face lit up.

The head of the Peace Corps in Peru visited Abancay soon after our conversation. I suggested to him that Antonio teach new, stateside volunteers about Peru and the Quechua language. The top boss said that the training programs' administrators hired the teachers of language and culture. He wasn't sure many of them saw a value in volunteers knowing the indigenous language. I disagreed with their priorities. Quechua-speaking Incan descendants were the majority population in the country's mountain areas. If Marie and I'd learned more Quechua, we might now be working to develop the indigenous communities in our area.

I wrote to a few of the universities that trained Peace Corps volunteers. Only one responded and its director had no interest in employing Antonio. Discouraged, I wondered why Antonio didn't have any ideas of his own if he wanted a future with me. I seemed to have taken charge of finding job possibilities for him. Maybe it didn't matter.

When my Peace Corps commitment concluded in a year, I would leave this country and travel around South America and maybe Europe with Marie. We'd had exciting adventures going together to Lima, Machu Picchu, and Chile. We'd walked around ancient ruins and met fascinating people. Our experiences made us eager for more thrills in the rest of Peru and the world.

However, my growing feelings for Antonio made me vacillate. My affection for him increased, even when we fought. Most arguments occurred when we'd been separated for several weeks. Maybe being near one another would improve our communications. I loved being with my boyfriend, except when we quarreled. After each disagreement I moped for days. Several spats later we decided again to just be friends. Never before had a guy taken so much of my time and energy away from my goals.

Antonio said I acted emotionally distant. And I did. I didn't want to become attached to him if the prospect of our being together in the future didn't look good. I would miss my family in the States and couldn't stay in Peru after leaving the Peace Corps without a means of support. Antonio seemed to have no ideas about how to remedy our dilemma. The prospect of our being together for life didn't exist because he couldn't make the necessary plans.

"I have no way," Antonio said again, one day when we sat in Abancay's main plaza, "to provide for you if we married."

"Well," I said, feeling grateful for his help, "you helped me with my jobs."

I loved his involvement in my endeavors, though I wished he could come up with more solutions for work using skills he must have. Organizing girls' clubs was my work.

"What is it you'd like to do?" I said.

"I don't like studying economics, that's for sure."

"Then what is it you want to study?"

"I like physics and math," he said. "It was my stepfather's idea for me to major in economics."

The strike at the university concluded. The next day Antonio returned to Cusco and the university to continue his studies in a subject he didn't like. I missed him again.

Antonio helped me more than I assisted him. Our long talks increased my fluency in Spanish. He helped with some of my work duties. And he filled the emotional void I felt away from my family. Antonio and I ate, played, talked, and worked well together—when we were together. But he didn't make any arrangements for our future, and I had no more suggestions. Then, through the Peace Corps rumor mill, I heard about a job I might qualify for in Cusco.

Señor Ponce, the head of SIPA, needed a female volunteer to guide the agency-sponsored girls' clubs in Cusco. The work sounded like something I could do. I would let Lenny, a veteran Peace Corps volunteer with SIPA, know of my interest.

I traveled to Cusco and found the lanky, brown-haired volunteer who worked with the agricultural agency. Lenny was eating lunch at the Cuzco Café. I sat down and ordered a drink.

"Lenny," I said, sipping my Inca Kola, "I like working with girls' clubs. I heard SIPA might have a job opening in Cusco."

"It would be full-time," Lenny said, taking a bite of his chicken dish, "and require a lot of work, patience, and sacrifice.

188 ❖ Between Inca Walls

If you want the job just to be closer to your boyfriend, forget it."
He sounded skeptical.

Lenny's mention of my boyfriend surprised me. Strange
that he knew how close I felt to Antonio. But the volunteer rumor
mill was as rampant with gossip as with job opportunities.

I thought over my situation. I didn't feel I'd accomplished
much community development in the past year, and it didn't look
as though I'd do a great deal more in the next. I wanted to achieve
more than teach PE, run one girls' club, and advance public relations for the U.S. The SIPA job might give me an opportunity
to have a greater impact during my time in Peru. I could work
with numerous clubs to develop the leadership skills of more of
the area's poorest young women. And, living in Cusco I could see
Antonio more often than I did now living in Abancay.

Two days later I met Lenny at the Cusco SIPA office for the
interview he'd arranged. I needed to convince him, Señor Ponce,
and eventually Mr. Cavendish, that I would be the right person
to supervise girls' clubs in the Cusco area.

We sat down on the wooden chairs in Señor Ponce's sparsely
furnished office. I barely listened to the initial small talk. I focused
on the points I needed to make to prove my ability for the job. I
knew how to run a successful girls' club. And I related well to my
fellow Peace Corps members and the local SIPA agency personnel.
Thanks to Antonio's tutelage during our long conversations, I now
had a good grasp of Spanish.

Señor Ponce turned his brown eyes to me. I jolted alert.
The head of the agency rubbed his hand over his balding head
and smiled.

"I hear you are taking a trip to the jungle," the SIPA engineer said. "On the way back you could look over the 4-H Club
office in Lima to get ideas for the new job."

Señor Ponce hadn't said I had the wrong motivation or

didn't qualify. Could I be hearing correctly? He sounded like he was pitching the job to me.

"Then," the older man continued, "you'd accompany Lenny and me to the national 4-H Club convention in Trujillo."

"It would be your duty," Lenny said, unsmiling, "to work with Peace Corps volunteers stationed throughout the Cusco area."

I suspected the men looked for discouragement in my demeanor. I showed none. On the contrary, I felt elated.

"You can give us your answer," the SIPA rep said, "after you've cleared it with the regional director."

Travel around the country *and* do something that mattered—enticements hard to resist. And, I could be closer to Antonio. I couldn't believe my luck. Most likely, the regional director wouldn't care what I did. He never did. The entire scenario sounded like more than I'd hoped for. I wondered if my excitement showed.

The next morning, I arrived early at the Peace Corps office. Mr. Cavendish had no time to discuss my new job offer with me. He needed to be somewhere and only had time to exchange a few words.

"And what," Mr. C said, walking out of his office, "will Marie do without you?"

"You could," I shouted down the stairs after him, "send a replacement volunteer to Abancay."

In the distance I heard him say we would talk more the next morning. But the director's comment about Marie made me question my decision. I had to confer with my roommate and evaluate the stakes.

I liked living with Marie most of the time. I became upset when she didn't wash her share of dishes or pick up her clothes. She spent too much time applying mascara to her dark lashes. But we shared laughs over the ways Peruvian guys came on to us.

Marie made delicious chocolate éclairs and apple turnovers from scratch. We filled in for one another when one of us had a pressing engagement. Marie's humor, camaraderie, flexibility, and her cooking were only a few things I'd miss if I left her.

Marie's college major in elementary education enabled us to use techniques she had learned. Neither of us spent money frivolously—unless won over by a pretty copper-colored oven set. We saw eye-to-eye on our assignment and said we'd work where the needs seemed greatest. Marie and I had similar values and concurred on most major decisions. We were more than compatible. If I accepted the Cusco job, I'd not just leave Marie, but also my pleasant life in Abancay.

Abancay's friendly residents included Marie and me in their social and professional lives, insisting we visit their stores or classrooms and sing American songs at their birthday parties. We received requests to attend local classes, theater performances, and radio productions. Invitations to special fiestas, the movies, dances, and picnics came our way several times a week. Youths threw flour and water on us during Carnivale. This messy aspect of the town's tradition before Lent annoyed us, but signified acceptance as real members of our adopted community.

Friends lent us anything we needed—an iron, a sewing machine, records, or a tape recorder. Our best friends, Zoila and Zulma, frequently brought us fruits and desserts they thought we'd like. We invited them to enjoy our Fourth of July party and the cake we'd decorated like the U.S. flag. The doctors at the hospital gave us more medical training than we could use. We had settled into teaching PE and running a 4-H Club in poor areas. We paid no rent for our little storeroom-sized house. I felt comfortable living in Abancay.

Cusco, though not as friendly as little Abancay, had one advantage. In Antonio's city full of tourists, he and I felt freer to display our growing affection in public. The wagging tongues in

Abancay, which speculated about our relationship, bothered me.
But I also had to think of Antonio.

He needed to spend his time studying, not being distracted
by me. I'd not yet told him that I'd applied for and been offered
work in his city. When he poked his head into the Cuzco Café that
evening, he said he would be dining with his parents, who were
in town. Therefore, I couldn't get his opinion about my job offer.

I loved Antonio, but I also loved my life in Abancay with
Marie. The deep feelings I'd developed for both Marie and Antonio weren't planned. Connecting with them just happened—like
so many pleasant occurrences in my life. The longer I knew my
roommate and my boyfriend, the closer I'd become to them both.
My world was richer with my roommate and my *enamorado* in it.
How could I choose between them?

I'd discuss my decision to leave Abancay with Marie when
she joined me in Cusco. I'd tell her of my decision after the Peace
Corps farewell party for the Harmons, a volunteer couple at the
end of their two-year commitment.

◇·◇·◇·◇

Marie arrived that afternoon, and we took a taxi to the party at the
home of the Peace Corps secretary. The secretary often let me use
her sewing machine if I needed to make myself a new outfit when
in Cusco. We knocked on the door, and those who'd planned the
surprise party ushered us into the living room to hide. When the
door opened again, the guests of honor walked in—with Antonio.

Other volunteers had invited him. Not only did he know
the Harmons, but he knew most of the volunteers present. In fact,
Antonio knew more volunteers than I did. Throughout the night
I saw him in long conversations with them all. They, too, seemed
to like him. He might do just fine living in the States.

I became self-conscious. The slacks I'd worn were too casual for this party. So I detoured to the bedroom where I stored my sewing supplies and tacked a collar onto the green sweater I wore. I slipped into the green tweed skirt I'd finished making earlier. Now I was presentable. When I exited, Antonio had disappeared.

"Where's Antonio?" I said. My heart sank to think he had gone. "He was just here."

"Oh," Bill said, "Antonio thought you'd left, so he left too."

Volunteers nearby laughed. I didn't. Why was Antonio gone?

"He went out to get some ice," Bill said when he saw the look on my face.

I relaxed. My boyfriend fit in well enough with my compatriots that they could joke about him. Antonio returned and playfully put a piece of ice down my back. Relieved he had reappeared, I didn't protest.

Antonio was unusually dance-shy this night, and because of my being his girlfriend, no other guy asked me to dance. I hid my disappointment. I loved dancing, especially with Antonio. He moved with the grace of a soccer player. He felt the beat of the music. At Abancay's festivities, we danced until dawn. Our bodies merged as one as we whirled around the floor dancing a cumbia, a merengue, or a huayno. But this night he sat by me and talked.

He'd come to the party to give me a gift. He took a record out of a bag he'd brought. He handed me the 45-rpm record of "Moon River" in Quechua. I put the small black disc on the turntable. The music and the thoughtfulness behind it touched me. I listened again to the record while Antonio went to the kitchen to converse with other Peace Corps volunteers. Marie didn't hear the beautiful rendition. She was too drunk.

◇·◇·◇·◇

Marie bumped into the bed in our hotel room. I awoke, sat up and turned on the light. It was 3 a.m. Time to break the news of my leaving to my roommate. Maybe in her inebriated condition Marie could accept what I had to tell her.

"Marie," I said, rubbing my eyes, "I'm going to take the SIPA job in Cusco. I think I can accomplish more there—and be closer to Antonio."

Marie burst into tears. Her shoulders slumped and her mouth drooped. Her sad hazel eyes focused on me as best they could.

"You can't leave me and Abancay," she said, slurring her words between sobs. "We live in a Shangri-La. What we're doing is important too. What about all our plans?"

"Another girl," I said, trying to reassure her, "will be assigned to live with you."

But Marie's reaction made me doubt my decision. I hadn't thought it through. A comparison of the quality of life in Cusco versus that in Abancay had to be factored into the equation. Maybe I was sacrificing an ideal situation for one that would be far less pleasant. I'd no longer have Marie to share observations, ideas, and travel. When it came right down to it, Marie had plans for us, Antonio didn't.

The flowers, rivers, and mountains in our valley beckoned me. I'd take the smell of Abancay's abundant vegetation over the dust, exhaust, and noise of Cusco any day. I'd committed to work in Abancay, with its friendly people, perfect climate, and breathable air. Besides, Antonio came to Abancay on a regular basis. In the end, I couldn't leave Abancay any more than I could desert Marie. I turned down the offer to work in Cusco.

Retreating

I bowed my head at the end of Friday morning mass in Abancay's cathedral. Father Repullés turned to the ten of us in attendance and pronounced in Spanish, "Go in peace," and exited the altar. I sat back in the wooden pew with my head down, not praying or leaving. I hoped no one noticed the tears streaming down my face. Antonio had returned to the university in Cusco, and Marie was 1,000 miles north at the 4-H convention in Trujillo. I hadn't been chosen to go because I didn't take the job supervising the Cusco area girls' clubs. I assumed Marie was chosen because of her better Spanish. I felt rebuffed and sorry for myself.

The pew jiggled. I stopped dabbing the moisture from my cheeks and looked up. The lanky, frizzy-haired Spanish curate who'd been at the altar sat down beside me and smiled.

I liked this tall friendly new priest, even though we'd conversed only a few times. He had a ready wit and a twinkle in his dark eyes. He'd recently been assigned to our small Peruvian town and showed an eagerness to relay any profound thoughts he assumed a foreigner like me needed to hear. Father had an accent

straight from Spain where they pronounced "s" with a lisp. Peruvians spoke Castilian Spanish, a high-quality form of the language,
pronouncing the "s" sound. I understood both styles of Spanish
and found my new language more beautiful than English for communicating with God.

"I have a special invitation for you, dear," Father said
taking my hand. "I'm giving a weekend retreat at the Santa Rosa
Women Teachers College, beginning this afternoon. Why don't
you attend?"

I'd participated in the meditation-type retreats several times
a year during my seven years in Sacred Heart High School and
Holy Names College. From one to three days at a time I'd listened
to clerics' lectures followed by hours in silent contemplation. Like
then, I could now use a few days' respite from the outside world.
A retreat might take my mind off my sadness and yearning for
Antonio.

"You could eat and sleep at the convent for free," Father
said, sensing my hesitation.

"I guess I could." I said, eager to be with people, even silent
ones. "Where do I go and when?"

"Just pack your rosary and enough clothes for the weekend,"
Father said, "and report to the Santa Rosa convent at two this
afternoon."

◁·◺·◻·◺·◻

A bell rang in the hall on the convent side of the Teachers College
at midnight. I jolted awake from a restless sleep, pushed back the
thin wool blanket, and turned on the lamp. My watch showed just
two hours since I'd entered the sparse, unheated convent room. I
couldn't believe I had to get up so soon. Shivering, I arose, threw
on my dress, and fished my shoes out from under the hard bed.

My head ached and my knees throbbed from the hours I'd spent kneeling the previous evening. How would I get through two more days of this? The retreats at Sacred Heart High or Holy Names College didn't wake me up this early to pray. I chalked up my discomfort as penance for the long embraces I'd allowed between my boyfriend and me.

Thirty-five young women entered the dimly lit nuns' chapel ahead of me. Damn! I mean darn! I'd arrived last. Two hours earlier, half the group had fallen asleep during Father Repullés's evening talk, so he had released us to go to bed at 10 p.m. Father said he had to keep us up late so we wouldn't chatter with each other all night.

After the midnight lecture, I stumbled back to bed to get a few more hours of sleep. Too soon the bell rang at 6 a.m., signaling the first meal of the day. I salivated like Pavlov's dog. I'd found it difficult to eat the tough stew meat at supper the evening before, and my stomach now growled with hunger. But for breakfast we received three pieces of bread, an orange, and a piece of chocolate. My stomach rumbled its disappointment. Half an hour later, another ringing bell called us back to the wooden pews in the chapel.

Today, Father's talk focused on male–female relationships and sin. He asked who had a *novio*, a boyfriend whom we planned to marry. Most of the twenty-something aged women, including me, raised our hands.

"It is wrong to arouse a man's passions," Father said. "Latin men are easier to excite than American men."

I looked up in surprise. Father must be directing his comparison of the two types of men to me. Certainly, I was the only young woman present who had dated both American and Latin men. Maybe the priest knew I favored Latin men. Guys I'd dated in the States didn't stir my emotions like the ones in Mexico and Peru. The Latinos had passion for whatever they did—surfing, dancing, singing—or me. Dozens had said they loved me. I liked their fun-loving ways. My fondness for these dark-eyed, dark-haired guys, however, didn't extend to marrying one—until I met Antonio.

"The number one sin of the youth of Abancay," the priest said, "is putting oneself in the occasion of sin. To use sex for pleasure is misuse of a God-given gift. God put the pleasure in sex to encourage reproduction. It is wrong to have sex outside of marriage."

I'd heard the no-sex warning many times during three years at Sacred Heart High and four more at Holy Names College. My father had said the same at the supper table when I was twelve and embarrassed me with an awkward lecture. Now, on my own at age twenty-two, I'd started questioning some of my parents' and the Church's rules. Father Repullés brought me back to the church's many prohibitions about sex.

"Worse than impurity," Father said in his noontime talk over an unappetizing lunch, "is the sin of stopping the birth of an innocent, helpless unborn child. This sin happens at least once a week in Abancay."

I was certain my face registered shock. Did anyone I know kill her unborn child? Most families here had three to seven children. I wondered about those couples who had few or no children. Or did Father refer to the use of birth control? I knew nothing about that subject except that the Church also forbade preventing pregnancy with the pill.

"Go out with boys in groups," the holy man said. "In this small town, when a girl and boy are seen talking alone together frequently, there is gossip, and the couple is forced to get married without love."

Now I knew Father was directing his comments at me. Antonio and I spent hours walking and talking around Abancay, and more evening hours petting heavily behind the big wooden

198 ❖ Between Inca Walls

door of the closed education office. No workers remained in the offices in the evening, so we had the indoor corridor to ourselves. Antonio and I tried to be discreet by not showing affection in public. We didn't even hold hands when we thought we might be observed. Did Father mean that just talking with Antonio made me a marked woman? No way could the priest know of our more intimate contact when my *novio* and I said goodnight.

Adults I met in stores or at parties often suggested I marry "that young man I see you with." But their recommendations hadn't sounded like judgments. I vowed to be more careful in the future so townspeople wouldn't suspect I desired Antonio with my heart, soul, and body.

"I recommend you attend daily mass," Father said, "to dispel temptation, and say the rosary regularly. By doing these things, some of you may even find you desire to enter the religious life."

I'd been a devout practitioner of the many religious rituals and rites I'd been taught since childhood. I'd often said I wanted to enter the convent. Since college graduation, however, I'd put the nun idea on hold. The compulsory vow of poverty that religious communities took didn't bother me. I'd always been poor. But their vow of obedience would be impossible for me, a headstrong, independent woman. People telling me what to do brought out my rebellious side. Then there was the religious life's third vow—chastity. Falling in love with Antonio made me realize I couldn't maintain a lifetime of no sex.

During my time in Abancay, I'd continued to perform the recommended holy activities like attending weekday and Sunday mass, going to confession, and saying the rosary. And I was attending this retreat. Everything added up to my still being a holy person, didn't it?

The retreat wound down on the third day. Father gave a blessing and suggested we make sacrifices to keep the religious spirit going after we left the protective environment of the retreat. Several of the young women promised to give up cigarettes, sugar, breakfast, or the movies. Some said outright they'd sleep on the floor, get up at 5 a.m., or pray for an hour with their arms extended. I didn't go that far. I silently vowed to go to mass and take communion six times a week and say the rosary three times weekly. I would examine my conscience and make three sacrifices a day. And I'd change my ways with Antonio.

The retreat had given me time to reflect on my future. No longer could I put my *novio* and myself in compromising moral situations. I resolved to be strong. Going forward, I would think less about my love life and more about my work. How many times had I vowed that?

Torn between Father's admonitions and my strong drive to be with Antonio, my life had become confusing. Maybe I wanted what I'd observed between my parents in their early married life, not what Father Repullés and my father had warned me against.

Growing Up

One winter Sunday evening, after I'd turned eight, our family gathered in the living room of our house across from the Catholic Church. My two younger sisters, Daddy, and I sat on the floor playing cards while my baby brother jumped in his jumper chair. My five-year-old sister, Charlene, had just won at canasta again. Mama, still wearing the red cotton dress with tiny white flowers she'd worn to church that morning, stood warming herself over the radiator grate in the floor.

A sudden burst of hot air blew up from the basement furnace and lifted the skirt of her dress thigh high exposing Mama's white slip. I hadn't noticed the small rip near the waistband of Mama's dress but Daddy had. He crossed the room, hooked his finger in the hole and tore the skirt in two. His impulsive action startled me.

"Charlie, don't," Mama said with a half-hearted laugh. "This is my good dress."

Daddy ignored Mama's protest and twirled her around and around tearing off more and more of her Sunday dress. My siblings shouted and tried to pull Daddy away. A strange smile on Mama's face showed amusement, so I didn't get upset. When Daddy stopped, remnants of Mama's dress lay all around like the carpet of tiny white flowers that covered Montana hills in spring.

Now, at age twenty-two, I recognized the scene between my parents as a game of passion like I'd seen in movies. My parents' inter-action seemed private yet I now saw that lust between two loving individuals didn't have to be feared. Nevertheless, the messages I received about sex in my childhood were not all positive.

◇·◇·◇·◇

On a hot July evening when I was twelve, our family sat around the circular oak table eating supper in the family kitchen of our second Ismay house. Daddy dug into the chicken and corn on his plate.

"Our crop," Daddy said as he took a bite of corn on the cob, "sure is good this year,"

Home-churned butter dripped onto the blue willow pattern of his dish. He exchanged the corn for a leg of Crisco-fried chicken, filling his mouth. Meanwhile, Mama itemized what clothes we girls might enter in the sewing contests at the upcoming Custer County Fair. Daddy listened but kept chewing.

"Evelyn," Mama said, "why don't you enter that slenderiz-ing A-line jumper you're making from green sailcloth? You know, the one that goes with the red and white puffed-sleeve blouse you made."

Daddy put down his chicken leg and looked at me. I could feel intensity in his gaze and squirmed in my chair. Something was coming, but I hoped he'd say more about our garden. I'd never known my father to be interested in what I wore.

"Strong feelings will drive you to want to do it," Daddy said in a serious voice. "It'll be hard to resist. But you have to be strong and hold back until you're married."

I glanced away, embarrassed and confused. Why would he mention marriage when we were talking about sewing clothes? Then it occurred to me that "it" referred to the uncomfortable subject of sex—a taboo topic in our Catholic family. I could say nothing and an awkward silence followed.

"You'll have feelings you'll want to act on," Daddy continued, his blue eyes staring in my direction. "But you have to wait for the right time."

His gaze then moved to the buttermilk biscuit on his plate. He added chokecherry jelly to the top and took a bite. Mama, my younger sisters, and brother chewed their suppers in silence. This had been all about twelve-year-old me. I felt embarrassed and now had no appetite. I jumped up and gathered dirty dishes from the table. My father's words of warning made me ill at ease and fearful of sex, much like the priest's lectures about our developing bodies in our summer Catechism classes.

◦·◦·◦·◦

Seminarians and priests taught summer religion classes and lectured us Catholic students about doing "it" much as my father had. And they informed us in greater detail about the anatomical differences between young men and women.

One summer they sent the boys to one room and the girls to another to listen to phonograph records where detached voices explained the male and female reproductive systems. For days after these sex education classes, members of the two different gender groups could barely look at one another.

I remained uncertain about the mechanics of just how "it" worked. My uneasiness about the subject didn't allow me to ask clarifying questions. But I didn't need to know. I planned to become a nun. Still, my curiosity had been stimulated. I heard the titillating topic of girls being "in a family way" talked about a great deal the fall I turned thirteen.

Three of the five high school senior girls became pregnant at the same time. The news was whispered about all over town. The scandal grew as big as the girls' bellies. Parents of the couples set winter wedding dates and the three new brides attended classes up through their spring graduation day. And we underclassmen at the Ismay school received some real-life sex education. I attributed the erroneous judgment of the young parents-to-be to the fact that they hadn't heard the phonograph records I'd listened to in my summer catechism classes.

Pregnancy wouldn't be in my teenage future. I was over-weight, and boys didn't ask me out. My first-grade picture showed me smiling coyly with a double chin and rolls around my middle. Mama called me "pleasingly plump." Boys in my elementary school classes called me "Heavy Evie." I hated being called insult-ing names and shouted back.

"My name is Evelyn," I shouted, my face becoming hot.

But my anger served to entertain the boys and didn't stop their taunts. My love of sweets increased my weight. I had a weak-ness for Mama's juicy rolls and sneaked them off our baked goods shelf often when I returned home from school. The sweet taste of caramelized brown sugar and butter melted in my mouth as I bit into each freshly baked bun. Sweets rewarded me for surviving the day and contributed to the "spare tires" around my stomach. I enjoyed eating confections, so I became skilled at baking them.

From ages twelve to fifteen, I earned blue ribbons at the Custer County Fair for my chocolate brownies, oatmeal cook-ies, and banana bread, all made with our home-churned butter. I received a "Best of Fair" ribbon for my angel food cake with hobnail icing—a testament to my expertise as a dessert maker. My growing size proved I was also an avid dessert eater.

204 ❖ Between Inca Walls

My nighttime prayers begged God to rid me of my rolls of fat. I fantasized cutting off my spare tires with a butcher knife. Instead, I took to wearing a three-inch wide, red, elastic cinch belt under my jeans to minimize my protruding stomach. The girdle-like device gave me away when I had to use the bathroom at a friend's birthday party. Other girls, freshening up, crowded in with me as I lowered my jeans. Peggy saw the red belt covering my panties.

"What's a cinch belt doing around your belly?" Peggy said.

"It's holding in my stomach," I said, feeling my face turn the color of the belt.

Peggy shrugged. The others girls said nothing. These thin girls never would comprehend my desperation to look slender like them.

In my preteen years, food and a vivid imagination brought me contentment. Boy–girl relationships became interesting topics of gossip and fun to read about in fiction, but only in my imagination was I with a flesh-and-blood boyfriend. I dreamed I was lithe and slim like the women in the novels I read or the movies I saw. I envisioned myself as Marcellus Gallo's Diana in *The Robe*, or Catana, the love of Pedro de Vargas's life in *Captain from Castile*, or Deanna Durbin in *For the Love of Mary*. But reality hit the year before I entered high school.

"If you're fat," Mama said, "you won't be popular in high school."

Mama hadn't always thought me too fat to be appealing. At age two she'd taken advantage of my cute roundness and paid for a portfolio of professional photographs. With my plump cheeks, blue-gray eyes, and long, curly light brown hair, Mama thought me pretty enough to be in baby shampoo ads. Then the birth of my sister Charlene, plus a move from Chicago to Arkansas to follow my Navy seaman father, changed that. Mama had no time to spend on my modeling career, and I didn't become another Shirley Temple.

Six months before I entered the ninth grade Mama said no more fried chicken, bread, or sweets. Instead, she put me on a diet of skinless chicken breasts, salads, skim milk, and fruit desserts. Though the new food lacked flavor, my "spare tires" melted off. At the end of four months I was slim.

"Wow, Evelyn," Mr. Leach, the school janitor, said as he rang the school bell one morning in June. "You look so good I wouldn't have recognized you."

The thrill of another accomplishment tingled past my flat stomach all the way to my toes. I mumbled my thanks and floated up to my second-floor classroom. Maybe I could be attractive to boys. Though that wouldn't matter if I stuck to my plan to become a nun.

But I'd think about the convent later. For now, in Peru, I'd take Father Repellez's admonitions to heart and focus on work.

Competitions

arie returned from the SIPA 4-H Club conference inspired
to work with the youth of Peru. I, too, wanted to throw
myself into fulfilling activities. We were immediately given a
new opportunity. Our PE students could compete in the annual
school-drill championships, if we could get them ready in time.

Each October, Abancay hosted athletic competitions for
the area's students. Any school could enter the drill team contests.
The administrators of the school where we taught PE in Villa
Gloria suggested we ready sixty of our best students in two groups
to perform synchronized movements in front of a reviewing stand
of judges. We accepted the challenge believing our students had as
much right to participate in the town's competitions as Abancay's
middle-class students.

Twice a week, Marie and I instructed our elementary
school-aged pupils in drills we'd devised for them. But we had
problems. At our second session, half the specially selected marchers didn't arrive. Other students we'd not picked came instead. I
grumbled my upset under my breath. Teachers had overridden

our choices of the most agile performers and either sent us their selections or the rambunctious students they wanted out of their classes. With the competition looming three weeks away, we had no choice but to train the new group.

At the third practice, half the kids ran off to play soccer instead of staying until we finished. Exasperated, I enlisted the help of Carlos, a good friend. When we next met with our groups, the tall, imposing Carlos spoke Quechua to our students in a booming voice. Our students looked fearful. I understood Carlos' angry demeanor, though not his words. To us he recommended that the marchers perform eight simple exercises instead of the twelve more complicated ones we'd devised. Carlos further suggested we teach our charges to salute the judges but didn't say how. He said we had to demand the teachers' cooperation, or we'd never succeed with their students. The next day we told the teachers to send only our selected students to each practice. They did, and we made progress.

The next obstacle became the clothing requirement. Our teams would have to wear matching uniforms and shoes. Many of the students had never worn shoes. They walked to school and functioned in their classrooms and in our PE activities, barefoot. Their parents had little money with which to buy school uniforms or shoes. We couldn't ask them to spend money they didn't have on special clothing for one competition. Marie and I decided to absorb the cost of the exercise outfits for the October 10 contest. I would sew the sixty costumes on the Singer sewing machine I'd borrowed from a friend. We would figure out a solution for the shoe requirement later.

I bought two bolts of light-blue cotton cloth at a bargain price and found a pattern in Cusco for a one-piece sleeveless top and bloomer-type bottom combination that would work for the girls. The side opening had snaps, no zipper—simple and easy to make. A gathered skirt of navy blue would make the girls' uniforms more stylish, but add to the cost. Marie and I couldn't afford the extra yardage for the skirts on our $100 a month stipend. So we eliminated them. I designed simple slip-on shorts for the boys to wear with their white shirts. I started sewing.

For the next two weeks our one-room home looked like a clothing factory. Piles of sixty partially completed outfits lay stacked on our beds. Boxes of snaps sat next to the plates on our kitchen table. In between teaching PE classes, marching practice, and the girls' club meetings, I sewed fast. I had sixty uniforms to finish in nine days. The sewing machine was whirring away when I heard a knock on our door. I opened it to five nice-looking young men.

"Congratulations!" one of the youths said. "You've been elected Queen of Miguel Grau High School."

I knew about Miguel Grau, the local boys' high school. Hordes of young men from the school often invaded the field where my boys' soccer team practiced. The Grau students must have noticed my unqueen-like yelling behavior when coaching my boys. I eyed the entourage awaiting my answer. Being chosen felt like an honor, yet I wondered what responsibilities the position would entail. Did it mean contributing money? I had little left over after paying for the uniforms.

"I'm deeply honored," I said feeling my face turn hot. I felt embarrassed by the five sets of eyes on me. "What must I do?"

"You need to find four young ladies for your court," one of the older students said, "to ride on the float with you this coming Thursday."

I'd been a chubby princess sitting atop my aunt's float in New England, North Dakota's Fourth of July parade at age eight. Back then my two younger sisters and three girl cousins had been my court. What a thrill to ride on the two-tiered display pulled by a big tractor from Aunt Sue's John Deere showroom. Now the request to be queen came from the local boys' high school—an opportunity for me to be an honored part of festivities in the Abancay community. I accepted.

I loved the idea of dressing up like a queen—until reality sunk in. With the parade a week away and the marching competition three days after that, how could I be ready? I needed a special dress fit for a queen.

No clothing stores existed in small Abancay and even if one did, I couldn't have afforded the elegant type of ball gown local women wore for important festivals. I couldn't ask to borrow a nice dress. I'd already borrowed too many household items from our girlfriends. None of them seemed my exact size anyway. Now, besides the uniforms, I'd need to sew myself a gown.

I dug through my dress patterns and found one with a scooped neckline, long sleeves and gathered skirt. Abancay had two fabric stores. At one, I bought yards of white satin—enough to make a floor-length formal. Lace-like material cost too much, so I purchased the minimum needed to cover just the bodice and the sleeves.

I asked four of my best Peruvian girlfriends to be members of my court. Nilda said she couldn't because she would be on her own float as queen of the Miguel Grau night school. María Pilar reacted with disgust. She believed Miguel Grau boys to be spoiled brats and wanted nothing to do with them. Our best friends, sisters Zoila and Zulma, also said no. They'd had enough experience being queens of other events. Each one had been expensive. Marie and I agreed she couldn't be the only attendant and thereby have only Americans on the float. So I reported my failure to the principal of the school. He shrugged his shoulders and said I could ride alone atop the float without a court, but I'd still need to supply a scepter and a crown.

Creativity took over. I covered a stick with aluminum foil for my scepter. The girls' school had a rhinestone tiara. Usually, the crown sat atop the statue of the Blessed Virgin in the school chapel. But I could borrow the sparkly halo for my own virginal head.

Invitations to have fun at the pre-competition games, food booths, and evening dances tempted me in the days prior to Thursday's parade. I especially hated to turn down the many requests to attend the dances. But besides making a fancy dress, I had to finish the last twenty exercise uniforms in time for the following Sunday's marching competition. I had no time to party. I couldn't have enjoyed the dances anyway without Antonio.

Luckily, the electricity stayed on Wednesday night. The Singer whined like an angry cat as I sewed thin piping along the front waistline of my gown. I finished hemming the white satin creation at midnight and tried it on. The bodice fit perfectly. Twirling in front of our small mirror in my flowing white gown, I looked like a bride.

The principal of Miguel Grau said a student would drive me to the school at eleven on the big day. I'd had my hair done and was dressed and ready at ten-thirty. I put the borrowed crown on top of my upswept hair and waited. I continued to wait until noon when Marie came back from a meeting. She'd heard that I'd be collected at three, not eleven. How inconsiderate of my subjects. No one had come by to tell me the changed pickup time. Indignation swelled under my beautiful gown. I wanted to make heads roll.

Word about the hour change came through at the same time Marie and I learned of a new requirement for our marching competition. The education office needed a list of our participants' ages or our team would be disqualified. I changed out of my regal clothes and ran downstairs to the education office to look up student rosters. At 2 p.m., when a teacher from Miguel Grau came to escort me to his school for the festivities, I continued jotting

Queen of the Boys' School

212 ❖ Between Inca Walls

down the missing student information. I told the teacher I'd be
ready at two-thirty. Then I typed up the list of our sixty students
with their ages and changed back into my queen clothes.

The two sister friends, Zoila and Zulma, who'd refused to
be in my court, came by with a bouquet of sweet-smelling white
lilies wrapped in red paper for me. I thanked them, grabbed
the scepter, flowers and crown, and left with my escort ready
to reign.

I climbed inelegantly over the side of a pickup, pulling yards
of satin dress after me and sat on the wooden chair at the back of
my float. The theme had been changed. Instead of a swan carrying
a rose, like I'd been told, the pickup bed had been transformed into
a boat with swaying palms and crepe paper streamers that waved
behind in the breeze. No matter. I could be queen of an imaginary
island and ocean.

My friend Nilda's float came behind mine. She and her four
attendants wore matching long, pink chiffon dresses and sat in
comfortable red armchairs. In the rear of her huge truck stood a
big, painted, open book. A banner about learning completed the
attractive ensemble—very appropriate for a school. I eyed Nilda's
elaborate and impressive float with envy. Apparently, the older
evening students of Miguel Grau were more artistic and better
organized than the daytime youth.

Streamers and palm trees fluttered in the breeze around
me as the parade moved down Abancay's major avenues. I waved
from my chair holding my flowers and threw kisses to my little
pupils who ran after my vehicle shouting and laughing. Friends
and neighbors lined the streets clapping and waving back. I could
hear boisterous shouts and whistles from young men in the crowd.

The floats, music bands, and high-stepping uniformed students turned down the final lane after three hours. Billowing pink
clouds provided a stunning background to the golden setting sun

at the end of our route. The sunset was a lovely ending to an exasperating, yet exhilarating, day.

Marie watched it all from a friend's balcony. Back at home I asked her for her impression. I couldn't believe her observation.

"It was kind of embarrassing for Nilda," Marie said. "Your float came by first and everyone yelled and screamed with excitement. Then her court and her truck with the fancy decor, rolled in behind and there was silence. The moving streamers and palm trees made your float prettier."

Marie's words surprised and pleased me. My undependable high school students had come through after all. The day could only have been better if Antonio had been there. I went to bed exhausted but content.

◇◦◇◦◇◦◇

I finished sewing and pressing the sixty gymnastics uniforms Saturday evening. Early Sunday morning Marie and I carried the blue outfits to the school where our students waited. The cleaned and combed marchers looked impressive in the blue outfits, except for their footwear. Many students had borrowed shoes from noncompeting friends. Not all the shoes fit the feet they were on. More problematic—several pairs of shoes weren't the required white color. Someone found white shoe polish and in an instant transformed black and brown plastic shoes into white ones. Problem solved.

Though scheduled for a 7 a.m. start, the event got under way at 9 a.m. We had the challenge of keeping our contestants out of mischief during the two-hour wait. Finally, we heard our school's name called. The students regrouped and marched straight across the field. The routines we'd practiced were performed in relative unison, and our marchers proudly passed the reviewing stand looking sharp in their uniforms. We hugged one another at the finish line.

Marie and I watched an endless line of other groups march in after ours. All the teams turned their heads and saluted the officials in the reviewing stand. Marie and I looked at one another. We hadn't taught our students to salute because we didn't know a salute was required. Our students had marched boldly by the tribunal as big as they pleased. Our teams had slighted the judges, the equivalent of snubbing their noses at the officials. Despite our oversight, our groups won our praise and placed sixth out of twelve teams.

Wedding

The band played a rhythmic *cumbia*, my favorite dance. I was in heaven moving my body to the sensuous beat, dancing with Antonio. The wedding reception, in full swing at a historic hall in Cusco, had followed Catholic nuptials in Cusco's big cathedral. The celebration looked like one in the States, except instead of college friends, Peruvians and Peace Corps volunteers imbibed the free drinks at the open bar. I wished the wedding was mine, but it wasn't. It was Marcus's, a volunteer from our Cornell-trained group who'd married a girl from Cusco.

The Peace Corps rumor mill had never mentioned that Marcus had a Peruvian girlfriend. He'd never said anything about a *novia* the few times we saw him in Cusco. Marie and Marcus had dated, but parted ways at the end of training in Puerto Rico. Apparently, Marcus hadn't wanted to tell Marie that he'd become engaged. When informed, Marie said his marriage seemed premature.

I'd encountered the groom and his Peruvian friend, César, weeks before in a Cusco restaurant when Marcus had handed me an invitation to his upcoming nuptials. I'd been finishing a meal of *lomo saltado*, and choked on a potato when

I read the formal announcement. I regained my composure and congratulated Marcus. I had no objection to a fellow Peace Corps colleague marrying a Peruvian. Marcus said little about his bride-to-be or his thoughts on marriage, but his friend César had many ideas. César said he wanted to marry an educated woman who spoke English.

When I mentioned the upcoming wedding to Antonio, he said the bride had the reputation of being mentally unstable and had been engaged before. Nevertheless, Antonio knew her so would be going to the wedding celebration. Not prone to gossip, he didn't elaborate more about the bride. He also didn't invite me to go with him to the festivities.

Antonio looked attractive at the wedding reception in a dark suit that complemented his black hair. I wore a sleeveless black crepe number I'd dug out of my trunk for the occasion. I added a string of fake pearls for a dressy look. My favorite hairdresser in Cusco swept my shoulder-length, sun-bleached hair up into a sophisticated style using a container of hair spray. I felt more animated than usual, before I'd even had much champagne.

Alcohol didn't loosen Antonio's tongue, at least not with me. He seemed reticent, maybe because we were once more in the "just friends" stage. He waited several musical numbers before asking me to dance. I hoped we'd dance every dance and be more like a reconciled couple. Instead, Antonio swirled me around the floor for a couple of fun *cumbias,* then went outside to smoke a cigarette with male Peace Corps volunteers. After his last puff, through the open door, I saw him depart with fellow Abancay volunteer, Ken. Neither man reentered the hall to explain taking his leave. I hadn't come with Antonio, so couldn't object to his abrupt departure. Marie and I stood partnerless on the edge of the dance floor. That's when César and one of his friends walked up.

Tall, mustachioed César invited me to dance and we waltzed away. The buddy he'd come with asked Marie. The wedding became fun again. My dance partner started the conversation in a familiar way by stating how attractive he found me. I blushed. We spun around the floor a few times before César asked if I were hungry. I was famished, so the four of us paused our dancing, and the guys went to the banquet table and brought back plates of food.

We'd finished off the *Ají de gallina* spicy chicken dish when César suggested we go to a better party—the Firemen's Ball across town. He pulled an official invitation from his pocket that said Miss Cusco and Miss Peru would be there. The new dance sounded more enticing than the wedding reception. I hadn't come with Antonio and anyway, he'd disappeared. So Marie and I accepted the invitation. Ken and Antonio returned just as we exited.

"We've been invited," I shouted above the music to our two returning friends, "to the Firemen's Ball." Their looks of surprise followed us out the door.

The Firemen's Ball had a livelier band than the wedding reception, though Miss Cusco and Miss Peru didn't look like the knockouts I expected. Their makeup made them pretty, though not gorgeous.

César spoke English as well as he danced. He guided me around the floor and informed me that he worked as the chief mechanical engineer at the local fertilizer plant and earned good money. Speaking great English, he revealed that he was twenty-four and ready to settle down with someone experienced in life like me. We found we had similar views on everything from married women working to the number of children a family should have. But I didn't feel the strong chemistry with César that I'd felt with Antonio. César had everything I thought I wanted in a man—attractive physique, good job, modern thinker, excellent dancer, and an offer of marriage. I wanted to fall for him.

218 ❖ *Between Inca Walls*

I'd often heard sweet talk like César's from other Latin American men, but this time I seriously considered his tempting words. Then César said he wanted to go to the United States and I became suspicious of his motives. He held me close during the last waltz and whispered in my ear.

"You need to come to Cusco to see me every weekend."

He made no mention of him making the trip to Abancay to see me. His desires sounded one way—his way. No way would I ride the eight hours in an uncomfortable bus every weekend to see César. His remark offended me. My interest in him fizzled. No guy could tell me what to do.

⌖⌖⌖⌖

I dragged myself from my hotel bed to 11:00 a.m. mass the next morning. After getting in from the dance at 4:30 a.m., I'd managed to get five hours of sleep. Marie slept in and looked perky at breakfast. I had bags under my eyes and felt like I'd been put through a clothes ringer—which implement I hadn't seen since leaving the States a year ago.

Ken and Antonio invited us to their table at the Cuzco Restaurant at lunchtime. They looked well rested and suggested we all go to an afternoon soccer match. My spirits rallied after eating, and I agreed with Marie that we should accompany our two friends.

Antonio was ecstatic when his university team scored a goal. He said nothing about my leaving the wedding reception with César. After the game, when Antonio and I finally sat alone in Father Repullés's jeep that Ken, Marie and I had driven to Cusco, I started talking. I wanted to know where I stood in Antonio's life. I was in a vulnerable state from too little rest. Then, too, I felt guilty for having left the wedding reception with César. I began by explaining my disappearing act from the wedding reception the previous night.

"I think I should tell you," I said, eyes downcast, "why I left you at the dance last night."

"No, you don't owe me an explanation," Antonio said, hurt in his voice. "Don't even talk about it."

"I wanted to see Miss Cusco and Miss Peru," I said, stammering in halting Spanish, "and have fun."

"It doesn't matter to me," he said. "It's of no importance."

I persisted, knowing my words charged into dangerous territory. I'd always been honest with Antonio and felt compelled to justify my actions. I also wanted to understand the status of our relationship.

"You hadn't brought me to the reception," I said, trying to defend my actions, "and we weren't even dancing that much together."

"You," Antonio said in a judgmental tone, "have a lot of German in you." He careened off subject. "You are very cold. You think only of yourself. You seek pleasure from my companionship, which you'll continue to do until you leave and no longer need me. Things will be more difficult for me when you're gone."

"I've been trying to help you find a way to the U.S.," I said, hoping to encourage him, "but I don't want to help anyone who won't help himself."

"You think," he said, fire in his eyes, "that I don't try?"

I wanted him to list the efforts he'd made so I could see positive movement toward a future we might have. But Antonio sat in the jeep, silent, making no mention of any actions he'd taken.

I didn't like being characterized as unemotional or having to justify my actions. A wave of exhaustion swept through me. I hurt and needed sleep, but I plowed ahead anyway with my defenses down.

"I just like to have fun," I said again, lowering my voice, "and I don't want to tie you down."

"I like to have fun too," Antonio said, his face getting red. "I'm nothing but an animal, and will always be that because, like all Latinos, being animal-like is more fun. I am nothing to you or anyone."

It pained me to hear him talk about himself in a degrading way. He had never taken advantage of me physically, like he implied a red-blooded Peruvian would. He was mad at me and at himself—and probably mad at the world.

"I've been an idiot," Antonio continued, angry and defeated. "I'll never again be so stupid as to fall for someone who doesn't care about me."

"You are important," I said, pleading, "to me, to Ken, and to Marie."

In my defenseless state, the thought of losing him as a friend brought me to the edge of tears. Antonio noticed.

"Don't waste your tears on someone so insignificant," he said. He exited the jeep, slammed the door, and bid me a cold, "*adios*," before sprinting down the street.

In a few words I'd destroyed the caring feelings we'd developed for one another. I had been the slayer, the stupid one to force Antonio to see the hopelessness of our coupling. I knew why I'd said what I had. Antonio was still young and lacked self-confidence. Maybe he didn't want to plan on a future with me because I'd leave Peru in eight months. We both had lives too unsettled to see a future together. But Antonio had been more than a good friend, and now I had wounded him with my actions at the dance and my words of explanation. I hated the hurt I'd caused us both. I wished I could control the feeling part of me and deny my emotional pain. But I was so depressed I could hardly function. My inner turmoil mirrored that of my freshman year of college. Then, emotional pressures had crescendoed and led to a physical mishap.

Tensions

My parents had purchased an orange Renault Dauphin car for my thirty-mile daily commute to classes for my freshman year in 1960. I steered the tiny car onto College of the Holy Names' modern, new campus nestled among eucalyptus and redwood trees high in the hills above Oakland. My folks had moved from Montana to California so they could afford their children's higher education by having them live at home while attending a local college. Gas, at thirty cents a gallon, added up to less than the one thousand dollars a year it cost to live in the college dorms.

Three years before, students at my college had attended classes on a site in downtown Oakland that overlooked Lake Merritt. The new campus boasted a panorama of the Bay Area. But I had no time to stop and admire the scenery. I needed to get to my classes and then to a job downtown.

I sat in Russian, my first course of the day, attempting to translate the strange Cyrillic letters that would reveal the clever plot of one of Chekhov's short stories. The Greek-like letters swam before my eyes. I'd enrolled in Russian 101 because with the ongoing Cold War it seemed like a good idea—and I liked new and unusual challenges. Chekhov's tales fascinated me, but the grading system put me at the lower end of the curve. My little Russian dictionary and I had been spending too many hours together.

I'd signed up for eighteen units, instead of the usual fifteen, full of confidence. But the homework, term papers, and foreign language translations overwhelmed me. I inched my way through Chekhov and struggled in English class to comprehend Beowulf, a different kind of foreign language. The body systems in physiology didn't interest me, so I couldn't memorize their parts. I did poorly on tests and earned grades lower than I should have in all but sociology and psychology classes.

At least I could win top grades in the classes of my majors. For sociology, I read the textbook before class and parroted back answers to Sister Antonia's questions. I wrote detailed, well-researched term papers. But Sister never gave me anything above a *B* grade. The marks disappointed me, but I kept trying to please her. I earned good grades in Sister Paulina's psychology classes, however. With five younger siblings, the textbooks couldn't teach me much I didn't already know about child development.

I amazed my philosophy professor and myself by writing an *A* paper on Descartes. I produced the well-reasoned piece by conducting research in the big San Francisco Public Library over Christmas vacation. I couldn't concentrate, study, or write at home. Growing tensions between my parents had made the atmosphere there unbearable. With the birth of child number six, a cute, blonde-haired baby boy with crossed blue eyes and colic, everyone seemed stressed.

My ten-year-old brother, Buddy, didn't like school, made no friends, and often cried and asked to return to Montana. Daddy converted the garage into a family room with a bedroom for Buddy, hoping he'd be happy with a room of his own. But my brother lay in bed tracing imaginary figures in the ceiling with his finger for hours. If he spoke to anyone, it ended in an argument. Sometimes he refused to eat. He couldn't adjust to life in California. Buddy needed the freedom of the open countryside that the pet dog we'd left back in Montana had.

When Mama went back to work, her new job was a mixed blessing. She beat out fifty-two other applicants for a position as a clerk with the Newark Police Department. Mama looked authoritative in her blue-and-white uniform with the badge on the front. The job paid well and allowed her to work close to home. But Daddy found problems with Mama's new job.

Daddy had been assigned the night shift at the Federal Aviation Administration, FAA, which made him free in the daytime. He said he'd driven by the police station and seen Mama and male police officers embracing. He accused Mama of all manner of sexual improprieties with her male coworkers. The mother I knew was religious and shy around men. Her faith didn't permit her to look at another man in a sexual way so Daddy's accusations sounded ridiculous. But nothing changed his imagined perception of Mama's infidelities. My parents argued nonstop.

The males of the family hadn't fared well with the move to California. Their moods and outbursts caused us females more stress than did our work and studies. The ever-present tensions put everyone in the house on edge. Mama said she'd married a Catholic because Catholics didn't believe in divorce. So divorce was out of the question. Our family couldn't go on with so much conflict between a suspicious father and a withdrawn mother.

I couldn't concentrate on my college homework. Every day I had an upset stomach. To keep my scholarship I needed to maintain a *B* average. My grades took a precipitous decline. I could lose my scholarship if the family conflicts didn't soon find a resolution.

One day I drove with Daddy in the old Studebaker pickup. The state of our household had worried me for months. I gathered the courage to speak up.

"I think," I said, "you and Mama should see a counselor. The hostility in the house makes it impossible for me to study. We're all upset with the constant arguing."

"I don't need a psychiatrist," Daddy said, staring at the road ahead. "I know what I've seen. Besides, we can't afford therapy."

I hesitated to say much more for fear Daddy might explode. But I sensed his fragile mental door opening a crack so I pushed. The tranquility of the household and my scholarship were at stake. I needed to effect some change.

"I have the name of a therapist in Fremont who Sister Paulina recommends," I said. "I'll make the appointment and pay for it, if you'll go."

Daddy thought. I waited in silence. I didn't know what to do if Daddy refused my offer. Counseling seemed the only way out of this uncomfortable discord. I needed him to agree.

"Okay, if you're paying," he said in a quiet voice. "I guess we could give it a try."

I breathed easier. Maybe now home life wouldn't be so tumultuous. I made the appointment, and Mama and Daddy went. Mama returned in tears. She hesitated to tell me what happened. The counselor had asked about my parents' sex life. Daddy said his sex life was private and none of the counselor's business. He stomped out of the office and refused to return.

When Daddy handed me the bill a few weeks later, the cost shocked me. I wished the improved peace in the house matched the amount on the bill. I sent the psychologist his fifty dollars, money I'd earned from one hundred hours of babysitting.

A few weeks later, Daddy transferred to the day shift at the FAA and his jealous paranoia diminished. When the Newark

Police Department moved into a new building with no windows, Daddy's accusations of infidelity ceased. Our family life regained a measure of tranquility.

Compared to Montana, my family's material advancements in California—a new house, good-paying jobs, educational opportunities, and tons of places to have fun—had improved our lives. However, I often yearned for the stability of the simpler, more boring life in the less-populated state. I hated how vulnerable my family had become in this busy and intense place.

❖❖❖❖

After a full day of college classes, I steered my little Renault down the hill to the center of Oakland to Capwell's Department Store— four stories high and a city block wide. The biggest store I'd ever seen. After graduating from high school, I'd started selling nylons during Capwell's big July sale. The fall I entered college, the head of the notions department lured me away from hosiery to her more varied and interesting department. Ten to twenty hours a week I helped shoppers select the right buttons from the bins and match thread and zippers to their fabrics. My shift ended when the store closed at nine. The twenty-five dollars a week I earned helped buy my college textbooks. Any remaining money went for fashionable school outfits from Capwell's Women's Department. Unfortunately, my 20 percent store discount encouraged me to buy more clothes.

I didn't mind the long days, but there were drawbacks. Between the job, the commute to school, and the tensions at home, my grades had decreased further. Then, in April, I did a stupid thing. At the end of a Friday physical education class, for no reason other than I'd seen it done on TV, I took a running leap to jump over a tennis net. The professional tennis players made it look effortless. But my feet got tangled in the top of the net so my body didn't soar over it. Then my hands didn't go down soon enough to break my fall. I crashed hard on my mouth and right hip. Teeth scattered in different directions and my hip hurt, though I could still get up and walk.

The nun in charge ran to check me for broken bones. Only my teeth were broken. Blood poured from my mouth. The sister stopped the bleeding then found my eyetooth near one wall and a front tooth near the net. She wrapped both in a cotton square, put them in my hand and told me to call my dentist. I didn't have one. I'd never had so much as a cavity.

The only dentist I knew was a high school friend's. One of the sisters drove me to the dentist's office, teeth in hand. He reinserted them in their sockets and wired the loose ones to nearby stable teeth. I sat in the dentist's chair and stared up at the ceiling contemplating what had happened. Fortunately, the PE class had been in the gymnasium and not outside on the concrete courts. The foot-long purple bruise on my hip and my throbbing mouth sent me to bed for the weekend. For many years my chipped front tooth reminded me of my impulsive nature.

This reckless act later played out when, in January 1965, I spent five days in a Cusco dentist's chair getting a root canal on my front tooth. Two months after the drilling and filling, I returned to Cusco for a dental checkup and my relationship with Antonio ignited. Sometimes decisions made in an instant have repercussions that last a lifetime.

Letters

Wooden shutters and iron bars covered the windows on the ground floor of the Abancay post office. The barriers kept out both sun and thieves. But the big timber doors of the two-story adobe building stood open in a welcoming gesture to me. Inside, I waited for my eyes to adjust to the darkness. Apartado 25 beckoned from the wall of mailboxes. Through the small glass door of Marie's and my post office box, I could see a two-inch stack of fat airmail envelopes—letters from the States. Last week's mail strike had deprived me of a principal source of emotional nourishment. With the strike over, I looked forward to the contents of the mailbox to refresh my spirit. I inserted the key in the lock and took out five red and blue striped envelopes and one cream-colored letter. The air mail dispatches, no doubt, had been sent weeks ago.

Cards for my November 5 birthday had greeted me on November 24. Christmas gifts had arrived in February. Nevertheless, I welcomed communication from family and friends anytime. Loved ones had put pen to paper thinking of me and awaited my response. Their words reminded me of the life I'd left behind and pushed back homesickness. No matter how long it took the mail to reach me, I loved receiving it.

Today two letters came from my family. Outside the post office, I opened the one with my mother's handwriting on the envelope and unfolded the sheets of paper inside. Something dropped to the sidewalk. Two sticks of Juicy Fruit gum. I smiled. My five-year-old brother, Randy, had wrapped my favorite flavor of gum inside a page marked with Xs. One of my three sisters had drawn an arrow to Randy's pencil scratches and written "kisses." My youngest brother must have learned to hold a pencil since I'd left him over a year ago. No doubt he enjoyed drawing crossed lines. A twinge of sadness enveloped me for a moment when I realized that by now I'd likely been replaced as my baby brother's favorite sister. Still, Randy's gift and his attempt to write my name meant he retained some memory of me.

With Randy's letter were messages from both my parents. I hurried home to read them. Mama wondered how I coped without convenient access to phones, electricity, and flush toilets. As always, she reminded me to be careful on the mountain roads and say my prayers. I hadn't informed her about the jeep blowing a tire and almost plunging me down a steep cliff into the Apurimac River.

Daddy said he wrote because Mama told him to. He continued to enjoy the bottle of Puerto Rican rum I'd brought him when I'd briefly returned home at the end of Peace Corps training. Did I need an oxygen mask to breathe at 12,000 feet? Was I going to get a cow? If I kept it downstairs, it would warm the upstairs. For electricity, he said, I could hook up a paddle wheel or wind charger to a generator. Daddy, always the electrician and farmer, advised me to grow alfalfa, oats, and barley and wondered if I had a plow. I sat on my bed consuming every word of Daddy's amusing questions and suggestions.

From their inquiries and remarks I could tell my parents still had little idea of my Peruvian life, though my letters over the past twelve months had described it in detail. I didn't mention my growing affection for Antonio, just that I wanted their help in finding a job for him in the U.S. No matter what people wrote, I loved hearing whatever they had to say. A wave of nostalgia rolled over me.

One letter of the five I opened came from an older man who'd sat next to me on the flight from Mexico City to San Francisco when I'd returned from Peace Corps training the previous year. His lengthy missive said he was deeply concerned about the continued conflict in Vietnam and the rising number of deaths on both sides. He hinted at a successful business and considerable wealth—and regrets about his impending divorce and not traveling when young. I took note of his disappointments and vowed not to be as remorseful when I reached an advanced age.

Another older acquaintance, with whom I'd worked at the library in my hometown, also penned his complaints. His letter railed at the injustices he'd suffered at the hands of authoritarian bureaucracies. Changing employers and cities hadn't improved his bitter feelings. I skimmed over his four-page dispatch, wondering how someone with a good education, a full-time job, and two small children could feel so wronged. The *campesinos* of Peru had none of either of these Americans' advantages yet appeared more content.

Neither middle-aged man who corresponded with me seemed to have a satisfactory marriage. I couldn't tell if they wrote personal diatribes to me because I would understand or if they wanted a relationship with a younger woman. Most likely, writing to me gave them an outlet for their frustrations because I was a sympathetic ear a safe world away. Their views helped me see with greater clarity the despair I'd often noticed in materialistic, American men. I wrote back to them sharing information about Peru and my current primitive, though satisfactory, living situation.

More than information was on the minds of the five young Latin men who wrote to me in Spanish long after I'd first met them in Mexico and Puerto Rico. I'd become fluent enough in Spanish to understand what these dark-haired, dark-eyed Romeos wrote in their letters. They all hoped for a romantic relationship with me.

The five *amigos* and a new one in Lima said they were studying or working and desired to eventually have a life with me. My heart beat fast whenever I read their sweet words. It touched me to know such kind, considerate young men cared enough to pour out their feeling on paper. They hoped I would return their affections.

Flavio said he was leaving Guadalajara for California and hoped to meet my parents. My parents had forwarded his letter. I quickly wrote back to inform Flavio that I now lived in Peru. Much to my relief, he later penned a response saying he'd made it as far as Los Angeles, not to Newark where my parents lived, before returning to Mexico.

Sergio and Juan, helpers from Apaseo, Mexico, where I'd lived for a summer, let me know the library I'd founded continued to function. Both recalled our days fondly. Juan continued his medical studies but Sergio had stopped his university classes to work and save more money. I hoped he wasn't saving money to visit me.

Inocente, the tall, slender engineering student I'd met in Acapulco, sent me Spanish books to further my language learning. I sent him books to help him with English. He hoped I'd visit him in Mexico City after my time in Peru as I'd done on my way home from Peace Corps training the previous September. I knew I wouldn't.

Eduardo was in college in Puerto Rico. He also wanted to meet my parents. He missed me and still had the worn-out tennis shoes I'd left him in Aguada.

Julio wrote me from Lima. He had serenaded me with his guitar at his sisters' home in Abancay. I'd suggested we correspond after he returned to Lima to complete his medical studies. But the French kiss he'd attempted with a mouth full of gum hadn't impressed me any more than did his romantic songs. My heart now belonged elsewhere.

The words in the letters of my Latin male friends ranged from polite affection to outpourings of love. I answered their heartfelt entreaties with news of Abancay and my current exciting activities. I could offer them no more than sincere friendship.

Reports I sent to my college advisor, Sister Antonia Marie, described the girls' club Marie and I had started and the boys PE class I trained to compete in the marching competition. I stressed that both groups lived in the poor areas around Abancay, and I hoped to help these impoverished students develop leadership skills. As a sociology professor, Sister could appreciate my attempt at community development. She quoted my letter verbatim in an article published in the *Oakland Tribune*.

"I've been given the invaluable opportunity to know, understand, and love a people different from me in culture, language, and values," I'd written my college professor. "I've been made to feel a part of a culture which a year ago seemed strange."

Truth was, my quote looked better in the newspaper than I felt living it. At the time I struggled to coach a soccer team without having any knowledge of the game's rules. And my PE classes were often unruly.

The high school and college friends I'd left behind wrote about which stage of graduate school, marriage, or child-bearing they were in—none of which I could relate to. The stateside person I connected with most was my twenty-three-year-old North Dakota cousin, Barbara Ann. She was spending a second year teaching Eskimo children in Alaska and wrote of riding a dogsled along silent snow paths for hours to reach her town in the wilderness. Her trip sounded like a colder, quieter version of my journeys around the Andes. Barbara Ann asked for every detail of my exploits. More than anyone, she wanted to be part of my adventures and to share hers with me.

My roommate Marie's parents wrote to her every few months. I received five to ten letters a week compared with Marie's one or two. The support from correspondence I had eluded Marie. I felt guilty at my good fortune, so I asked my family to send Marie's favorite candy, Tootsie Rolls, for her October birthday. They did.

Marie received more than candy for her twenty-third birthday the end of October, 1965—her parents and unmarried aunt came for a weeklong visit. At first her family's trip to Peru delighted my roommate, until she realized she'd need to plan a week's worth of activities for them.

First she whisked them off to Machu Picchu, then to Abancay so they could see how we lived. I marveled at how comfortable and knowledgeable her parents were in a foreign country. They could communicate in Spanish because of the twelve years the family had lived near Guadalajara, Mexico. Maybe her family didn't write often, but they certainly seemed to comprehend life in an undeveloped Latin American country better than my parents.

Marie's parents didn't find much to talk about with Darcy when they met him in Abancay. Yet all three of her relatives were at ease talking to Antonio when they returned to Cusco and took Marie, Antonio, and me to the tourist hotel for dinner. They liked my boyfriend—thought he was handsome and very nice. Antonio seemed comfortable talking with Marie's family. My heart quickened. I could envision this intelligent Peruvian living in the States. Marie's spinster aunt pulled me aside as we left the hotel restaurant.

"Be particular about who you marry," she said with a twinkle in her eye, "but not too particular, or you'll end up unmarried like me."

An airmail envelope, separate from that of my parents, contained greetings from my two teenaged sisters. I opened Patty's letter first. At eighteen, she lived at home while studying at Cal State, Hayward. She lamented that her poor grades meant she might flunk out of school. She'd been spending too much time taking guitar lessons and playing the bass viola in the town orchestra. Though she diagnosed herself as depressed, she still managed to be her usual lighthearted self.

"I've come into a large sum of money," she joked. "I robbed a bank so I quit school and will see you shortly."

I'd written both sisters about my growing affection for Antonio. Charlene, nineteen, worked and lived in a dorm at Santa Clara University. She clearly sensed my dilemma and wrote back:

> *Since I've lived at school I've found myself questioning the church a great deal. You've got to find the answers that really apply to your life and what you see as significant in your life. What I'm saying is "do what comes naturally." Don't be a coward. Don't be satisfied with half answers or accept others' decisions only because they are our superiors. When you admit you've become more aware of the physical aspect of life, you've begun living like a human, not some spiritual textbook being.*

I welcomed Charlene's sage words. Her letters gave me the courage I needed to charge ahead with Antonio. Both my sisters asked my advice about dating and attracting boys. I wrote back telling them they should go to a Latin American country where they'd have no problem meeting attractive, caring guys who'd pursue them. Some might even be sincere.

Love Letters

My misspelled name on the cream-colored envelope stared up at me, daring me to open it. "Señorita Evelyn Kolh," not Kohl, was typed on the front. The unfamiliar silent "h" often caused Peruvians to misspell my name. No return address, but "Cusco" was stamped in the right corner. I'd carried the letter, along with the airmail ones, from the Abancay Post Office. Pages of the delicious news and greetings I hungered for from family and friends spread around me on my cot. I'd devoured the letters from home like a starving beggar. I might not like the taste of what was inside this last envelope. It looked bland enough on the outside, but I shuddered, fearful of what might pour out from the inside. I hesitated to open the letter I recognized from Antonio.

Our last conversation replayed in my head. He had been angrier than I'd ever seen him when we'd parted in Cusco after Marcus's wedding. His rage seemed the size of an Andean mountain and just as insurmountable—with Antonio on one side and me on the other. His ire had been directed at himself, but he'd also accused me of being cold and unfeeling. His words from our shouting match in the jeep still stung—maybe because they were true.

Now, barely two weeks after the worst uncoupling yet, he'd sent me a letter. I unfolded the two pages of onionskin paper covered with line after straight line of Antonio's familiar neat cursive in blue ink.

"I'm sorry and in pain for the way I treated you when I last saw you in Cusco," his letter read." The thin paper shook in my hands, and my heart beat fast. "You can't imagine how I feel, as I don't have the way to ask forgiveness for what I said."

Joy filled my heart. Maybe his angry words at our last parting hadn't destroyed the bond we'd developed over the past seven months. Perhaps our relationship wasn't over because of the way I had left Marcus's wedding reception with César. Tension drained out of my body. I couldn't believe the writing before my eyes. By the end of the first paragraph Antonio's lovely words had wooed me back. My body quivered, overjoyed to be back in his good graces.

The letter ended with "I want to be in Abancay to ask your forgiveness personally and to calm my spirit. I miss you."

I couldn't understand the rush of feeling that filled me. One moment I was self-sufficient and didn't need Antonio in my life. The next moment I craved his gentleness and authenticity. He lacked self-confidence and a vision for his life, unlike me. Nevertheless, he always wanted the best for me, never exploited our relationship, and he loved me. How could my emotions for him whip so fast back and forth between uncaring and love?

❖❖❖

Two weeks after receiving the letter, on a Saturday in mid-September, Antonio caught the bus back to me for a weeklong stay. I was not certain how to act when I saw him. My ambivalence made me awkward. I took my cue from the movies I went to almost every evening at Abancay's El Nilo movie theater. I threw my arms around Antonio at the Abancay bus station and played the adoring girlfriend, happy to see her true love. I acted the part until I believed, once again, that he was the only man for me.

Antonio may have sensed some falseness in my behavior. The next day, when we huddled together talking on a bench in Abancay's flower-filled main plaza, he said something I was afraid might be true—that I didn't really love him and never had.

"I'm a diversion for you," Antonio said in hour two of a three-hour soul-bearing session.

"I do want to help you," I said, "to make something of your life."

"But you want to help me," he said, "out of pity. Then you'll just go away and forget that I exist."

"I don't pity you," I protested. "I want you to use your intelligence to plan for a future that could include me."

"You have the picture of an ideal man in your head," Antonio said, "and you'll never find him in real life."

"Okay," I said, thinking I could fluster him, "why do you love me?"

"Because you're good, you're intelligent, and you're sincere," he said without hesitating. "No other girl I've ever met has been so frank about everything. But we need to stop being so close, or we'll both get hurt."

Now was my chance to agree again to yet another cooling-off period. I needed time to decide what I wanted. Continually going back and forth between friendship and love whipped me to and fro like the switchbacks to Machu Picchu. I needed to stop hoping for a permanent life with Antonio in the States.

But he wouldn't conform to my wishes. He wouldn't dance when I wanted, say what I thought he should, or perform up to my expectations of a serious companion. He didn't take the lead in any plans for our present or our future. Most of all, I wanted to stop missing him when he left me.

"The problem is my very existence," my boyfriend said, removing his arm from around my shoulders and looking down at the sidewalk. "We're both independent individuals with no obligations to each other. If I was smart, I'd have taken you to bed and be done with this cat-and-mouse game."

I wasn't surprised by his directness about having sex. We had spent too many hours caressing and kissing. The next step was obvious. But his reasoning didn't fool me. In his scenario a man had everything to gain and a woman had everything to lose.

"A man and a woman," he continued, "can seal their love with their actions."

"My body might be tempted to violate the 'no sex before marriage' rule," I said, "but I doubt you can convince my mind. You just want pleasure without any of the responsibility that goes with it."

"No," he said, "I don't want to hurt you in any way, and I will, too, if we keep arousing one another, because I'm Latin. I'm afraid I'd make you suffer if you made your life with me."

"I'm not afraid of material hardships," I said. "I grew up poor in Montana without many things. I worked summers on ranches from the time I was eleven to buy my clothes and shoes."

"No, but you are afraid of the emotional hardships, and I know I'll make you suffer."

Once again, I had the panicky feeling that my *amor* wanted to end our relationship before I wanted it to end. Antonio spoke more honestly, with more sincerity than any man I had ever known. He'd won over my heart with how he seemed to care more for me than for himself.

"I'm willing to take the risk of emotional hurt," I said, lowering my head to hide the tears streaming down my face.

"But I don't ever want to hurt you," Antonio said, gently cupping my chin in his hands, making me look into his tear-filled eyes. "I'll never love anyone as much as you. I've wanted to fool myself into thinking things could work out, but they won't. We are from two different worlds. The one you belong to holds much opportunity for you. Mine contains nothing. My life has been like a living death and will continue that way."

I hated Antonio's fatalistic thinking. His depressing statements seemed to mean that he thought he shouldn't have been born because of the circumstances of his early life. I always found life worth living, and I hoped he would someday come to the same conclusion. I couldn't decide his fate for him. He had to determine what he wanted and go for it, like I did.

"Promise me one thing," he said, as we left the plaza and he walked me the few blocks home, "that you will leave Peru as pure as you came to it. Some day you will find the man you deserve in the U.S., and when that day comes, you'll be able to have pleasant memories of Peru without any regrets."

We walked in silence with my mind churning. There was no way to convince him that life could be wonderful if he'd never experienced hope. He seemed to be mired in a belief that he had no future anywhere.

"And I want you to promise me," I said, "that you'll look into yourself and decide what you are capable of and then persevere to achieve whatever you decide."

We walked to my front door with a sense that this was the end to a beautiful relationship. I wanted so badly for him to give me one last goodbye kiss, but he just ran his finger tenderly up and down my cheek and looked deep into my eyes.

"*Adios*," he said, and left.

This time I didn't dash off a letter trying to convince Antonio that we should keep being *novios*. He had said it would be better to try and forget him rather than go through the same hurt over and over. I didn't really believe in the emotionally ruthless path he'd insisted we take. But I had to believe it to go on.

Despite our parting, I continued to search for a job for Antonio in the U.S. I obtained letters of recommendation from Cusco area Peace Corps volunteers who could vouch for Antonio's Quechua language abilities. Requests to six universities, recommending they hire Antonio in their Peru training programs came back explaining the bureaucracy that handled all hiring, but no job offers. A future for Antonio in the States through my efforts seemed impossible.

In one of our personal discussions in Cusco, months before, Antonio had said that his biological father, Frank, lived in Ohio. Twenty-two years before, Frank's upper-class-lawyer family hadn't allowed him to marry Livia Ochoa, the sixteen-year-old "Miss Cusco" sweetheart, pregnant with his child. Instead, the LaTorre family rushed their enamored son back to Lima. Antonio was born without his father present. Frank moved to the U.S. and never married.

Antonio's maternal grandparents and mother cared for Antonio in his early years. He stayed with assorted relatives when he came to Cusco for high school and college. He'd seen his biological father twice, at ages five and twelve, before Frank migrated to the United States. Once, Mr. LaTorre had visited Cusco and given his twelve-year-old son a pair of soccer shoes. But his father didn't stay around long enough to watch Antonio play. Soon after, someone stole the shoes. Discouraged, Antonio never again played on a soccer team.

I had encouraged Antonio to write and ask his father to help him study in the States. Antonio showed me his father's answer. Frank said Antonio would have to be fluent in English and have a job skill and a means of support before going to live in the U.S. His father's stipulations were impossible for Antonio to meet while living in Peru.

I'd scribbled down Frank's address when Antonio shared his father's response and, in desperation, wrote to Mr. LaTorre. I explained that he had an intelligent son who had no future in Peru. In a neatly printed response, his father wrote back, repeating the same conditions for going to the States that he'd written to his son. I couldn't comprehend how a parent could be so unfeeling as to refuse to help his own flesh and blood. But then, Antonio didn't speak about Frank like a son who felt loved by his father.

In early October, two weeks after Antonio returned to his studies in Cusco, another plain cream-colored envelope with familiar handwriting arrived in Apartado 25. The last time we'd been together, Antonio and I had agreed for the umpteenth time that we would try to forget one another. So I was surprised to hear from him.

"That night I told you it's better to forget me," he wrote, "I thought it would be for the best. But in this moment when many kilometers separate us, I realize the magnitude of my love for you."

The poetry of his tender words massaged my aching heart. How could I resist such a wonderful love? I wanted to run into his waiting arms.

"I wish I could be indifferent to your words and forget everything completely," sang Antonio's letter, "and break with the past, but it's not possible. My mind is like a magnetic tape, everything from the past repeats, each time becoming clearer and stronger. Your words echo and hit me over and over. I want to stop them but I can't, so I am convinced that my heart is not the same as months ago. It is encumbered and full of a grand love."

He explained that he'd wanted me to forget him because we might never have a life together. The connection we had forged, he feared, would be left behind if we moved to the United States.

"But like the rules of war—conquer or be conquered," he wrote. "I'm ready for the biggest risk of my life. You can't comprehend how much I love you—with the same intensity that I try to disengage from you. I don't know if you understand this, I hardly comprehend it myself. You are the grandest thing I have, the most sublime, purest, and indescribable. I can't stand that I might lose you."

His words captured my heart—again. I, too, agreed on paper, like he had, that we should be together.

Demonstrating

Attendance at our weekly girls' club meetings in Tamburco varied between seven and twenty preteen and teenage girls since we'd begun meeting in April. We'd scheduled the weekly get-togethers around educators' strikes, holidays, special events, and our travels. I'd taught the girls to sew potholders, simple skirts, and aprons, using a borrowed portable sewing machine. Together, we'd cooked banana bread, apple pie, and chocolate chip cookies in our ugly black oven that we carted the two miles uphill. Our club members had learned about sanitation, health, and hygiene. The girls had taught Marie and me their huayno and merengue dances, many Quechua words, and how to barbeque beef heart. Marie and I were proud of our girls' club.

Paulina had been elected by her peers to be president of the Michaela Bastidas 4-H club of Tamburco. In the seven months of the club's existence we'd seen the stout girl's confidence grow. She'd become comfortable running the meetings. Now she would represent her club in the annual three-province demonstration competition.

In four days, on October 30, 1965, Paulina would give a demonstration on how to make potato pancakes at the regional competition. For the twentieth time, she began her practice peering down at her tire-tread sandals trying to find the words she needed. We adults waited. Paulina started, then stopped again. The presentation hadn't come together.

Two teachers from the Tamburco area school, whom we'd asked to be a practice audience, shifted uneasily in their chairs. Our star club member fidgeted and looked at us searching for help. If Paulina couldn't function with only four people observing her, how would she perform in the spotlight in Cusco under the gaze of judges and scores of fellow competitors? Her performance would reflect on Marie and me as club leaders. As ambassadors from the United States, we wanted to show that we could do our job of developing young leaders by producing one who could give a good demonstration.

Paulina's thick black braids swished back and forth, brushing the back of the green and white apron I'd helped her make. She snatched the script Marie had written for her from the table in a desperate gesture and began to read.

"Use your own words," I said. "You won't be allowed to read your lines in the competition."

"But my words," Pauline countered, "don't come out sounding good."

She was right. In her world the way she talked was fine. But compared to the way her teachers, and even we foreigners spoke, Paulina didn't use correct Spanish. Her words came from the uneducated country folk where she lived. But we'd selected Paulina to represent the 4-H club in the demonstration contest because of her fortitude.

Three days prior to the big day, Paulina, with her younger sister, walked the two-and-a-half miles from their home to our place to practice her demonstration. We would do all we could to help her live up to her potential. She showed dedication.

We made visuals to assist her and instruct the audience. The recipe, printed on a large poster, noted the nutritional values of the eggs, potato, and the surprise ingredient, beer. I stenciled in the cost of each item and Marie drew a diagram of a potato with all its parts. We'd set all in motion for Paulina to succeed.

Two days before leaving for the contest, Paulina still hesitated, attempting to recall the right words for showing how *Panqueques de Papas* are made. We invited three of our women friends to observe what must have been practice number twenty-five. Our dark-eyed leader sailed through her demonstration using her own words, smiling like we'd taught her, and looking like she enjoyed the process. We couldn't believe our ears. Paulina impressed our friends. I breathed easier. We'd made progress.

The next day, the head of Abancay's sponsoring agricultural agency, SIPA, scheduled local boys' and girls' club contestants to present their demonstrations in the agency's offices. Marie and I dragged the charts, cooking pots, grater, and primus burner to downtown Abancay. Paulina gave her demonstration first, and after becoming confused twice, she recovered and finished her presentation. Two boys gave demonstrations so disorganized I couldn't comprehend what they wanted to show.

On Friday, the day before the big contest, we loaded the equipment plus Paulina, her mother and sister, and several club members into the back of the SIPA pickup and headed for Cusco. Marie and I rode in front with the SIPA engineer driver and, during the six-hour trip, learned more about his love life than we needed to know. We arrived around 2:30 p.m. and treated our girls to dinner before settling them into a hotel. Few had ever stayed in such a luxurious place, with electric lights that stayed on and hot and cold running water. They giggled with delight at having indoor toilets.

The big day arrived. Paulina would be the fifth presenter—ideal because she could compare her pace with that of the demonstrators who went before her. When her name was announced, she marched smiling to the front of the church hall. Marie and I had the charts, pans, and cooking burner set up for her.

Paulina began by pointing out the ingredients in her recipe, their nutritional values and low cost. She reminded the audience that Peru grows over 3,000 types of potatoes, many in the Abancay–Cusco areas. She looked like the intelligent person we knew, and seemed comfortable teaching her specialty to the crowd. Then she reached for the potato to grate it. There was no potato. Marie had peeled it, put it in a cup of water to keep it from discoloring, and then left it in the back room. We'd forgotten to gather up the potato when we brought in the rest of the equipment.

Thinking quickly, Marie ran back, grabbed the cup with the potato, and raced up the center aisle to hand the main ingredient to Paulina. The audience and judges laughed. The missing potato and Paulina's mention of the secret component, beer, seemed to relax the audience.

After Paulina fried up a few potato pancakes, Marie and I helped give out samples to the judges. They gobbled up the tasty morsels with gusto. Then we sat back to enjoy the remaining demonstrations. No one presented as well as Paulina. We had to wait to hear who had won until the following afternoon. The extra time gave us an opportunity to provide new experiences for our rural girls on Sunday morning.

We took our charges to the airport to watch airplanes land and take off. They had viewed the winged machines flying high above their mountains but never up close. Their eyes opened wide in wonder. Next came a special mass, to which we arrived late. A trip to a church museum followed. After looking at a couple of the religious vestments on display, the girls wandered into the nearby central plaza to watch the colorful vendors. The award ceremony came after lunch.

At the church hall, a young girl who'd given her demonstration the previous day, sat talking in the row in front of me. She was next to Señora Margarita, an important SIPA employee and leader of a local Cusco-based club. After a long series of introductions, the Master of Ceremonies announced the second-place winner. The talkative girl in front looked startled when she heard her name. She looked as displeased as her club leader.

"I really should have won first," the girl said, trying her best not to cry when handed the second-place prize, an electric hotplate. Then came the pronouncement of the first-place winner.

"For demonstrating . . ." I held my breath, "how to make potato pancakes, first place goes to . . . Paulina from Tamburco's Michaela Bastidas Club." Everyone except the two people in front of me burst into applause. Our club president beamed as she received a trophy and two large cooking pots—a more practical gift for her than the hotplate.

Marie received a certificate for going to the 4-H leaders' convention in Trujillo and I received one for serving as a club organizer. All participants received certificates, including Peace Corps members in attendance who had no presenters in the contest. The excessive number of awards didn't surprise me. Some kind of recognition was awarded to everyone at most events.

Marie and I received more applause than anyone. We thought it was because we'd been friendly. The unhappiest person appeared to be the SIPA home demonstration agent whose club member had won second place. She refused to speak to us because our Paulina had won first place. Two weeks later, our three colleagues in Compone were featured in the local newspaper because Robert Kennedy visited their worksite. Marie and I weren't written up in the newspapers, but we were proud that our club member had won an important competition. I would continue working with Peru's young people in whatever capacity I could.

Touchy Situation

In December 1965 a landslide took out a section of the road between Abancay and Cusco. Rocks and boulders blocked the narrow dirt thoroughfare, and vehicles couldn't pass in either direction. The *derumbe*, as the natives called it, gave me a legitimate excuse to back out of a promise I'd made months ago to help fellow volunteer, Larry, with a January summer camp in his town of Quillabamba. Volunteers often ran summer camps that provided recreational and educational events for the youth of our towns. I'd recently returned from a three-week approved vacation to Chile, and didn't want to leave Abancay again, so soon.

With the road out, reaching Larry's town, one hundred thirty-three miles away and on the other side of Cusco, would be difficult. I'd have to do what we always did to get around a slide—disembark from the bus carrying my luggage, trudge down the mountain's rough terrain, balance on rocks to cross the river, climb up the steep riverbank, and board the bus on the other side.

Larry's December letter to me said that the Quillabamba municipality had employed several townspeople, but he needed me and another local Peace Corps volunteer to assist with the seventy students he expected would attend the January camp. I'd promised to work the first two weeks of the six-week camp. I shouldn't back out now. Larry wanted my assistance and I'd given my word. I didn't renege on my commitments. I packed light.

An incentive awaited me if I left a few days early. I could spend time with Antonio as I passed through Cusco. My heart and body ached for him. I'd climb crumbling mountains and ford roaring streams to be by his side. My motivation got me to Cusco but resulted in other questionable activities.

❖❖❖❖

In Cusco, Antonio lent me his typewriter and encouraged me to complete the applications I'd brought with me for graduate schools of social welfare. He championed my desire for a master's degree. He'd never have my opportunities, he said, and I should take advantage of those given me. Personnel at the University of Wisconsin had expressed an interest in my attending their institution and suggested I apply for a scholarship. Antonio and I spent an afternoon in his university library while I filled out the scholarship form and wrote requests for letters of recommendation—when we could keep our hands off one another.

At dusk of my final day in Cusco, Antonio said he knew of a place where we could be alone. The offer was confusing and appealing. I liked what we did when alone. When he wrapped me in an embrace and kissed me, I felt loved. We couldn't show our affection in public because I felt judged as another loose American girl. Still, there was safety when others were present. I knew what could happen if we were alone for very long—and I feared that greater intimacy.

Antonio took my arm and guided me off the city's main street through a dark corridor and down a few steps. I followed him with trepidation, not knowing where we went. He stopped in front of a rough-hewn wooden door.

"My family owns this storeroom," he said, turning a key in the lock.

He signaled for me to enter through the opening. I stood in the doorway, hesitating. I trusted Antonio, but didn't know if I could trust myself.

Brisk mountain air flowed from the open street-level window across to the unbolted door of the basement-type room. I felt a chill. Light from Cusco's dim streetlamps filtered through dried mud on the small, transom-topped open window and fell onto a wood floor. Inside the room I could make out discarded furniture: a small table, a cupboard, and a couple of upended chairs. Everything seemed to have been tossed into the dusty room without regard for order.

"It smells like a dirt cellar," I said.

"I know," Antonio said, taking my face gently in his cupped hands like he often did, "but it's the only place we can be alone."

Antonio sat down on a dusty wooden chair and motioned for me to sit in his lap. I did. My body warmed again pressed against his slender frame. I felt passion welling up inside me. I recognized desire in Antonio and recalled the time my father tore Mama's dress off her at our house in Ismay. Now we were in the throes of it.

Soles scraped on the concrete sidewalks outside as Cusco's workers hurried home for their evening meals—all oblivious to the two in the room below them entwined in each other's arms. During the next hour, if a walker had stopped to look through the few transparent spots on the dirty window, he would have seen two young lovers lost in the ecstasy of one another's touch, becoming more aroused with each kiss.

"I love you," I said, coming up for air, "but I don't want our first time to be in a junk room. We need to stop."

We wrenched ourselves apart. I stood up and pulled down my blouse. Antonio righted himself and zipped his pants. Fortunately for us, no bed existed among the tumble of furniture. My body tingled and my face felt hot as I walked toward the exit.

"I'm going to try," Antonio said opening the door for me, "to dominate my animal urges with my mind."

I, too, needed to dominate my sexual urges. A partial solution was to leave town. Who knew what would happen if I stayed in Cusco with Antonio like I longed to? I boarded the train for Quillabamba early the next morning.

❖ ❖ ❖

The *click-click-click* of little rat's feet on the wooden floor of my room awakened me my first morning in Larry's jungle town. I turned on the lamp. A gray rodent scurried across the floor from a hole in the baseboard. I hopped from my bed, grabbed a nearby baseball bat, and in three steps crossed the room. The rat ducked back into its hole. I slammed the large end of the bat into the rat's front door blocking it. That should keep the pesky varmint away—until I needed the bat for my recreation classes.

Larry had scheduled the bus going to the camp to leave the main plaza at 9 a.m. By 10:30 a.m., less than half the number of expected campers had arrived. Larry, another volunteer, and I accompanied the twenty-five students to the school outside town. When we arrived at our camp base, the local paid helpers we expected were nowhere to be seen. I focused my attention on lunch and got to work.

I found the school kitchen filthy. No one had cleaned it at the end of the school year. I spent the morning scrubbing it down. The local employees didn't arrive in time to perform their assigned jobs, even though we'd had a planning session with them the night before. Explicit instructions had been given to come to work at 11 a.m. Even the director, Padre José, hadn't appeared by noon. Good that so few children had come.

I'd gone to the market with the supply person at 6:30 a.m. to buy food for lunch. He didn't bring our purchases to the school until 12:30 p.m. Summer camp was not beginning well.

"Where's the cook?" I said from the camp kitchen at 11:30, an hour before the hungry elementary-age campers were due to come in from playing.

"Oh, I'm sure she'll be here soon," Larry hollered from the yard where he was sweeping up debris.

"Well, no one else came on time," I shouted back, frustrated, "so why would we expect the cook to get here before lunch?"

The cook arrived at one o'clock and prepared a lunch with insufficient meat. As a result, everyone received a one-tablespoon portion of the main dish, so we supplemented the meal with loads of rice, vegetables, and fruit.

I organized the campers to wash the dishes, then took the girls out to play baseball. At least the girls didn't try stopping the baseball with their feet the way the boys in my PE classes did. Padre José had offered to bring sodas and take the boys to play soccer. But when he didn't arrive, Larry performed the Padre's duty. After sixty minutes of running in 90 percent humidity, thirst overcame us all. But, because Padre José hadn't brought the drinks he'd promised, Larry and I ran to the nearest soda stand and bought Fantas and Cokes for everyone.

When Padre José honored us with his presence that after-noon, he alternated between sitting on his rump reading a book and playing chess with one of the boys. Apparently, the Padre had come for rest and relaxation. I certainly hadn't.

I rested fitfully in the humidity of my room that night, dreaming of a better life. In my fantasy, Antonio's priest friend,

Father Gálvez, had married us in his church in Cusco. Few guests attended since we couldn't afford a big reception. I imagined we went to Machu Picchu for our honeymoon, then to Lima for my Peace Corps termination conference and to obtain a U.S. spousal visa for Antonio. To save money, the two of us traveled by land from Lima, through Central America to Mexico, and arrived in California at the end of July. Antonio studied English at an adult school near my hometown while I worked until we left for the University of Wisconsin. I'd been given a scholarship with the extra $500 stipend the university allotted for a spouse. We helped one another study until we graduated. I had our lives all figured out—in my dream.

I awakened from my half-sleep to again face the rat instead of my love. Beady black eyes above twitching whiskers stared at me when I turned on the lamp. I found a loose board and blocked the hole. I wanted to be gone from here and rush into Antonio's waiting arms. But duty called.

By day three, there still seemed to be no one in charge of the summer camp. I provided as much organization as I could by reminding others what needed to be done by when. Few workers followed through with my orders. I thought the disorder couldn't get worse, but it did. I confronted Padre José.

"You promised to bring drinks after recreation time," I said in Spanish, hands on my hips, "but for two days Larry and I have been buying them."

"Oh," Father said, glancing toward his jeep, "I asked Larry to do that."

"Everyone is shoving his duties onto someone else," I said, my face getting hot with frustration. "No one is in charge. No one is following through on his assigned responsibilities."

Father backed away and disappeared after our encounter. I later saw him riding around in his jeep. He never brought drinks to the kids.

I took every chance to tell the others what they should do, even though I had no authority. I was an outsider, so my orders were ignored. The other female Peace Corps volunteer told me I was too bossy. She was right, but how else would the camp run? Then, too, maybe Padre José stayed away because he didn't like me reminding him of his obligations.

Though irritated that the adults weren't doing right by the children, I couldn't desert the kids. I'd been raised to not expect pleasure from hard work. "Work before pleasure," my father always said. No pleasure followed this work.

By day four, sixty-five students rode on the bus to our camp, and the lack of coordination created one mess after another. Larry had the foresight to reserve two buses to drive all of us to a park with a museum. Before everyone piled in, I suggested we pack tuna fish and buy bread to make sandwiches for lunch at the site. The kids would be ravenous by noon. The female volunteer disagreed and said okay to taking the tuna fish, but we wouldn't need to purchase bread because "Padre José said he was bringing it."

I knew how that would be. Against her wishes, I insisted the bus stop so I could buy bread on our way to the park. Good thing. Padre José later said he knew nothing of his duty to bring the bread. The female volunteer never said she was wrong.

Rain poured down on our way back. As we arrived at camp, Larry rushed over to my bus. I was ready to call it a day.

"Would you entertain the campers in the gym?" he said. "I need a rest."

I needed a rest too. But Larry had done well to plan the first part of the day, so I guessed I could take care of the afternoon. I got creative.

First, I led our charges in songs we all knew. Then I made up a game where they had to shoot balls into wastebaskets. When the students became bored with that game, I switched to teaching them how to make the alphabet letters with their arms while singing the song I'd learned from my Cri-Cri records. The final half hour I had the bus drivers transport us around the countryside.

By evening I had caught a cold and was exhausted. Still, I helped plan the evening campfire with one of the local staff. On the way back to my rat-infested room I checked at the bus station for tickets to Cusco. I would do a Padre José and leave. The ticket office was closed. Maybe tomorrow would be better.

A young man and woman from another organization joined us on day five and Larry put Elvira, the blue-eyed young woman, in charge of my 3 p.m. recreation classes. The change surprised me, but I needed to rest to get rid of my cold. At 2:45 p.m., after my siesta, I went to check with Elvira, in case she wanted some pointers on what to teach. I found her fast asleep. I decided then that if the kids weren't being tended to by 3:30, I would quit the next day. When I returned, Elvira was out in the yard with the girls and had a question for me.

"Are the girls going to have their class?" Elvira said batting her baby blues, "I think this is the time."

"You were assigned to teach them," I said, trying not to sound sarcastic, and left.

When I returned that afternoon, Padre José had brought cases of Fanta and Coke, flashlights for all the volunteers, and a special larger one for me. I welcomed Padre's delayed responsibility. His stepping up gave me an excuse to leave. I couldn't take another five days of fighting for the kids. My mental and physical health would suffer.

No one seemed to care about the camp as much as me. The other adults would be better off without my constant grouchiness and complaining while trying to organize them. I felt proud that some volunteers now used my suggestions, after they had rejected them in our planning meetings. Enough volunteers remained, and the camp had a bit more organization. I would miss the children, for whom I had genuine affection, but not the adults. On the way back to my room I bought a ticket to Cusco for the next morning's bus.

In between blowing my nose and writing a note to Larry, I packed. The note I slipped under Larry's door before the sun rose read, "I'm leaving because I need to complete more graduate school applications before the February 1 deadline. Also, I miss Antonio."

The next morning I said goodbye to the rat and boarded the 4:30 a.m. bus eager to get home.

Birthday Present for Daddy

A ntonio had left Cusco to spend his summer vacation with his parents in Abancay, so I didn't want to stop there. Also, I didn't want the director of the Peace Corps regional office to know I'd left my camp assignment early. But I arrived in Cusco too late to catch a bus to Abancay. I'd stay in Cusco but have to stay out of sight.

Once in the Inca capital, I put on the glasses I rarely wore. I hoped they'd disguise me in case I encountered anyone I knew. I ate at restaurants not frequented by other volunteers. When I saw a colleague on the street, I darted into the rear of a nearby store and became fascinated with its wares. After a day of successful hiding, I felt emboldened to approach Peace Corps headquarters to collect the correspondence from our mailbox.

I peeked inside the office. The director's door was open, but I couldn't see Mr. Cavendish. I stopped holding my breath. The secretary typed noisily with her back to the door. Great luck. I slid my hand into the Abancay box and quietly pulled out a magazine and several college catalogs. I turned to leave, gloating at my success, when a male voice called out, "Hello, Evelyn."

I'd forgotten that Chuck, from my group, spent most of his days perched on a table in the office, waiting to talk to anyone who entered. He apparently had no work to do. I didn't respond to his greeting, hoping he would ignore me.

"If you don't want to talk," Chuck shouted as I hurried away, "don't."

"*Hola*," I said turning my head toward him and whispering, "I'm just out of breath."

I fled down the hall only to be stopped by Hilda, another office employee. My getaway wasn't working. I stood facing Hilda, ready to run.

"You looked so nice in your new outfit at the New Year's Eve party," Hilda said, smiling.

I thanked her and kept going. I expected someone to appear and shout, "But you're supposed to be in Quillabamba! That's why we paid you 104 *soles* for your transportation and other expenses."

When no one appeared, I thanked my lucky stars that I wouldn't have to give back my hard-earned money. I was free to get on my way to my Shangri-La and Antonio.

❖❖❖❖

The next day, my punishment came in the form of nine hours on the hot Tagli Cusco-to-Abancay bus. During six of those hours I devoured every article in Ken's *Harper's Bazaar* magazine that I'd rescued from our Peace Corps mailbox. For the past two years I'd been deprived of the intellectual stimulation that well-written literary articles provided. At 5:30 p.m. I walked in the door of our little room behind the Education Department. Marie looked up from her hotdog supper, surprised.

"What are you doing back here?" she said, still chewing.

"I made a wish to be in Abancay," I said, "and, poof, suddenly in a cloud of dust I was here."

I spoke the truth. As always, the trip had been dusty. Flying over the narrow landslide-prone roads, though, was pure fantasy.

The next day Antonio came running up the stairs and gave me a big welcome hug. That evening we greeted one another too warmly for over an hour, embracing inside the dark stairwell of the empty Education Department offices. My resistance to full body contact had lessened, disappointing myself. I needed to set some rules. When I told them to Antonio, he smiled and gave me a knowing look. My new rules were:

Only ten-minute goodnights.

No going to private rooms like Ken's apartment.

Spend more time talking and less in close bodily contact.

That evening we followed rule 3 and had a two-hour talk in the park. Our conversation followed a familiar pattern.

"You are really beautiful," Antonio said, looking into my eyes. "You should have someone better than me."

"You could do anything you want," I said, my heart melting.

"I know I could have gotten a perfect score on my math final," he said looking at his feet, "but I didn't study enough."

His math final happened the day after I'd visited him in Cusco. I wondered if he had neglected his studies to be with me. I felt guilty. We walked toward home where I would invoke rule 1.

"I went to talk to my mother about going to the States," Antonio continued, "but I just couldn't. I don't want to ask her to contact my father. My primary goal now is to get there, but I don't think my father will come through for me. He never has."

Tears rolled down my cheeks. I thought for the hundredth time that a life together would never be. Antonio took me gently into his arms. I molded to his body.

"I'd be very, very happy living with you," he said, kissing me in the dark hallway.

We kissed and embraced for ninety minutes before he left. We'd complied with rule 2 but my weakening body couldn't enforce rule 1.

I needed to focus my attention on something other than Antonio. I busied myself with several new projects. I could still accomplish a lot in the four months I had left, even if Antonio couldn't.

Marie had started a new girls' club in the nearby fringe community of Pueblo Libre. Girls from our Tamburco Club met with the new club members to orient them. At the ensuing weekly meetings I taught the five new 4-H club members to sew and cook.

At home I began making a Monopoly game in Spanish, something to distract us. I copied one lent to me by a newly arrived family of Protestant missionaries. Our artistic teenage neighbor, Alfonso, eagerly spent hours by my side drawing the train figures for *Ferrocarril Reading*, Reading Railroad. He sketched with perfection shapes for the *Compañía de Electricidad*, the Electric Company, and the *Compañía de Agua*, the Water Company. The avenues remained similar: *Avenida Vermont*, *Avenida Báltica*, and *Plaza Park*. A card pulled from the Treasure Chest, or *Fortuna*, pile stated a Jail Visit as "*De Visita en la Cárcel, no mas*." "Go Directly to Jail" became "*Vaya a la Cárcel*" and the Chance card to get out of jail free became, "*Salir de la Cárcel Gratis*." I typed the Community Chest cards and found unique buttons to use as tokens. We made monopoly money from green and yellow construction paper, with different denominations on them. We could now use the completed game to fight boredom, have fun, and promote a knowledge of capitalism.

Ken, Antonio, Marie, and I inaugurated the board one lazy afternoon. Antonio lost the first game—probably because the basis of the game included the concept of buying up real estate, not an activity in his experience. Either because I won the game, or because I maintained more physical distance between us, Antonio stopped talking to me for two days.

When we resumed communicating, as well as our long goodnights, I felt like a hypocrite. I went to mass most mornings, then engaged in heavy petting each evening. I needed to come clean about what I'd been doing. I went to confession at church.

The old Spanish priest at the cathedral down the hill from our house where I attended daily mass heard my confession. I described in Spanish how Antonio and I had been saying goodnight. Padre wasn't pleased. He warned me not to go alone to places with my *novio*. Then the elderly priest became angry when I couldn't say the entire Act of Contrition in Spanish. So I changed confessors.

The next week I made the trip up the hill to the American missionaries' new church. The two Maryknoll priests came from Boston, and I didn't know either one very well. However, Father O'Brien had to know it was me behind the screen in the confessional. Who else in this Spanish-and-Quechua-speaking town would recount her sins in English? I began as I'd done regularly for the past sixteen years.

"Bless me Father for I have sinned," I said, relieved to be using English.

"How have you sinned, my child?" Father answered.

"I have allowed my boyfriend to touch me in inappropriate ways when we are alone," I said, expecting the wrath of God to come down on me.

"Do you plan to marry your boyfriend?" Father asked.

What a surprising question. Antonio and I wanted to marry. Was that the same as planning to marry? I was silent and then answered the truth, as I wished it to be.

"Yes," I said.

"Then you are only doing what comes naturally," Father said. "Say three Hail Marys and three Our Fathers and go in peace."

Father's words were a revelation. A load of guilt lifted from me. I couldn't believe what I'd heard. Father O'Brien reinforced what my sister, Charlene, had written in her letter months ago. Her reasoning came from her Jesuit instructors at the University of Santa Clara.

My parents' response was very different from my sister's message. I'd been writing to them about Antonio for a few months. My letters mentioned that I cared deeply for a certain Peruvian university student.

"Don't make any rash decisions," my mother wrote. "You are in a strange country and haven't been in the States for a long time. You aren't seeing the entire situation."

Mama reminded me that I'd have to live in Peru if that was what Antonio wanted. She also wanted to know if Antonio drank. And, did he want children?

"The man is the head of the family," she added. "Is he a sincere Catholic?"

Daddy was certain Antonio was taking advantage of me to obtain a green card to come to the United States. Daddy never had much trust in people. I could sense his fear that his first-born might get hurt.

◇·◇·◇·◇

At the end of January 1966, both Marie and Ken developed bad cases of "the turistas." When their runs to the outdoor bathrooms hadn't subsided after a few days, the new Peace Corps doctor directed them to come to Cusco to be examined. Ken left me the key to his place so I could hang the curtains I'd sewn for his apartment.

I felt unwell myself, though not with "turistas." Feelings of emotional upset welled up inside me. I often felt like crying. The turmoil caught me off guard. I thought I had a handle on my emotions. Now I felt anxious and confused. Antonio said he knew the right prescription for my "illness." We'd talk about it when he came by in the evening.

It would be improper to let my *novio* sit and talk at my place at 8:30 p.m. because I was home alone. So we walked arm in arm to Abancay's central plaza and sat on a bench under the palm trees. We talked frankly about our differences.

"I'm concerned," I said, thinking I had to broach the sensitive topic sometime, "that you were not brought up in a home with your mother and father."

Studies in my college majors of sociology and psychology led me to believe that I took a chance marrying someone who'd not been raised in a stable nuclear family. Most likely, Antonio didn't have a good father role model. On the other hand, he seemed very devoted to his mother.

"Not having a father to live with is not my fault," Antonio said. "Besides, I had my grandfather until I turned eighteen and he passed away. You are being very short-sighted."

"There are so many things from my life," I said, "that you've never known, like baseball and *Time* magazine."

Antonio had no answer to that. I didn't add that in my college genetics class I'd learned that gene pools from two separate countries often produced the healthiest offspring. I needed to look at a permanent linking with this Peruvian from all angles.

It began to sprinkle, then rain hard. Antonio suggested we seek shelter at Ken's place, which was closer than my house. I had the key to Ken's apartment in my purse and was eager to get out of the downpour as soon as possible.

We didn't turn the lights on at Ken's place. In the dimness of an outdoor light, Antonio slowly removed my wet skirt and blouse leaving me in my slip. He took off his damp shirt and ushered me to Ken's narrow bed. I had never seen Antonio shirtless. He looked so young, white, and hairless. He pressed his naked skin against mine. His nakedness repulsed me. I wanted to leave.

"You are cold as a stone," he said, taunting. "I think you have a psychological block against physical relations."

True. I was physically cold, uncomfortable, and very reticent. But mostly I could hear my father's and the priests' warnings, about "needing to wait to do 'it.'" I needed to heed their words and get out of this dangerous situation.

Determined to leave, I searched for my clothes. I didn't want to do "it." I wanted to cry.

"Oh, the stone is going to shed a tear," he teased. "I'll have to get another girl to help me celebrate Carnivale."

His words tried to make me jealous, but instead made me angry. I wanted to flee this uncomfortable situation, but the darkness outside stopped me. And I didn't want to be seen walking Abancay's streets alone. The doors to the Education Department offices where I lived would be latched from the inside by now, so I couldn't get in anyway.

As quickly as Antonio's mood turned cruel, he smiled. Maybe he wanted to comfort me. But he didn't. He rolled over in Ken's cot and went to sleep. I got in next to him. I wanted to fall asleep in his arms. When that didn't happen, I decided to risk going out into the darkness. But when I got up to leave, I accidently kicked over Ken's primus burner. The loud bang awoke Antonio.

"Where are you going?" he whispered.

"Home, where I belong," I said in a lowered voice searching the end railing of the bed where he'd hung my wet clothes.

"Don't be silly. Come back here," Antonio said gently pulling on the hem of my slip, reeling me back to him. "Your fear of intimacy is causing a conflict between your mind and body. This back-and-forth game is bad for you and for me too."

Charlene's letter and Father O'Brien's question had now convinced my mind that I should follow what my body had wanted for over a year. Yet faced with the reality of losing my virginity, I became afraid and shy.

"I'm embarrassed to be naked with you," I said, shivering.

"There is nothing embarrassing or shameful about the human body," Antonio said, holding me tight.

That night in Ken's apartment, we consummated our relationship. I rested peacefully in Antonio's protective arms as a new day dawned. It was January 28, my father's birthday. I wouldn't be telling him about this present.

Worry and Work

There were more opportunities to be intimate since my first taste of Antonio on my father's birthday. Marie and Ken traveled out of Abancay, leaving apartments where Antonio and I could be alone. I felt no guilt about our behavior, which surprised me. But I ceased attending daily mass and now only went on Sundays. No amount of praying saved me from doing with Antonio what church rules forbade. No walls kept me from falling all the way for him.

I bathed in the pleasures of feeling like a woman. Since age twelve, I'd been warned of the evils of sex. No one had ever told me it could be enjoyable. Still, Antonio and I needed to limit this pleasurable activity. I'd never been instructed on how to prevent a pregnancy. My *novio* said he'd take the responsibility to prevent any unwanted consequences. I didn't ask exactly what measures Antonio was taking.

I expected our new physical closeness would make us more emotionally compatible. However, our relationship switched between hot and cold as before. One February 1966 evening in

Abancay, we stood in front of the Education Department. We were saying goodnight outside the big doors instead of inside. Antonio droned on about Peru's economic problems. I yawned.

"It never fails," Antonio said, "whenever I talk about a deep topic, you become tired. If I begin discussing sex, you perk right up."

"That isn't true," I said. "I just didn't get a good night's sleep."

"You know very well," he said, in an accusing tone, "you'd rather be on the other side of that door saying goodnight with more passion. If you didn't want me inside, you'd have gone in already."

Antonio's words were right about us touching one another more when we were out of view of others. Usually, for hours we pressed together tucked into a dark corner of the hall inside the Education Department's doors before forcing ourselves apart. I'd become addicted to melting into Antonio's body, folded into his embrace. I needed to limit our excessive body contact—for our own good. But by his statement Antonio insinuated I no longer had control of my emotions.

"Well," I said, my pride hurt, "I can go in anytime I like with or without you." I pushed the door open and stepped into the long hallway that led upstairs to my place. Antonio's hand reached for the heavy wooden door, but was too late. I slammed and latched the entry from the inside.

Who was he to judge me? My interest in him wasn't just sexual, though I did enjoy that new part of our relationship. I stomped up the steps with no regrets. I didn't need Antonio and his critical remarks. In a few months I'd leave him and his country behind and start a new chapter of my life. I'd join Marie and some of her volunteer friends on a trip around South America on our way back to the States.

After the door-slam incident Antonio pouted for days. I heard him criticize his mother for listening to the *novella* soap operas she enjoyed on the radio. He said she shouldn't read her books with their crummy love stories. His mother protested and defended her choices. She said she had a right to her diversions and had already read all the good books in the house. Then Antonio switched to disapproving of his mother's devotion to her Catholic religion. This disparaging side of him surprised me. He usually seemed to revere his mother.

At least he'd stopped arguing with me. He didn't talk to me at all. He acted too busy to respond to my greeting when I took Marie's pressure cooker to the Eguiluzes for Livia to use. But then, at lunch, out of the corner of my eye, I saw Antonio squelch a smile in my direction. He still had feelings for me.

Abancay's intense Carnivale celebrations finally broke the tension between us. Water-filled balloons could hit anyone anywhere at any time during this pre-Lenten merriment. One day, after having lunch there, Antonio's siblings and I threw water bombs at one another in the yard of his parents' apartment. Antonio joined the fight and landed a couple of big wet balloons on me. I retaliated with the same. The throwing and splatting was all in good humor. Later that evening, all dried off, Antonio walked me home and we talked.

"You had no reason to slam the door in my face," he said, his hands in his pockets. "I'm not the one who has to beg forgiveness this time."

"You put me in an impossible position," I said unsmiling, my arms akimbo. "I had to show you that you can't guess at my motives, then criticize what you imagine."

He turned to leave. "I'm not a toy that can be played with and tossed aside," he said.

We clearly didn't understand one another. For the next few days, my pride still smarting, I matched his reserved demeanor. Maybe we finally had reached the end—and for the best. He'd gotten what he wanted from me. But then, why did I still want to spend time with him, and he with me? We continued to walk around town together, but I felt like crying most of the way.

We were saying goodnight outside the Education Department doors one evening when I decided to forget my ego. I guessed that Antonio wanted what I wanted. I leaned against him, put my arms around his waist, and touched his cheek with a gentle kiss.

"I don't want to lose you," I said, afraid he'd rebuff me and walk away.

"I couldn't have lived long without you," Antonio said, embracing me.

I didn't care if the townspeople saw us.

❖❖❖❖

Valentine's Day was our last night together for several weeks. Marie and I would leave the next day to help staff a summer youth camp in Ollantytambo, outside of Cusco. I welcomed the opportunity to be part of a camp team. And I needed to get away from temptations of the flesh. What Antonio and I did together might create a future neither of us had planned.

I knew very little about birth control. Peace Corps medical personnel hadn't offered contraceptives, and I hadn't asked for any. Years of Catholic education had taught me that preventing pregnancy through artificial means was a mortal sin. I suspected that Antonio and I tempted fate using what he called the "early withdrawal" method. Venturing off for two weeks to work in a summer youth camp was a way to prevent actions that could have calamitous results.

I'd been requested to teach sewing and recreation skills to 4-H club members for two weeks at the Ollantytambo camp run by two new Peace Corps volunteers. My work would benefit seventy youth of the area, including five girls from our clubs in

Abancay. Involvement in this endeavor would serve as an antidote to my craving for Antonio. But getting to the camp turned out to be the biggest challenge.

Two side-by-side trucks blocked the narrow Abancay–Cusco dirt thoroughfare. One empty truck tottered on the edge of the mountain road, its front tire stuck in a pothole. A second truck parked next to the leaning one, and a taut rope tied between them, kept the teetering vehicle from plummeting 1,500 feet down the embankment into the Apurimac River. Fifteen vehicles stood waiting in both directions behind the two trucks. For half an hour, dust-covered men walked around the two stuck trucks scratching their heads. My bus to camp and scores of travelers wouldn't be going anywhere soon.

Whenever my progress was thwarted, I looked for a way around the obstacle. But here a steep mountain rose on one side and a cliff as deep as the Grand Canyon descended on the other. There was no way through. An accurate picture of my life, I thought. Like my emotional dilemma, going around the obstruction of love didn't seem an option.

Then someone on the road had the bright idea to shove the tottering truck out of the hole. Several strong men held the rope taut so the truck wouldn't go over the edge while others pushed the vehicle from behind. After a few minutes of exertion and uncertainty, the tethered truck settled safely back onto a level part of the road. Traffic moved again. We arrived late to Ollantytambo, but we got there.

Gracie and Phil, the two new Peace Corps volunteers in charge of all Cusco area 4-H clubs, were organized. They'd arranged for personnel, food, and equipment and gave everyone specific assignments. Those campers not in sewing classes learned to cook nutritious meals. Local 4-H leaders demonstrated how to put meals together, using the homegrown products of quinoa, corn, or potatoes. This time, unlike in Quillabamba, I was part of a functional organization. All my energies went into leading morning exercises and sewing classes, not pining for Antonio.

The leaders mixed the participants from different towns into two teams. At first, the campers complained about not being with their friends, but after a few days they seemed happy making new acquaintances. Points were awarded to teams based on their members' behavior and helpfulness. Activities ran like clockwork because everyone performed his or her assigned job. Work at this camp was a pleasure.

Physical calisthenics with thirty-five girls began my day at 5:30 a.m. After breakfast, I taught sewing to two groups of girls on three borrowed machines. Every girl in the class wanted to use a sewing machine all the time. So I developed a schedule. One group cut out their potholders or aprons while another group sewed or ironed them. Constant calls for me to fix a problem, like a machine running backwards, presented a challenge. But I used my skills and surmounted all difficulties. Then I had a more serious concern.

I'd gained weight and my period was several weeks late. Could eating too much starchy food at the camp be the reason? I hoped so. When I'd skipped my period for two months in college, a hormone shot got me back on schedule. Stress and poor food choices most likely explained my lateness now. Thankfully, the well-oiled camp system kept me too busy to dwell on my physical irregularities.

Each evening a volunteer with a guitar led the boys and girls in a sing-along of Peruvian favorites. I heard *"Déjame que te cuente, Limeña,"* words of a catchy Peruvian waltz, sung by campers throughout the next day and on field trips to various Incan ruins and the fertilizer factory. Our participants and staff remained enthusiastic and friendly up to the last day. What a difference from my experience in the Quillabamba camp.

We instructors cried along with our students when our session came to an end. From early morning until late in the evening everyone worked and played well together. My students asked if they could write to me. I loved the idea. At the camp I no longer participated in dramatic emotional games with Antonio. Arguments between my mind and my body diminished when I was away from his enticing presence. I'd been too occupied to miss him. And I hadn't encountered a single rat.

◦◦◦◦◦◦

Before returning to Abancay, I stopped by Cusco to purchase some final souvenirs in preparation for my return to California. My trunk awaited at the Peace Corps warehouse in town. When full, the Peace Corps would ship the container to my home in the States via sea freighter. I purchased alpaca sweaters for everyone in my family. I hoped they wouldn't be too warm for California winters. Besides alpaca rugs, carved gourds, and an alpaca blanket, I bought some baby-sized clothes—a tiny gray sweater, socks, and a hat. They'd look good on someone's baby, and they'd been a bargain. I wanted to take back as much memorabilia as I could.

Marie and I bargained for two typical bright-colored native outfits that included vivid-red and bright-blue disc-shaped hats. I braided nylon stockings and pinned them under my hat to make me look like a local indigenous woman. Then we walked up to the stone Incan fortress of Saksaywaman in our costumes and snapped photographs of one another posing barefoot as native women on top of the huge boulder walls. Afterwards, I put my ensemble into my U.S.-bound trunk.

Antonio returned to Cusco the same day I traveled back to Abancay. Our buses must have crossed somewhere on the road. Though disappointed I'd not seen him, I counted on the distance between us to calm my romantic desires. It didn't. I longed for Antonio's gentle touch. Twice during the next two weeks, I packed a bag and found a ride that would take me to him. Before my transportation left, however, I reconsidered. If my only reason for going to Cusco was to be with Antonio, I shouldn't go. I valued my independence. My happiness didn't depend on a man. I could do what I wanted with my life. I remained in Abancay.

When Antonio returned to my town for a few days in March, I couldn't believe my behavior. I didn't care who saw me holding hands with the man I loved. He, on the other hand, became concerned about displaying affection in public. Our attitudes had reversed.

He showed concern when I said my stomach had been bothering me. I dismissed any thought that I might be carrying within me someone who could use the baby clothes in the trunk. I mentioned to Antonio what my stomach problem could be.

"What will you do," he said as we sat on a bench in Abancay's main plaza, "if you're pregnant?"

"I think," I said, not wanting to worry him, "the Peace Corps would help me."

"We need to be more careful." he said. "We don't want to begin our lives together with an accident. If anything happens, I'll be by your side. But you deserve someone who can make a better life for you. I will only keep you from taking advantage of the many opportunities that await you in the States."

I didn't say so, but I agreed. I wanted to travel many more places and have more adventures. I planned to see more of South America after I left the Peace Corps in June, then go to graduate school in the fall. And a stomachache wouldn't stop me.

Selling and Packing

The same day that Antonio returned to Cusco to continue his third year of university studies, I received a "Permit to Register" certificate in the mail. It allowed me to begin studying for a master's degree at the University of Wisconsin at Madison in September 1966. Also in our Abancay mailbox came letters from home expressing my family's eagerness for my return. I needed to tie up my Peruvian life and get ready for life in the States.

Marie and I began to sell or give away anything we didn't want to ship back. I made a long list of my possessions—phonograph records, a record player, a typewriter, a never-used hectograph contraption, and assorted household items. Dresses I'd sewn and didn't want to pack sold first. By the end of March my savings amounted to $500, enough for a trip to Argentina and Brazil.

Local young men with whom I'd danced at fiestas bought many of my sale items without bargaining. I didn't know if they wanted my records, piano books, and slippers to use or as mementos. A few inquired about my relationship with Antonio.

"We're *novios*, engaged," I answered.

"What will Antonio do when you leave?" they asked, concerned about one of their own.

"He will come to the States," I said, not knowing how or when that might happen. I wished for this to be true, though I didn't think Antonio had taken any action to get there. He had vacillated between finishing his final two years of university studies in Peru or trying again to convince his biological father to help him study in the U.S. Though I thought I was in love with Antonio, I didn't have a ring or a wedding date. I just had my doubts.

When I spoke about Antonio to my American friends, I judged him through their eyes—immature and unable to be responsible for anyone but himself. He didn't know who he was or what he wanted in life. He had no goals other than finishing his studies and sometimes he said he might quit the university. He didn't like studying economics, his major. He wished he could study physics and mathematics. Maybe I couldn't have the secure life I thought I wanted with Antonio. When with him, though, I'd see the warm, caring, playful man who loved me.

Most of March I spent packing in Abancay while Antonio stayed in Cusco studying. A future with him alternated between a nightmare and a dream. The nightmare left me anxious about my physical condition. Could I be pregnant? Not possible. I could count on one hand the number of times we'd slept together. My good dreams left me content and in a loving relationship with him. But a dream is what Antonio seemed to be. I hadn't seen him in a month. I imagined he might be dating other girls by now. Nevertheless, I missed him and needed to talk to him. I took the night bus to Cusco at the end of March.

◇⁃◇⁃◇⁃◇

Antonio was an hour late meeting me in the main plaza the morning after I arrived. A school exam had run late. I spent the hour shopping for the last of my souvenirs. We went together to the warehouse to add my purchases to the trunk the Peace Corps would ship home for me. I showed Antonio the baby clothes I'd bargained for. He laughed and gave me a hug. I felt ashamed but blithely mentioned that I was now over a month late. He gave me another hug and invited me for tea.

We walked hand in hand up the stairs to the second floor of a small coffee shop on the Plaza de Armas. I thought we might continue to discuss the possibility of my condition, but Antonio had another topic on his mind.

"Could you love a communist?" he said.

"Probably not." I said. "I guess it would depend if his belief was a big enough part of his life to affect my way of living. I don't think two people with strongly opposite political philosophies would fall in love in the first place."

I didn't think he believed in the same communism I'd been taught to hate. But my comment turned him cold. Shortly thereafter he dropped me off at my hotel with a curt "Bye."

I'd had it with his inattention to my concerns. On the verge of tears I went to retrieve a room key from the front desk. Unexpectedly, from around the corner, Antonio returned to invite me for a cup of chocolate. I accepted, though his earlier behavior displeased me.

"Why do you enjoy playing with me like a cat plays with a mouse?" I said as we walked back to the café. "You act in ways you know will hurt me. You must not love me very much if you can torture me so."

"Please forgive me," Antonio said.

"Okay," I said, "but this is the last time."

We climbed back to the second floor of the small café. In the next breath he taunted me again.

"Americans marry for convenience's sake," he said. "And if love comes out of that, okay. If not, okay too. The average American father is more interested in his work than anything else. And American women don't like to raise their own children."

"You exaggerate," I said. "Americans aren't that rigid about marital roles. And marriage isn't any better in Peru where the husband doesn't stay in love with his wife, and the kids are raised by servants while the wife sits idly in the home bored with nothing to do but boss around the help."

Maybe Antonio formed his ideas of American parenthood from the movies he'd seen. He had met Americans who lived and visited Cusco, but I didn't think he knew how their families operated. My observations came from living in Peru and discussing male-female relationships with a wide variety of single and married Peruvians of both sexes. We'd both made gross generalizations, not knowing their accuracy.

As we walked back to the hotel, Antonio said he'd given up all hope and desire of going to the States. He could offer me nothing, so I should stop thinking of him as anything but a friend. I shouldn't have any trouble forgetting him, he said. I answered that we shouldn't give up hope until June.

"But if you are pregnant," he said giving me a quick peck on the cheek, "don't take any extreme measures."

"I don't believe in abortion," I said.

"Give the baby to me," he said, tears in his eyes. "It would give me something to live for."

Back on Track

April began with a feeling of freedom. My period came and I wasn't pregnant. A burst of liberation swept through me like melting snow surging around sagebrush. I'd narrowly escaped parenthood, for which neither Antonio nor I were prepared. I'd be leaving Peru the first part of June, and my adventurous life could continue unfettered.

I had plans for more travels, but Antonio couldn't work toward the only goal I knew he had—completing his university studies. The students at the university were on strike again, so Antonio was back in Abancay. We resumed our evening walks around the plaza.

Antonio was sad to know I wasn't expecting. He'd become fond of our imaginary child. I was touched by his sentimentality but disappointed he'd not told me how he would support a wife and baby. Maybe the *idea* of fatherhood was more pleasant for him than the actual responsibilities required. For me, chagrin surfaced over the actions that had nearly brought me to motherhood.

"I'm ashamed," I said, hanging my head as I sat down on a plaza bench, "when I think of my parents and friends ever knowing what I've done with you."

"There's no reason," he said, with no hint of remorse, "why anyone would ever know. I certainly wouldn't say anything."

It was true. Antonio didn't brag about his relationship with one of the *gringas*. Ken kept us informed about rumors he thought we should know. Other men lied about which of us they had bedded, but not Antonio. I respected him for that.

Antonio sat down far away from me on the plaza bench. I began to weep. If he loved me, he would take me in his arms and say he'd take care of me no matter what. Except he couldn't reassure me because he had no way to take care of anyone. Besides, now that I wasn't pregnant, I could take care of myself. Still, I wanted him to feel some of the guilt I felt about the chances we'd taken being intimate.

"Everything we've done," he said, his voice cold as ice, "you can easily forget."

"I don't know that I can," I said feeling tears flow down my face.

Forgetting him wouldn't be easy. I pictured myself reading my journal in future years, wondering how he was and whom he'd married. I hoped I wouldn't look back on this time together and regret everything we'd been for each other. Despite his alternating moods, I still had strong feelings for him. Our lives were going their separate ways, and I wanted us to part as friends.

I pulled a handkerchief from my sweater pocket and blew my nose, then dried my tears. Soon I'd be home in California with a family who loved me. For the past year, Antonio had filled the void of someone who treasured me—when we weren't at odds with one another.

Antonio's body stiffened. He rose from the bench and stood

over me. His face was stern. I sensed that something I'd said irritated him.

"Tell me," he said with increasing vehemence, "why the U.S. sticks its nose in every place from Vietnam to the Dominican Republic."

I hadn't seen that coming. Why bring up now how my government conducted its foreign affairs? I wished he wouldn't badger me with these controversial topics when I was feeling sorry for myself. Maybe he interpreted my embarrassment over having slept with him as regret for having had any connection with him.

"I don't know that much about U.S. foreign matters," I said, trying to drop the subject, "but neither my country nor Peru is perfect."

"Peace Corps volunteers think that every South American, including me, is just dying to get into the U.S.," he said, his face getting red. "Well, I'd rather go to almost any other country."

"Fine," I said, standing to face him, becoming irritated too. "I wouldn't dream of making you go to the States."

Antonio had everything to gain by going to the U.S., but he'd said he didn't want to go without assurance that I'd be his when he got there. I loved him, but in my world and in the novels I'd read, the man had goals for a future before he asked the woman he loved to marry him. Antonio should do the right thing and make a plan. Still, knowing he needed me made me more reluctant to leave him.

❧ ❧ ❧ ❧

The next morning Marie and I sorted through items we wanted to either sell or ship home. I had twenty-five prepaid aerograms I didn't need to take back. Marie wanted to unload the clothes hangers we'd used. Antonio came in and sat on a chair, watching. He looked sullen.

"The United States should have intervened in Hungary," he said, raising his voice. "Your country didn't help the Hungarians and it gave in to Russia by agreeing to divide Germany and Korea."

He continued his rant from the night before. I still didn't know for certain where his anger came from. I wasn't eager to respond. Marie continued to remove clothes from hangers. We had important packing and selling to do.

"You shouldn't have intervened," Antonio said, "in the Dominican Republic, Cuba, or Vietnam."

Did he think my country should intervene in other countries or not? Yesterday he'd been critical of the United States for not taking action. Now he was complaining we'd intervened. Why was he so adamant about U.S. foreign policy anyway? And why was he making Marie and me account for our government's decisions?

"You make no sense," Marie said, finally able to get in a word. "What do you believe? Better yet, what is it you want in life?"

I knew he couldn't answer. Antonio didn't know what he wanted in life. I'd not heard him talk about what he would do after college. Often, he lamented that he'd never amount to much. He seemed confused and insecure. One minute he said he could do anything if I helped him. The next minute he said no woman would put up with his moodiness and I should leave him alone in his misery. Maybe he was right. I didn't have time to play psychologist to him—and he didn't want that anyway.

From my point of view, until he found who he was and what he wanted, he couldn't be happy with anyone. He needed to discover some purpose that made life worthwhile—besides me. That's what real men in the United States did. They had careers and accomplished things. That's what my father did. He worked to provide for his six offspring, even though the stress messed with his head. My mother bore the children, cared for them, and suffered in silence. Though I never wanted as limited a life as my mother's, I still expected the man I married to have an occupation and a means of support.

I didn't know how many more days of my last two months we could spend together. Antonio would return to his classes in Cusco when the student strike was over. And there were a few more cities in Peru I wanted to see. After Antonio's afternoon of complaints, we took our usual evening stroll.

"I'm realizing too late," he said with tears in his eyes, "that through my own fault, I am losing the most precious thing I've ever had in my life. I'm sorry if I've taken something from you that I can never return. I hope our relationship won't have any adverse effects on your future."

"You didn't take anything," I said, my heart breaking, "that I wasn't willing to give."

Chance Card

Antonio and I were no longer engaged *novios*, just close friends. His presence wasn't a reason to keep me in Abancay. In fact, my desire to be where he was waned. The new school year had just begun, and Marie and I determined we shouldn't resume our PE classes or girls' clubs because we'd leave Peru in a couple of months.

Both of us wanted to explore more of the country before we left. The many Peace Corps volunteers who lived in Ayacucho boasted about how spectacular Holy Week was in their central Peruvian city. We decided to spend Easter week there.

A doctor friend offered the perfect mode of transportation for the long trip. He said we could fly the 231 miles from Abancay to Ayacucho in a helicopter used by the physicians at the local hospital where we'd trained. The helicopter would save us two days' travel over narrow mountain roads. We looked forward to the prospect of exchanging the usual bumpy roads for a smooth airplane ride over the Andes.

At 6:30 a.m., ten days before Easter, the helicopter sat at the football stadium. We waited at home. The pilot needed to receive a weather report from our destination before he could lift off. We would be notified when to report to the departure pad. At 8:30, the pilot's wife called the education office to tell us the trip remained on hold. By noon, word still hadn't come for us to go to the stadium, so we went to lunch. We were at a local restaurant when fellow volunteer, Ken, walked in.

"What?" he said, doing a double take when he saw us. "You're still here?"

"Why?" Marie asked.

"Because the helicopter left at 10:45," Ken said. "I thought you were on it."

Marie's face dropped. I was stunned. At that point I hated Peru and all Peruvians. Why were they so undependable? On the phone, the doctor friend repeated Ken's statement of surprise.

"Weren't you on it?" the doctor asked.

So many of our trips had begun in the same disappointing way. With two months left in Peru, it couldn't happen too many more times. We returned home, moping and complaining. There was nothing to do but distract ourselves and invite Ken and Antonio to play the Spanish-language version of Monopoly with us on the set I'd made.

I felt strangely content playing the real estate game with Antonio. Knowing about this typically American game might motivate him. Perhaps pretending to buy, sell, and rent properties would inspire him to find ways to earn an income.

Ken and Marie landed on *Váyase a la cárcel*, and often went directly to jail without collecting $200. Antonio and I alighted on *Parcada Libre*, or Free Parking, more than our friends and were the final players to keep our properties. I was surprised at how fast Antonio had picked up the strategies of a game that so symbolized

American values. Then he won. We switched to checkers and he beat me at that too. He didn't inform me of any ways he might be inspired to earn an income that could support a family.

◦·◦·◦·◦

The next day Marie and I renewed our search for transportation to Ayacucho. Antonio knew of someone with a truck that could get us to the next town of Andahuaylas where we could catch a plane to Ayacucho. The ride fell through. Days later, on Saturday morning, we finally left Abancay in the cab of the mail truck.

That night Marie and I stayed with Bill, a Peace Corps friend in Andahuaylas who worked setting up cooperatives in the area. Precautions to hide our coed housing with Bill no longer seemed necessary. We would soon terminate our stay in the country, so rumors about our sleeping arrangements wouldn't bother us.

The next day, Sunday, I went to confession, then mass, in Andahuaylas's big adobe cathedral. I had a talk with the kind priest. When I mentioned my closeness with Antonio, Father opined that after a year together a couple should get married. I wondered what magic wand the kind cleric would wave to make that happen.

I took the opportunity to give Father my observations that the indigenous population treated church rituals as if they were magic. On Palm Sunday, for example, I'd witnessed a near riot at the Abancay Cathedral when local farmers clambered over me and everyone else in their way to obtain the palm fronds being distributed. The emotionality of the scene repulsed me.

Father cautioned me. I should understand and learn from the church here and not criticize it. After all, the priest remarked, I'd had considerable religious education. Still, the type of passionate Catholicism I'd witnessed in my part of Peru I found disquieting. I had been reared in a family, church, and culture not prone to outward displays of sentiment over anything, especially the imagined power of religious artifacts. I preferred a rational to an emotional Catholicism.

❖❖❖❖

A small twin-engine plane whisked Marie and me the one-hundred-thirty-seven miles from Bill's small mountain town to our destination of Ayacucho in fifteen minutes. By 11:00 a.m. we were at our friend Yvonne's old chapel house with the bell tower. Yvonne came to the door yawning. We'd awakened her and her two hung over male guests. I looked at our sleepy host with skepticism. I hadn't come for late-night drinking parties. I was here to see the religious pageants.

Each day of Holy Week, a different colorful procession filled the streets of town. The parades had miles of floats covered with flowers, candles, and wooden statues of saints. The smell of incense filled the city streets. Most events were about as entertaining as the religious pageants I'd seen in Abancay. However, one was downright scary.

In the main cathedral seven priests in long flowing black robes and matching hoods covering their bowed heads walked at a slow pace down the main aisle of the Ayacucho cathedral. The priest in front swung a huge black flag with a red *X* on it from side to side thirty-three times, Christ's age when he died. He repeated the flag-waving ritual from the altar's three other sides. Then the six men following him prostrated themselves on the floor at the front of the church for over ten minutes. All the while, dissonant music played on the organ while two blind men sang. The entire spectacle was strange-sounding, ominous, and even horrifying to me. Certainly the Pope must have forbidden this kind of scary ritual.

On Saturday, our new Regional Peace Corps Director, Steve, arrived by car from Cusco and suggested we all go to the big outdoor *feria* market. I loved being tempted by so many colorful handmade items when walking among the hundreds of vendors selling blankets, rugs, and handicrafts of all kinds. A two-foot-high wood carving of a bent-over little peasant man leaning on a cane caught my eye. The figure looked exactly like the indigenous man in a photo I'd taken on a Cusco street. I had to have it. The female vendor wanted 500 *soles*, around $18. If I paid more than 400 *soles*, I wouldn't have bus fare to get from Andahuaylas back to Abancay. I offered 250 *soles*. She scoffed at my offer, so I feigned a lack of interest in the little man by looking at less expensive items. I upped my offer by fifty *soles* as we talked.

The woman said that her son, a taxi driver who'd lost his legs in a car accident, had carved the wooden figure from a tree stump. The story, true or not, impressed me. After an hour of bartering we were friends and the woman said she'd accept 400 *soles* for the sculpture. Overjoyed at my prize, I was digging the money out of my purse, when Steve, my new boss, walked by. He casually asked the vendor how much she wanted for the carving. She answered, "500 *soles*." I informed Steve that I was about to get it for less. He didn't care. Steve whipped 500 *soles* from his pocket and took the figure for himself. He walked away with my statue under his arm, leaving me in tears. His act was the insensitive type of behavior Antonio had criticized in American men. This time I agreed with my ex-boyfriend.

Every night liquor flowed at a party. Twenty guests now stayed at Yvonne's monastery home. Marie celebrated with the Bobbsey clique she'd run with during training. I stayed in my bedroom loft. Marie said I was subdued and not having fun because I missed Antonio. True, but I also didn't care to get drunk every night like the others. I'd had more Pisco Sours than I could count since coming to Peru and didn't like my reduced control and dizziness afterwards. Besides, the drinks cost money that I preferred to save and spend on Peruvian artistry.

Local young Peruvians joined us at the final party of Holy Week. I loved dancing with the fleet-footed Peruvian guys—until they began with the familiar line, "I love you and want to marry you." When they persisted with their insincere pickup lines, I left the celebration and went to bed early . . . alone.

Marie and I attended 4 a.m. mass on Easter morning with hordes of others packed inside the cathedral. Outside, after mass, we followed the platform with a statue of Christ surrounded by hundreds of candles at the base. To my surprise, Bill and Director Steve were among those carrying the religious display on their backs around the plaza. I watched in wonder as faint pink streaks colored the morning sky and the sun rose over the Andes. The devout and beautiful awe-inspiring scene gave me goose bumps. I no longer judged the elaborate church rituals by the level of emotion they provoked.

The next day my roommate and I flew back to Andahuaylas. Steve left earlier in his van and unexpectedly met us at the Anda-huaylas airport to offer Marie and me a ride to Abancay. Though still smarting from my boss's underhanded dealing at the *feria*, I accepted his offer. The free ride saved me bus fare. The wooden statue Steve had purchased out from under me lay forlorn and upside-down in a corner of his van. I did a slow burn thinking how little consideration he had for the fine work of art or my feelings.

Much like his predecessor, Mr. Cavendish, Steve had the power and the money. I didn't.

◁・◁・◁・◁

Back in Abancay, Antonio and I greeted one another like more than good friends. We had missed each other, which showed in our private displays of affection. When I'd left for Ayacucho, I'd been certain I could get along fine without him. Now, after a week apart, I realized I wanted to be with Antonio for as much time as I had left. My motivation was stronger than ever to get him to the States.

I sent out twenty-eight more inquiries to the directors of Peace Corps training sites where Spanish or Quechua would be taught. Twenty-three responded, saying they weren't in a position to hire Antonio. I wrote another letter to his biological father in Ohio and asked him to help his intelligent son with airfare to the U.S. I said that if Antonio remained in Cusco, where there were few work opportunities, he would waste away his life. Antonio wrote once more asking his father to sponsor him in the U.S. No one offered Antonio anything.

One day in early April, Antonio's parents, Marie, and I were playing Monopoly at the Eguiluzes' house—without Antonio. I thought he should play with us one last time since he'd gotten so good at it and obviously enjoyed the game—and because I wanted to be with him. No one could say where he was. I offered to go search for him.

I found Antonio reading a math book alone in Ken's apartment. This would likely be the last time we'd be alone together. He abandoned his book as soon as he saw me. An hour later, flushed and out of breath, we rejoined the Monopoly game. As we sat down to play, I realized my love and I had once again drawn a "Chance" card that might send us directly to parenthood jail.

Goodbye Abancay

M arie and I had lived rent-free in a storeroom in back of
the Education Department for the past eighteen months.
At the end of April, an official from the Education Department
informed us that the department needed their room back by May
1. We were surprised. It was April 26, five-and-a-half weeks before
our final debriefing in Lima on June 8. The education officials must
not have realized we'd be leaving forever in a few weeks. Marie and
I scrambled to find a place we could move to for the next month.

Antonio's parents offered us a windowless storeroom near
their apartment that usually held Food for Peace products. Broom
in hand, I went to sweep it out. The room smelled of powdered
milk. A white cloud formed above my broom when I began brushing. Through the haze, two tiny black figures emerged—mice! Not
what I'd bargained for. All three of us squealed, and the mice raced
out the door. I dropped the broom and followed.

Marie and I returned to Señor Landao, head of the Education Department, and asked for a delay in vacating their facilities.
We informed him that we were leaving for good in just five weeks.

Our request was granted. This time, the *mañana* attitude I usually despised, worked in our favor.

Items to pack were piled high on the beds, the table, and the floor of our room. I stepped around the mess as I sewed the all-weather coat I'd take on my trip around South America. The black rainproof material was a lucky find. I added a warm zip-in lining from a coat whose outer shell I'd worn out. June was winter in the southern hemisphere, and southern Argentina could get cold this time of year. The black velvet collar and reversible hood added a stylish look to the coat. The borrowed electric sewing machine whirred as I finished the final stitches and handed the coat to Antonio. He voiced his approval and ironed my masterpiece. His university was on a hiatus, so he'd returned home to help me pack.

The Peace Corps would ship two chests per volunteer to the U.S. I looked at the piles of handicrafts, food, and souvenirs I planned to send back. I'd already filled one trunk in Cusco, and I still had enough souvenirs to fill three more. I publicized my baggage dilemma via the Peace Corps grapevine. A married couple from my training group, who hadn't found as much to take home as I had, came to my rescue. They gave me two of their luggage allotments. I'd send home four trunks.

Alpaca rugs, colorful wool blankets, hand-woven ponchos, and packages of quinoa grain given to me by our girls' club filled the chests. Antonio stenciled my name in white paint on two black metal trunk lids. He said I was taking half of Peru back to the States with me. His remark hit me right in the heart. How could I unpack my Peruvian treasures at home without him? I knew I'd break down when I saw his neat writing on my trunks back in California. Pangs of sorrow shot through me. I wished I could smuggle him inside one of my chests.

The pretty copper-colored oven and matching kerosene burner, purchased when we'd first arrived, no longer had to be dealt with. Neither appliance had ever worked, and we'd used the oven as a breadbox. A local man, as enchanted as we'd once been with the appliance's beauty, paid us the original price. We sold our beds, closet, table, and cupboards to neighbors and friends at low prices. We'd been offered 25 percent more by some townspeople, but our indigenous family next door, the Eguiluzes, and our teacher friends had been charitable to us, so they had first choice of whatever they wanted.

We gave our ugly, well-used, black oven and assorted kitchenware to Antonio's mother. She had been generous, feeding us lunch and often dinner for months—without compensation. We hoped it might make her endless cooking duties easier.

From all the sales, I now had enough money to lend Antonio airfare to the States. But I still wanted him to find his own way—and life—and not depend on me. However, I could assist him with a loan. He refused my offer.

We ordered a plaque and a wood frame for the map of the world that had covered a good portion of one of our walls. We'd plotted future trips on that map. On the lower edge of the frame we glued a plaque in Spanish that translated:

IN GRATITUDE TO THE DEPARTMENT OF
EDUCATION FROM MARIE HANNA AND EVELYN KOHL,
PEACE CORPS VOLUNTEERS 1964-66.

❖❖❖

One day Marie went to Cusco to see Regional Director Steve. As they conversed, Steve said he was interested in buying the *Joy of Cooking* cookbook I'd brought from the States. The tome had provided recipes for anything I wanted to prepare. It explained the adjustments needed for high altitude baking—reduce the baking powder and sugar and increase the liquid and cooking temperature. Steve was fond of Marie, and she must have used her charm to barter with him. To my delight, he agreed to exchange the wooden statue of the little peasant man that had been mine for a moment in Ayacucho, for the cookbook. I hugged Marie for her thoughtfulness. Never had she driven a better bargain.

Thirty of our closest friends came to an elaborate going-away party at the Club Abancay one afternoon in late May. Our three best girlfriends planned the delicious food, lively music, and farewell speeches. One spoke in perfect English to thank us for choosing to live and work in their little town for the past two years. Though we felt sad to leave the kind people who had made our stay so enjoyable, Marie and I were eager to see what exciting escapades lay around the corner.

Ken, our fellow Peace Corps colleague who had lived in Abancay almost as long as we had, didn't come to any of the farewell celebrations. He and another volunteer, Troy, had recently traveled to Argentina together and become close friends. Then Troy was killed in a plane crash in the Peruvian Andes. How ironic and sad. He might have come to Peru in the Peace Corps to avoid being killed fighting in Vietnam but then died in a plane crash in Peru. Ken took off for Bolivia before our parties began. He didn't want to be around to say goodbye. Ken said he couldn't take another loss.

I looked around for Antonio at our final party. I knew he'd been invited but he hadn't said if he was coming. My heart throbbed faster than the *cumbia* beat when I saw his V-shaped figure come through the club door. Other young women, maybe realizing Antonio would soon be available, asked him to dance, but, as usual, he danced only with me. He was his devilish self all afternoon and tried to hold me closer than I thought proper. I loved him but knew we'd soon be parting, so I began withdrawing—whenever I had the emotional strength. My coolness created problems between us. Antonio voiced his objections to my physical reserve as he walked me home.

"I'm going to look for a girl," he said, "who does what she sincerely feels. Someone who doesn't have so many scruples."

"Well," I said, my feelings hurt, "you go right ahead."

I didn't like him spending our remaining limited time together being mean. We had been saying goodbye for several nights the way he liked, without many scruples on my part. With so few days left together, I didn't want to waste them arguing. But I had my pride. I hurried ahead of him. He caught up to me at the entry to my place.

"I don't want to lose you," he said, clinging to me. "You are my life."

I felt the same about him—when he was considerate. I'd soon be flying miles away and he was doing nothing to stop me. I'd have my adventures and schooling and he'd stay right where I'd found him. I so wished he'd accept my offer to lend him enough money for airfare to get to the States. There, he could . . . well, I didn't know what he could do but I believed he'd have to do something on his own before he would be worthy of me. But his pride wouldn't allow him to use my money, so there was no way to begin forging a permanent life together.

That evening Antonio helped me deliver the last of our furniture to our friends' houses. Marie stayed with a girlfriend. I had sold my bed so had to sleep at Ken's place. Antonio stayed with me.

⚬·⚬·⚬·⚬

The head of the agricultural program we'd worked with gave us our final ride from Abancay to Cusco in his pickup. Marie and I rode in the cab. Antonio sat in the back with our suitcases, another of our male friends, and a group of rowdy area native men. Every few miles Antonio reached through my window to grab my hand.

"You'd make a good wife for a Peruvian," the SIPA head said observing us. "Most American women expect Peruvians to understand them, but you make the effort to understand Peruvians."

I would have discussed his observation with him, but the pickup stopped. A truck on the road in front had overturned and hung off the side of the mountain. To our amazement, Antonio's stepfather, Adolfo, climbed from the passenger side of the wounded vehicle, shaken but unhurt.

"Our vehicle's brakes failed," Señor Eguiluz said, his face pale.

"Are you alright?" Antonio asked, hopping down from the pickup.

"*Sí,*" our sponsor added before giving Marie and me a quick embrace.

The men got out of our pickup and pushed the slightly battered truck back onto the road. We waved goodbye as the lopsided vehicle continued on its way. My life in Peru was ending much like it had begun—treading on a dangerous thoroughfare with no guardrails or walls to keep me from falling off the precipice.

Between this accident and Troy's plane going down, I, too, felt vulnerable. For the past three weeks I had been fighting nausea and stomach pains. I couldn't eat and vomited up what little I managed to get down. I slept more than usual. I felt so bad that I'd stayed in bed for several entire days. Marie and Antonio said it was nerves. Life wasn't predictable. It could begin, be cut short, or be significantly changed without warning. I was uncertain how mine would be.

❖ ❖ ❖ ❖

The Peace Corps required a final medical checkup for volunteers at the end of their service. I saw the new Peace Corps doctor the day before my departure from Cusco. Dr. Marty said my stomach discomfort could be a case of worms. I told him I vomited mostly in the morning.

"Have you been doing anything," Doctor Marty asked me point blank, "that would get you pregnant?"

The very idea took my breath away. I didn't think Antonio and I'd had sex often enough for a pregnancy to occur. But then, my sex education was lacking.

"Yes," I said looking down at my feet. "I guess that could be possible."

"Well, I'll list the diagnosis as a probable case of worms," Marty said, "and arrange for you to get a pregnancy test by a Peruvian obstetrician in Lima."

I left the doctor's office confused. Antonio and I had been through this worry two months before and come out unscathed. I mentioned the doctor's pregnancy diagnosis to Antonio the night before I was to leave. He was certain Dr. Marty was wrong. I agreed, but still felt anxious. The doctor had to be wrong, or my life would be destroyed.

Leaving Peru

On June 7, 1966, I said goodbye to the love of my life with long embraces at the Cusco airport. Antonio's shoulders slumped. Before he turned away, I noticed tears flooding his dark eyes. I couldn't reassure him that we would see one another again. He needed to take the initiative if he wanted us to be together, but he hadn't. We'd met when I was twenty-two and he was nearly the same age. Now, after loving one another off and on for fifteen months, we were parting forever.

"Please find a way," I said, choking back tears, "to come be with me in the States."

Antonio said he would try. But what could he do that he hadn't already attempted? I knew I wouldn't see him again. I'd have to go on alone.

I clenched my teeth to avoid embarrassing displays of emotion. From the airplane stairs I waved farewell. Antonio looked thin, small, and defeated when he waved back. My heart was breaking as I entered the plane and sat next to fellow volunteer, Larry.

The plane taxied down Cusco's runway, then lifted through the narrow mountain passage, headed for Lima. I could no longer contain my despair. Emotional pain overwhelmed me. My body shook as I wept, trying to keep my sobs from being heard. Wet Kleenexes piled up at my feet. Larry sat reading a book, unmoved by my pain. Just as well. I was inconsolable.

∘·◌·∘·◌

One-hundred-two Peace Corps volunteers, including me, had begun community development training at Cornell in June 1964. Seventy of us had landed in Peru on October 1, 1964. The first day in the country, two young women from our group had returned to the States to get married. Rich, who hated mice, had lasted a month in his rat-infested rural hut before returning home on his own terms. The remaining sixty-seven of us from the original group had fulfilled our two-year obligation. We'd be debriefed for four days in Lima and write reports about our Peace Corps experience. We'd been immersed in Peruvian life in different regions since arriving. We had endured—and some of us had even thrived.

Swept up in a whirlwind of discussions and the excitement of reuniting with fellow volunteers, many of whom I'd not seen since we'd arrived, I was too busy to dwell on my upcoming visit to a Peruvian obstetrician. I submitted a report of what I'd accomplished in Abancay—girls' clubs, youth camps, and teaching physical education. I frowned when the final test of my Spanish showed me to be at the same level as the previous year. Between Antonio and my numerous Peruvian friends, I'd had a lot of practice in Spanish. I thought I'd score at level four or five, not level three, professional working proficiency. I began to worry what I'd get on my biggest final exam, the medical one.

Marty, the Cusco Peace Corps physician said we needed to determine the cause of the intestinal discomfort I'd felt over the past month. I agreed. He'd suggested that I could have a case of worms, a fairly common affliction here—or I could be pregnant. So he'd arranged an appointment with a Peruvian obstetrician for me. There'd be an easier solution for worms than for a pregnancy. I didn't know what I'd do if I were pregnant.

After the tests, I planned to say good-bye to most of my Peace Corps colleagues and fly off with Marie and her friends to tour South America. Later, I'd head back to California, and in the fall, I'd attend graduate school in Wisconsin.

I walked to the doctor's office alone, feeling out of place. A nurse in a starched white uniform ushered me into a bathroom and gave me a cup. After delivering the urine sample, I was whisked off to an examining room. I perched on the end of a cold plastic-covered examining table in a thin white gown. I shivered. Muffled voices in Spanish came from the other side of the heavy wooden door to the doctor's office. I strained to hear what was being said. When I couldn't, my thoughts turned inward. What was causing my morning nausea? Was it worms or something more life-changing?

I didn't want to have to explain any unwanted consequence of my actions with Antonio. My parents would be mortified if I was with child. My father had warned me to wait until marriage to do "it." The moral guardrails of church and parents hadn't kept me safe when on my own in the mountains of Peru.

The nurse reentered the room holding a syringe in one hand and a container with empty glass tubes in the other. I'd already given her my urine. Now she wanted my blood. She tightened a plastic band around my upper left arm and pricked my vein with the needle. I bit my lip and watched blood fill each small vial.

3

"*Pobrecita*," the nurse said as she capped the last tube. "Poor dear." She obviously knew I was unmarried, in a foreign land, and going through pregnancy tests.

The salty taste of tears, or maybe it was the blood from my lip, filled my mouth. She left, and I was alone again. She was right. *Pobrecita.* My eyes searched for something to calm my fears.

The small exam room looked like the one in my childhood at Garberson Clinic in Miles City, Montana. Dr. Treat had checked me there for swollen tonsils. Nurses had held me down for a spinal tap to check for rheumatic fever. Something then had not been right with my body. The uncertainty I'd felt at age twelve returned now at age twenty-three. Only this time my parents weren't nearby providing support. No one was.

I yearned for a touch of gentleness among this cold, clinical atmosphere.

After an eternity, the nurse returned to the room with the doctor. This time she wasn't all business. She put her hand on my shoulder in a comforting gesture. Hers was the first touch of caring I'd felt since leaving Antonio in Cusco.

"*Sí, usted está embarazada*," the doctor said. "Yes, you are pregnant."

The words felt like a slap in the face. My body shuddered. Sobs I'd been holding back hurtled out in a torrent. Unable to contain my passions, my life had taken the wrong turn. I was tumbling off the narrow mountain road into a tumultuous stream below. My world turned upside down.

"*¿Qué piensas hacer?*" the doctor asked. "What are you going to do?"

I couldn't answer his question. I didn't know. I was alone and confused. I had Antonio's baby growing inside me. Returning home to my parents would be a disgrace to them. Telling Antonio would force him to take on responsibilities I'd seen no proof he could assume. None of this felt like an adventure. At least not one I thought I could manage or enjoy.

The Peruvian medical staff asked me about the baby's father. I told them he was a university undergraduate. Their suggestions implied they knew students had little money even to support themselves. They were right. Antonio had no way to support a family. Being pregnant had severe consequences. The Peruvian doctor encouraged me to "take measures" to erase my mistake.

Options were spelled out in private meetings with Peace Corps personnel. Their recommendation was that I fly straight to Washington, D.C., without returning home. I could work in the Peace Corps offices in the nation's capital until my child was born, then give up the baby for adoption. Everything would be paid for. The Peace Corps had policies regarding such situations. I was startled. Apparently, they were prepared for situations like mine.

The Peace Corps officials said I needed to make a decision right away so my care could be arranged. Adoption seemed like a better option than abortion—the Peruvian doctor's solution. I couldn't agree to either action. I was in a daze.

Morning nausea weakened any resolve I had. Too many decisions had to be made too fast. My mind was too befuddled to decide anything. I'd brought this dilemma on myself. There was no sympathetic person with whom I could discuss my situation. Marie wasn't around. She was off with the Bobbseys planning her trip around South America. I, too, wanted to be planning my next trip. But in my present state I couldn't.

I hated to leave the country without talking to Antonio. Phone service was undependable. Besides, I was uncertain where to reach him. Mail delivery wasn't much better. I'd be gone by the time Antonio received my letter. I wrote to him anyway about the decision I'd come to.

Querido Antonio,

   I am pregnant with your baby. I can't explain how confused I am. Peace Corps people think I should give it up for adoption. I cry whenever I imagine giving it away after carrying it for nine months . . .

   I don't want to give you responsibilities that you aren't ready to take on—especially in a country you don't know.

   That's why I've decided to go to California first, then to Washington, D.C., where I'll wait for you. If you don't come, I'll do what I have to. If you come, we'll see. I'm enclosing a form you need to immigrate to the U.S.

Love, Evelyn

P.S. I still might travel around South America with the others.

❖ ❖ ❖ ❖

Marie and I went to lunch one last time. She and the Bobbseys were set to catch a free ride to Rio on a Brazilian embassy airplane the next day. Reality hit me. I couldn't travel with them. I had responsibilities now. With all my misgivings, I still was overjoyed to bring Antonio's and my offspring into being. I wanted to shout out my baby news to my roommate and best friend of two years. Nevertheless, I remained quiet. Marie became suspicious of my silence and lack of enthusiasm for discussing travel plans.

   "Are you pregnant with Antonio's baby?" she asked outright.

   "Yes," I answered, feeling awkward. "And I'm happy about it. I just don't know what I'm going to do."

"Oh, Evelyn." She leaned toward me, tears spilling from her big hazel eyes. "You said goodbye to Antonio. Does he know about the baby?"

"No." I shook my head and imagined his dark eyes. "He knew it was a possibility. I think we thought this would be another false alarm like a couple months ago."

Marie looked surprised. Many times she and I had discussed how important it was to remain pure, despite temptations. I'd never told her what I was doing the last four months when alone with Antonio. I felt like a hypocrite.

"Oh, I'm so sorry," Marie said, giving me a hug. "I should have been there for you."

Marie and I had been virgins when we started our Peace Corps commitment. I assumed she still was. I was too—until four months ago. Antonio and I had been a couple off and on since we'd first met in Abancay sixteen months ago. Marie had been very understanding, considering all the time I'd left her alone and been with Antonio. I don't know what else she thought she could have done to help me.

That evening I went out for pizza with Larry. He had requested to stay in Quillabamba to teach English until the school year finished in December. Then he'd head back to Fresno to get a job—if his draft board didn't send him off to Vietnam. Most likely, I said, I'd look for work back in the San Francisco area. I knew my life would change drastically, but I didn't tell him.

The next morning Marie awakened me in the hotel room I shared with her and three fellow female volunteers. My roommate said there was an urgent phone call from Cusco. It was Antonio. I took the phone into the womblike pocket I made under the covers for privacy. My heart leapt at the sound of Antonio's voice through the scratchy telephone line. He had called the evening before, he said, but I hadn't been in. His sweet words were honey that glued my broken heart together.

"I don't care if you are pregnant or not," he shouted through the poor phone connection. "I want you to come back and marry me."

Around noon that same day, I cracked open the door of my Lima hotel room to a Peace Corps volunteer who said he'd come from Cusco and had a letter for me. My name was typed in neat blue letters on the envelope. I recognized the blue ink from Antonio's typewriter. My body flooded with warmth thinking of him. But why a letter? Antonio had called me that morning asking me to marry him.

I opened the envelope and looked at the date—Cuzco, 8 de Junio de 1966. Antonio had written the letter the day after I'd flown from Cusco to Lima. I didn't know why I was just receiving it now. Any word from Antonio was a comfort to me. He wrote,

> *Querida Evelyn,*
>
> *You can't know how despondent I am in these moments of almost infinite agony knowing that I can't reach you. Nor can I comprehend how great is my love for you. When you left, it was like a part of me left with you. I was so confused that I could do nothing. I can hardly write, even now, remembering that only a few days ago I could hold you and kiss you and I was so happy. And now I am so alone I can barely express it in words . . . I would marry you in a minute if you would return. I hope to receive word from you about our????? very soon.*
> *Yours for eternity,*
> *Antonio*

In one neatly typed page my *novio* had poured out his soul. It contained more heartfelt feelings than he'd had time to express in our too brief conversation over the phone that morning. I'd felt lost without him the past week. Antonio's call, the doctor's diagnosis, and now this letter—I knew what I needed to do.

Beginning in Ruins

The return trip to Cusco was happier than my departure from there had been the previous week. Still, I had doubts. What was I getting into? How could I have a wedding without my family? I was buoyed by necessity and love. But love didn't mean I had confidence that Antonio could plan what was needed for a ceremony, a reception—and a life together. I wondered if he had enough money to buy me a wedding ring.

We clung to one another at the Cusco airport elated with the miracle of being together again. For more than a year the odds hadn't favored a happy outcome to our romance. It still didn't. I'd almost left the country determined to go on alone. Had Antonio's call to Lima not reached me when it did, I might now be in Brazil or California. But here we were in Cusco, taking the most important step of our lives together.

Antonio escorted me to his cousin Elsa's apartment to stay. We planned for a civil marriage on June 18, followed by a religious ceremony on June 19. The government required the legal rite. We wanted the church ritual. Antonio arranged for his friend, Padre Gálvez, to perform the wedding in a historic Spanish Chapel in back of Cusco's La Compañía de Jesús Church. Antonio and his stepfather picked out wedding bands for both of us. Señor Equiluz paid for them. Our wedding—our marriage—was happening with or without material resources of our own.

❖❖❖❖

White taffeta with an embossed leaf print was the perfect material for my knee-length wedding dress. I longed for the full-length white formal with the lace bodice I'd made when elected queen of the boys' high school in Abancay the previous October. When I'd sewn that full-length dress, I'd fanaticized it as my wedding gown. But the red paper surrounding the bouquet of flowers I'd held during the three-hour parade had stained the lacy front. Laundering hadn't eliminated the paper's indelible red marks. I'd abandoned the dress in Abancay. Besides, it wasn't new.

I found a pattern for a short and simple A-line dress with an empire waistline and boat neckline. The size eight pattern was two sizes smaller than my usual dimensions. My body was the slimmest it had been since I'd gone on a strict diet at age thirteen. I'd not been able to keep down much food for the past month. A plastic bag in my pocket kept me from embarrassing episodes of upchucking in the street as I scurried around Cusco putting things together for the big day.

June was winter in Peru, and I thought fur trim would add the right accent to my bridal attire. I bargained all over town for lengths of white alpaca fur to sew around the neck and the hem of my new wedding dress. No one would sell me the trim at a good price, and I refused to pay the amount the vendors wanted. The dress went furless.

The Peace Corps secretary offered me the use of her electric sewing machine while she was at work. The machine's needle stitched across the taffeta yardage I'd begun shaping into my wedding garment. Three days after cutting it out, I hemmed up the bottom of my dress. I pricked my finger with the needle. A drop of blood spilled on the inside edge. Neither my dress nor I was pure.

Three times I drafted a letter to my family. Breaking the news of my marriage proved a challenge. I'd written often about Antonio in the past months, so I hoped my marriage in faraway Peru wouldn't shock them. There wasn't time to invite my family. They couldn't afford the trip anyway. My letter wouldn't prevent Mama from worrying or Daddy from being angry. I certainly couldn't tell them that their first grandchild was on the way. Their rules and my strong will had protected me like strong Inca walls. But I'd broken through the protective barriers of church and family and would live with the consequences. If this wasn't the wedding and life I'd dreamed of, maybe it was the partner I needed.

"By the time you get this letter I will be married to Antonio," my message home began. "This was not a last-minute decision as Antonio and I have been in love for over a year and can't bear the thought of being separated. I don't want to cause you worry."

The words I wrote wouldn't soften the message to my parents. Mama must have guessed I'd fallen in love because months ago she'd written cautioning me about marrying a man from another country. My sisters wrote that Daddy thought Antonio wanted easy entry into the U.S. Mail delivery between Cusco, Peru, and Newark, California, took three weeks. Even if my parents disapproved, it was too late for them to stop me.

◦·◦·◦·◦

On June 18, a day after Antonio's twenty-third birthday, we stood with our witnesses at the courthouse in Cusco. I looked into Antonio's eyes with affection and hope, eager to make our relationship official. He held my hand in a loving but strong way, as if to say, "I won't let you get away from me again."

Gracie, the only female Peace Corps volunteer around who knew me, signed as my witness. Antonio's stepfather had returned to Abancay for work, so Antonio's uncle, who lived in Cusco, was his witness. I wore the all-weather coat I'd made for my trip around South America. Antonio wore a tweed sports coat. We signed pages of legal documents that were then stamped by somber-looking officials. Everything was so legal-like that any expression of the contentment I felt would have been out of place. Maybe I wasn't getting the responsible man I thought I deserved, but I was getting a loving husband.

Later, eating lunch together, we held hands as a legally married couple. There was no laughter as we discussed what we thought were the steps to get Antonio to the States and then forge a life there together. He had no future in his own country, and I didn't plan to live my life so far from home. In the States we'd have more educational opportunities for our offspring and ourselves. We hoped our love was strong enough to see us through the rocky road ahead. We turned to plans for the next day. Being Catholic, we weren't married in the eyes of the church until we took our vows before a priest.

❖❖❖❖

The night between the civil procedure and the religious ritual, I stayed in Gracie's apartment. Through the thin wall of the bedroom I heard my name.

"Why isn't Evelyn sleeping with Antonio?" Gracie's roommate asked. "They made it legal today, didn't they?"

"I think," Gracie said, "it's some kind of religious rule or something."

I'd already slept with Antonio and was two months pregnant but hadn't told anyone. My flat stomach kept my secret. Only Antonio and I knew my condition. It was important to me to look like the good Catholic I wasn't.

Early Sunday morning, the Cusco salon where I'd had my hair styled for the past year, opened with me as its only customer. Hugo spent hours piling my medium-length hair on top of my head in an attractive style. Then on the top he and his assistant, fashioned a yard of white netting into a short veil. They were happy I was marrying a man from Cusco. I was too. I floated on a cloud of joy.

At ten o'clock on Sunday morning, June 19, 1966, Antonio and I walked down the center aisle of the ancient Spanish chapel. Padre Gálvez officiated in Spanish at the private mass. I understood the language that pledged us to one another as we exchanged rings. A few of Antonio's aunts, uncles, cousins, and his university friends watched us kneel at the altar. Antonio's mother was ill again, so his immediate family hadn't made the trip from Abancay. Members of my Peace Corps group were either traveling the world or had returned to the States, so no North American attended. The small number of attendees was just right. The vows spoken in the chapel that day were between Antonio and me. No one gave us wedding gifts. We didn't need anything more than our love for one another.

My husband was handsome in a new black striped suit that matched his shock of black hair. Thanks to my special hairdo and white dress, I looked the part of a modern bride. Antonio's youngest cousin took photos of us with my Instamatic camera. Those pictures would show a slim, attractive bride and a handsome groom standing in front of the historic altar, smiling.

Mass and photos concluded, Antonio and I emerged hand-in-hand from the sixteenth-century Spanish chapel built on top of Inca walls. Laughing, we ran down a centuries-old cobblestone street between the sturdy granite Inca walls that supported the big stone church and the chapel behind it. Antonio's relatives threw handfuls of rice as we raced to a waiting Volkswagen beetle. Was this real? It didn't feel like reality. I was a stranger in a foreign dream world. My marriage was beginning among ancient ruins. I hoped our love would sustain us while we made a family and a life together.

❖ ❖ ❖ ❖

At age six I'd trudged up a hill to seek the source of the waters that flooded the bridge in front of my schoolhouse in Montana. There, I saw rivulets join to form streams that created the river-like force that tumbled over the school bridge's planks each spring.

In my early twenties the same curiosity, paired with my desire for adventure, led me to Peru. There I traveled the high winding roads to work with some of the country's poorest natives. The mountain road between Cusco and Abancay crisscrosses the Apurimac River. The river is a principal water source to the mightiest of water flows, the Amazon River. It was there, at the beginning of the world's largest river system, that a great natural force captivated me.

Silent streams of curiosity in my childhood led me to a flood of passion sixteen years later. Forces of nature swept me into the arms of a loving husband where I've remained for over fifty years. Only time and the river will tell whether my journey will continue over rough or smooth waters.

Acknowledgments

I owe much gratitude to the generous residents of Abancay, Peru, who welcomed and cared for this foreigner like one of their own. Through their kindness and love, my life was forever changed. I couldn't have found a better roommate than fellow Peace Corpsman and friend, Marie Hanna. Together we took on the challenges of living in a foreign culture with laughter and camaraderie.

This book became a reality through the guidance and tutelage of Charlotte Cook, editor extraordinaire. Her classes on the writing craft, expert advice, and encouragement, brought this book to fruition. Her way of interpreting my life gave me insights I couldn't have appreciated on my own.

Special acknowledgment goes to members of The Night Writers critique group, Tish Davidson, Joyce Cortez, and Jan Salinas. Every two weeks over many years, they patiently assessed each chapter of the first, second, and third versions of my manuscript. Their cogent suggestions improved the book's emotional tone, ordering of events, and character development. Ideas from members and presenters at the Fremont Area Writers, a branch of the 2,000-member California Writers Club, helped me clarify numerous foreign concepts.

Thanks to all who spent hours reading my first manuscripts and questioned me about my choice of words and events. Your remarks enhanced the overall readability of this book.

About the Author

Evelyn Kohl LaTorre grew up in rural Southeastern Montana, surrounded by sheep and cattle ranches, before coming to California with her family at age sixteen. She holds a doctorate in multicultural education from the University of San Francisco, and a master's degree in social welfare from UC Berkeley. She worked as a bilingual school psychologist and school administrator in public education until her retirement. Evelyn loves to travel; to date, she and her husband have traveled to some 100 countries. You can view her stories and photos on her website, www.evelynlatorre. com. Her writing has appeared in *World View Magazine*, *The Delta Kappa Gamma Bulletin*, the *California Writers Club Literary Review*, the *Tri-City Voice*, *Dispatches*, and *Clever Magazine*. She is currently completing a second book about the struggles and triumphs of a bicultural marriage in the US. Evelyn lives in Fremont, California.

Author photo © Bejay's Photography

SELECTED TITLES FROM SHE WRITES PRESS

She Writes Press is an independent publishing company founded to serve women writers everywhere. Visit us at www.shewritespress.com.

Nothing But Blue by Diane Lowman. $16.95, 978-1-63152-402-8. In the summer of 1979, Diane Meyer Lowman, a nineteen-year-old Middlebury College student, embarked on a ten-week working trip aboard a German container ship with a mostly male crew. The voyage would forever change her perspective on the world—and her place in it.

Accidental Soldier: A Memoir of Service and Sacrifice in the Israel Defense Forces by Dorit Sasson. $17.95, 978-1-63152-035-8. When nineteen-year-old Dorit Sasson realized she had no choice but to distance herself from her neurotic, worrywart of a mother in order to become her own person, she volunteered for the Israel Defense Forces—and found her path to freedom.

Fourteen: A Daughter's Memoir of Adventure, Sailing, and Survival by Leslie Johansen Nack. $16.95, 978-1-63152-941-2. A coming-of-age adventure story about a young girl who comes into her own power, fights back against abuse, becomes an accomplished sailor, and falls in love with the ocean and the natural world

Godmother: An Unexpected Journey, Perfect Timing, and Small Miracles by Odile Atthalin. $16.95, 978-1-63152-172-0. After thirty years of traveling the world, Odile Atthalin—a French intellectual from a well-to-do family in Paris—ends up in Berkeley, CA, where synchronicities abound and ultimately give her everything she has been looking for, including the gift of becoming a godmother.

Notes from the Bottom of the World by Suzanne Adam. $16.95, 978-1-63152-415-8. In this heartfelt collection of sixty-three personal essays, Adam considers how her American past and move to Chile have shaped her life and enriched her worldview, and explores with insight questions on aging, women's roles, spiritual life, friendship, love, and writers who inspire.